AIRCRAFT

COMPARED & CONTRASTED

AIRCRAFT
FROM 1914 TO THE PRESENT DAY

ROBERT JACKSON
JIM WINCHESTER

amber
BOOKS

First published in 2010 by Amber Books Ltd
Bradley's Close
74–77 White Lion Street
London N1 9PF
United Kingdom
www.amberbooks.co.uk

Previously published in 2006 in a landscape format

ISBN: 978-1-906626-99-0

Project Editor: James Bennett
Designer: Brian Rust and Keren Harragan
Picture Research: Terry Forshaw

Picture Credits:
All images courtesy of Art-Tech/Aerospace except:
Art-Tech/MARS: 10(t), 41, 130, 192, 213
TRH Pictures: 6(t), 7(both), 8, 10(b), 11(t), 13, 20, 25, 28, 32, 49, 54, 70, 71, 79, 88, 96, 97, 100, 117, 134,
139, 154, 158, 162, 163, 168, 173, 184, 193, 197, 200, 204, 212, 217
U.S. Department of Defense: 11(b), 112, 216, 220, 221
U.S. Air Force: 164

Printed and bound in China

CONTENTS

INTRODUCTION

What is it about aerial combat that endows it with a particular romance and fascination? Surely, and above all else, it is the personal identity of the pilots, the direct clash of individual qualities – courage, judgement, keenness of vision and reflex – and the ability to control machinery of immense complication and power.

For more than five centuries, from the time of the discovery of gunpowder until the invention of the aeroplane, the practice of warfare was about anonymity. The big battalions decided the issue, and as the use of explosives widened so the range at which combat encounters took place lengthened. The private bravery and accomplishment at arms of the participants consequently diminished in importance. Of course, there were savage hand-to-hand struggles, at Blenheim, at Waterloo, at Gettysburg, but the essential factors that determined the outcome were the deployment of firepower and

BELOW: The French air ace Roland Garros is seen here at the controls of the Morane-Saulnier Type N, holding a strip ready for the 7.6mm Hotchkiss machine gun.

mass. At Verdun, in World War I, tens of thousands of soldiers lost their lives crawling backwards and forwards through storms of high explosive remotely directed upon them by artillerymen whom they never saw, nor could ever hope to reach with their personal weapons.

But aerial combat was from the very outset – and remains even to this day – exclusively individualist, and the proliferation of high technology accentuates the roles of human intelligence and the virtues of bravery and calculated risk. There is a direct link between a World War I observer hammering desperately with gloved hand against the jammed magazine of his Lewis gun as the pursuing Fokker closes the range, and the pilot of a modern strike aircraft diving to low level as he tries to shake off a pursuing surface-to-air missile.

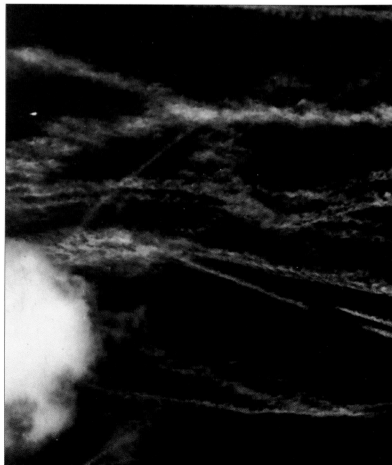

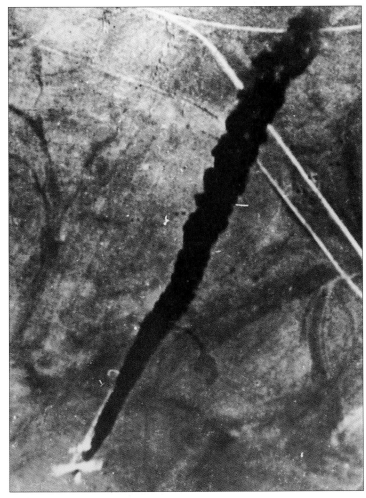

ABOVE: *United States Army Air Force P-51 Mustang pilots are briefed before a mission in April 1944. The Mustang would eventually provide full-mission fighter escort for USAAF bombing missions over Germany.*

LEFT: *A dogfight over the Western Front during WWI results in the destruction of an Allied fighter.*

BELOW: *Vapour trails from aerial combat lace the skies over southern England during the Battle of Britain, one of the few campaigns in history decided almost entirely by air power.*

INTRODUCTION

In aerial combat there is also a certain clinical detachment. The presence of one's opponent is always felt, and the intrusion of his willpower and cunning warps the contest, as it does over a chessboard. But his appearance, the many clues and inferences to a man's character that can be drawn from a scrutiny of his face and eyes, remain a mystery. Nor can the victor of an air combat ever see the actual effect of his prowess, those tenths of a second when a whiplash of bullets tears across the enemy's cockpit, smashing bone, leather and instruments; the sudden loss of pressurization as the canopy shatters at altitude; the rapid and catastrophic failure of the flying surfaces; the deluge of coolant; the orange blast of ignited fuel – even this last effect is observed only remotely, a minute gyrating speck signifying a transient triumph and a momentary lifting of danger.

Airmen, then, are different from other soldiers. They have to be navigators, mathematicians, experts in meteorology and geography. They have to be marksmen and athletes. But without the killer instinct, the animal tenacity that holds the jaws clenched for those critical seconds longer than seems physically possible, their survival is at risk. They are above all others an élite, and their tales are the tales of heroes.

The aim of this book is partly to permit the reader to share in the experiences of the pilots who have flown in combat over the past century, from the twisting dogfights over Flanders in World War I to the faster-than-sound encounters of modern jet fighters. The aircraft are arranged in pairs, mostly as combat adversaries, but some as combat

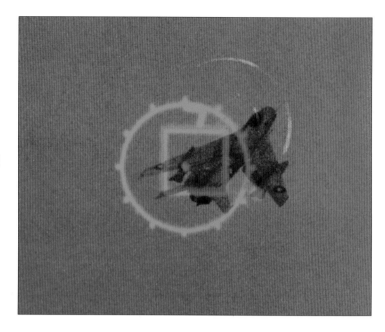

ABOVE: *A Shenyang F-6 – a Chinese-built version of the Mikoyan-Gurevich MiG-19 – is here seen caught in the gunsight of its adversary. MiG fighters of the Cold War era were extremely manoeuvrable and were a serious threat to faster and more advanced fighters such as the F4 Phantom II.*

BELOW: *A Nakajima 'Kate' torpedo bomber erupts in flames after being hit by anti-aircraft fire from the USS* Yorktown. *Air power was the deciding factor in naval supremacy in the Pacific theatre.*

ABOVE: *USAF fighter pilots, standing in front of a McDonnell Douglas F4 Phantom II, indicate the number of air combat kills following an operation during the Vietnam War. The Phantom was introduced into Vietnam purely with air-to-air missile armament, but a cannon was later added to the nose section after it was acknowledged that lack of gun weaponry was a serious deficiency when dogfighting with manoeuvrable Russian-designed fighters.*

competitors – types that were on the same side but were in competition with one another. Others are paired for purposes of comparison – types that were designed to perform a specific task but performed it in very different environments and combat circumstances.

The story begins over Flanders in 1918, with the Fokker Triplane made famous as the mount of Manfred von Richthofen – the famous Red Baron. This is compared to the Spad XIII that was used to such good effect by all the Allied flying services, and which provided the means for the newly arrived pilots of the United States Air Service to stand a chance in air combat against their highly experienced and battle-hardened German adversaries. This was the aircraft that saw the rise of the first American air aces, founding a tradition of gallantry that was to be the hallmark of American aviators for decades to come.

The first part of the book follows the progress of aircraft design from the biplane era to the monoplane fighters and bombers that were the mainstay of all the principal air forces in the early years of World War II – aircraft like Italy's Savoia-Marchetti SM.79, Britain's famous Vickers Wellington and Supermarine Spitfire, and Germany's Messerschmitt Me 109. The latter part of the decade between the wars

ABOVE: *The McDonnell Douglas F-15 Eagle is arguably the defining fighter aircraft design of the late 20th century. It has a powerful rate of climb, a 2655km/h (1649mph) top speed and excellent manoeuvrability, and can perform roles ranging from air interception to ground attack.*

BELOW: *The F-16 Fighting Falcon is a lightweight fighter system built by General Dynamics. Its shape is aerodynamically unstable, but this allows for the tight manoeuvres demanded of dogfighting aircraft, and the F-16 can pull 9g even with weaponry on the underwing hardpoints.*

ABOVE: *The Sukhoi Su-27 Flanker entered service in the 1980s as a high-performance air-superiority fighter. With excellent manoeuvrability and a top speed of 2500km/h (1553mph/h), when it emerged onto the world stage it was seen as more than a match for even the F-15 Eagle.*

saw the emergence of aircraft that would become legendary, and would alter the pattern of air warfare – aircraft like the notorious Junkers Ju 87 Stuka dive-bomber that was to rampage across Europe and the Middle East in 1940–41, and the Douglas Dauntless, whose action at Midway in the Pacific would change the course of the war in that theatre.

The story moves on to the later war years, when new and revolutionary combat aircraft laid the foundation of a fast and highly technological type of air warfare that would dictate the course of air combat for decades to come. It devolved directly into the first and most dangerous decade of the Cold War, when air power doctrine was

dominated by the development of the nuclear-armed strategic jet bomber – and the means to shoot it down.

The remaining period of the Cold War era saw a further air power revolution, with the emphasis gradually moving away from weapons of mass destruction to 'smart' weapons, delivered by aircraft like the Grumman A-6 Intruder, that were the key to success in limited wars. The story of the combat aircraft, in the pages of this book, ends with those aircraft optimized to conduct aerial police actions around the world – actions in which former adversaries like the F-15 and the MiG-29 are often on the same side, and aircrews of NATO and the old Warsaw Pact stand firmly in alliance with one another.

BELOW: *The Northrop B-2 Spirit bomber costs in the region of $900 million (£640 million). Its 'stealth' technology renders it almost invisible to enemy radar systems, and it is designed to perform precision-strike operations deep within enemy territories.*

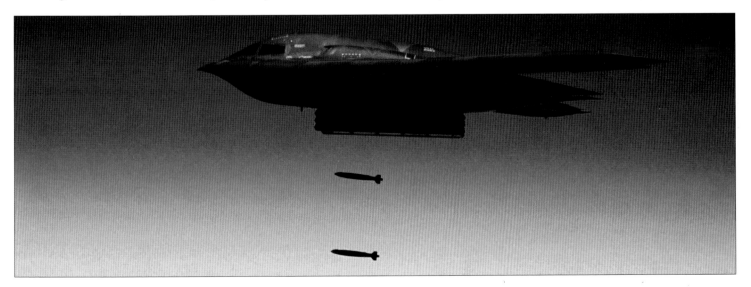

FROM BIPLANE TO DIVE-BOMBER

The two decades that separated World Wars I and II saw huge technological strides in the development of combat aircraft. Yet 15 of those years passed before designers finally accepted that the cantilever monoplane, with its single strong spar running from wingtip to wingtip and traversing the fuselage, was a far better proposition than the strut-and-wire-braced biplane. Consequently, it was the mid-1930s before the monoplane fighters and bombers that would play such an enormous part in the coming conflict began to leave the drawing boards of the world's leading aircraft manufacturers.

The key to the development of successful combat aircraft during this period was the high-performance aero-engine, and in this respect it seemed that the Americans and French had established commanding positions in the years immediately after World War I. Foreign record-breaking successes in the air spurred leading British aero-engine manufacturers into re-examining their engine design philosophy. From the Rolls-Royce stable came the Kestrel, which represented a considerable advance over previous engines and was selected to power the RAF's highly successful Hawker Hart light bomber and Hawker Fury fighter.

The Kestrel in its ultimate form – the Kestrel V – went on to be developed into the PV-12, the prototype of the engine that was to play such an enormous part in World War II – the Rolls-Royce Merlin. Ironically, it was an imported Rolls-Royce Kestrel that powered the prototype of Germany's most famous fighter, the Messerschmitt Bf 109.

ABOVE: *A Douglas SBD-3 Dauntless light bomber. The Dauntless began its military service in 1940 and was central to the US carrier victory in the Pacific.*

LEFT: *Aircrew of RAF No.23 Squadron at Kenley stand in front of a line of Gloster Gamecocks. The Gamecock had a 25 per cent loss rate to accidents.*

As far as radial engines were concerned, British efforts in the immediate post-war years were not particularly successful. The first generation of post-war British fighters – types such as the Siskin, Grebe and Flycatcher – were powered by the Armstrong Siddeley Jaguar, a heavy, complex and cumbersome two-row radial that suffered from a short running life and lubrication problems. The situation improved in 1925 with the introduction of the Bristol Jupiter; this powered the Gloster Gamecock, the first really viable British fighter of post-war design, and the later Bristol Bulldog. The Jupiter's successor, the Mercury, was installed in the RAF's last biplane fighter, the Gloster Gladiator, and in the Bristol Blenheim, which formed the backbone of the RAF's bomber force at the outbreak of World War II. A more powerful radial, the Bristol Hercules, was installed in the redoubtable Bristol Beaufighter, which was conceived just before the outbreak of war and which, together with airborne radar, went on to defeat the Luftwaffe's night bombers in 1941.

By the mid-1930s, Rolls-Royce had established a firm lead in high-performance liquid-cooled aero-engine development, and in 1934 their PV-12 was approved for installation in a new monoplane fighter then being developed by the Hawker Aircraft Company, the Fury Monoplane – later to be called the Hurricane. Similarly, it was the PV-12 that was chosen to power Supermarine's monoplane fighter design, based on the S.6 floatplane of Schneider Trophy fame – the aircraft that was to become the incomparable Spitfire.

In the United States, despite the success of the liquid-cooled Curtiss D.12, aero-engine manufacturers – notably Wright and Pratt & Whitney – concentrated on the development of radial engines for the new generation of combat aircraft such as the Douglas Dauntless naval dive-bomber. Both firms were to make an outstanding contribution to military aviation in World War II.

Fokker Dr.I

The success of the British Sopwith Triplane impressed the German High Command, and all the German aircraft makers were ordered to produce a triplane, or *Dreidecker*, design. Of all the designs that emerged, only two, the Pfalz Dr.I and the Fokker Dr.I, entered production, and only 10 of the former were built. Anthony Fokker was reluctant to spend time on a triplane, but produced an aircraft based around the fuselage of an experimental biplane named the V4. To this was added three fabric-covered wings and an aerofoil-section wheel axle. Two pre-production V4s were shipped to the front for evaluation in late August 1917 as the F.I, and these were evaluated by ace World War I pilots Manfred von Richthofen and Werner Voss. Richthofen's machine, F.I 102/17, was soon painted overall red, and he rapidly scored his sixtieth victory in it.

Werner Voss was shot down and killed on 23 September 1917 after an epic dogfight, and the 'Red Baron's F.I was lost with another pilot at the controls. Production Fokker Dr.Is entered service with JG 1, Richthofen's 'Flying Circus' in October. Only 320 production aircraft were built, and peak strength in the German Imperial Army Air Service (*Luftstreitkräfte*) never exceeded 170 aircraft.

FOKKER DR.I

Specification

Type: triplane fighter

Crew: 1

Powerplant: one 82.1kW (110hp) Oberursel UR.II, nine-cylinder rotary piston engine

Performance: max speed 185km/h (115mph); service ceiling 6100m (20,013ft); endurance 1 hour 30 minutes

Dimensions: wing span 7.19m (23ft 7in); length 7.19m (18ft 11in); height 2.9m (9ft 8in)

Weight: loaded 586kg (1292lb)

Armament: two synchronized 7.92mm (0.31in) LMG 08/15 machine guns

JASTA 11, JAGDGESCHWADER 1, LUFTSTREIKRÄFTE, CAPPY, FRANCE, 1918

The Dr.I was very successful in the German spring offensive of 1918 and achieved lasting fame in the hands of Richthofen, the 'Red Baron', who scored 20 of his 80 kills in at least three different examples, including 425/17 shown here. Richthofen himself was shot down in this aircraft on 21 April 1918. The remains of the Red Baron's Fokker Triplane were displayed in Berlin after World War I, but were destroyed by Allied bombing in 1944 during World War II.

SPAD XIII

In May 1917, the French Escadrilles de Chasse on the Western Front began to standardize on a new type, the SPAD XIII. Like its predecessor, it was an excellent gun platform and was extremely strong, although it was tricky to fly at low speeds. Powered by a Hispano-Suiza 8Ba engine and armed with two forward-firing Vickers guns, it had a maximum speed of nearly 225km/h (140mph) – quite exceptional for that time – and was capable of climbing to 6710m (22,000ft). The SPAD XIII subsequently equipped more than 80 escadrilles, and 8472 were built. The type also equipped 16 squadrons of the American Expeditionary Force,

which purchased 893 examples, and was supplied to Italy, which still had 100 in service in 1923. After World War I, surplus French SPAD XIIIs were sold to Belgium (37), Czechoslovakia, Japan and Poland (40).

The SPAD XIII was described by American air ace Captain Eddie Rickenbacker as 'the best ship I ever flew'. A rugged aircraft, well able to withstand the stresses of a dogfight, the SPAD XIII had a higher speed than any rotary-engined aircraft at the front during World War I. What the machine lacked in manoeuvrability, it more than made up for in rate of climb and maximum speed.

SPAD XIII

Specification

Type: scouting biplane

Crew: 1

Powerplant: one 164 kW (220hp) Hispano-Suiza 8BEc eight-cylinder Vee-type engine

Performance: max speed 224km/h (139mph); service ceiling 6650m (21,815ft); endurance 2 hrs

Dimensions: wing span 8.1m (26ft 7in); length 6.3m (20ft 8in); height 2.35m (7ft 8in)

Weight: 845kg (1863lb) loaded

Armament: two 7.62mm (0.30in) machine guns

ESCADRILLE SPA.48, ESCADRILLE DE CHASSE, AVIATION MILITAIRE WESTERN FRONT, 1917
The example of the SPAD XIII illustrated here bears the crowing cockerel emblem of SPA.48, derived from the unit's motto *Chante et Combat* ('Sing and Fight'). SPA.48 also used SPAD S.VIIs, which were generally uncamouflaged. This type was flown by French air ace Georges Guynemer, who scored 54 victories before being shot down and killed in September 1917. An example is preserved at the French Air Force Academy, Salon-de-Provence.

FOKKER DR.I VS SPAD XIII

MADE FAMOUS AS the red-painted mount of Baron Manfred von Richthofen, the Fokker Dr.I was introduced into service in October 1917.

Although the Dr.I was extremely manoeuvrable, it was already outclassed by a new generation of fighter biplanes, and it was never used in large numbers. The fact that it achieved success in combat was due more to the experienced pilots who flew it.

German Aces

It took an exceptional pilot to get the best out of the nimble and highly manoeuvrable Dr.I. Manfred von Richthofen was its main exponent, but there were others, the most notable being Werner Voss, known to his comrades as the 'Hussar of Krefeld' because of his cavalry background. In April 1917 Voss became one of the small band of top-ranking German pilots selected to test the DR.I, and when he took it up for the first time he knew instinctively that the little fighter was a thoroughbred.

It would be several weeks before the Dr.I reached the frontline squadrons, and in the meantime Voss was given command of a *Staffel* equipped with Albatros D.Vs, which he led in his triplane.

By the end of July 1917, when Voss's score had risen to 30 enemy aircraft destroyed, the whole *Staffel* had been equipped with the Dr.I, and in the first 10 days of August Voss destroyed five more Allied machines while flying the type. He accounted for a further four aircraft before the end of the month, and in September he demonstrated his prowess still further by achieving a series of multiple victories.

Voss adopted his own personal colour scheme, having his aircraft painted all black with a white skull and crossbones design on either side of the fuselage.

On the morning of the 5th he shot down a Sopwith Pup, and later that day destroyed a French Caudron reconnaissance aircraft. Five days later, he surprised a formation of three Sopwith Camels,

BELOW: The Fokker Triplane, mount of some of Germany's leading air aces, was inspired by Britain's Sopwith Triplane of 1916.

ABOVE: *This immaculate SPAD XIII is seen airborne in 1960. At the controls is American pilot Cole Palen, who owned a collection of vintage World War I types.*

shot one down with his first firing pass, put a burst into another that broke up in mid-air, and chased the third until it made its escape. He then sighted an FE.2d and attacked it; the wings were torn off the British biplane.

On 23 September, 1917, Werner Voss claimed his 48th victim, but after a furious dogfight he was himself shot down and killed by Lieutenant Arthur Rhys-Davids of No. 56 Squadron, Royal Flying Corps (RFC). A superb and fearless fighter in the air, Voss had achieved complete mastery over his aircraft.

French Adversary

The French ace of aces was René Fonck, who ended the war with 75 victories and who flew Spad XIIs and XIIIs with the famous Escadrille de Cigognes. Fonck was meticulous in his approach to air fighting. He constantly devised new methods of exercising his vision, heart, muscles and reflexes, as well as making sure that his machine and its armament were technically perfect.

Fonck brought his own brand of science to air combat, spending hours of his precious leisure time working out such things as relative speeds and deflection angles. He inspected as many shot-down enemy aircraft as possible, not because of any macabre fascination, but because he wanted to work out the 'dead spots' in the enemy's field of vision.

Correct positioning and superb marksmanship were Fonck's twin secrets; he could hit a one-franc piece with a rifle bullet when most other people could not even see the coin.

In the air, Fonck's economy in the use of ammunition was almost legendary; he seldom used more than a dozen bullets to despatch an adversary.

The Spad XIII was by no means as manoeuvrable as the Fokker Triplane, but it was faster and it had an excellent rate of climb, both of which were used to good advantage by Fonck and other leading Spad pilots. Fonck's tactics were simple enough. He would fly high, so that he was almost always above his opponent; then, choosing his moment carefully, he would use his height and speed advantage to achieve surprise. Thanks to his excellent aim, one firing pass was usually enough to send his enemy down. Avoiding a turning fight, he would then use his excess speed to climb back to altitude.

Fonck described one memorable air battle. It took place on 16 July 1918, as he was flying from Paris to join his unit at Trecon, having been recalled from leave.

'I sighted a pair of LVG two-seaters directly over the lines, with six Fokker D.VIIs 1500 feet [460m] higher up. Despite the fact that my Spad was encumbered by two suitcases and a case of wine, stuffed under my feet in the cockpit, I decided to attack. Ignoring the Fokkers, I made one pass against the two-seaters and sent both down in flames. The Fokkers pursued me, bent on revenge, but I out-ran them and made a safe landing at Trecon, my precious bottles intact...'

Bristol Bulldog II

Together with the Hawker Fury, the Bristol Bulldog epitomized Royal Air Force (RAF) Fighter Command in the 1930s. The prototype Bristol Type 105 Bulldog flew as a contender for an RAF fighter specification in May 1927. A 'fly-off' was arranged between the Bristol and the slightly superior Hawker Hawfinch, and the modified Type 105A was selected as the Bulldog II in 1928. Two factors in its favour were its more modern steel tube structure and cheaper Jupiter radial engine. The 92 Mk IIs were followed by 268 of the Mk IIA with a more powerful Jupiter as its powerplant.

Although possessing better handling than its predecessor, the Sopwith Snipe, the Bristol Bulldog was not very much faster or better climbing, and its armament of two machine guns was the same. The Bulldog did, however, introduce a radio and oxygen supply for the first time in an RAF fighter. Due to the conservative approach of the Air Ministry, which issued overcautious specifications, British fighter development was to progress little in the 1920s. The RAF's fighters remained biplanes with two or four rifle-calibre machine guns until the Hurricane and Spitfire entered service in 1937–38.

BRISTOL BULLDOG II

Specification

Type: single-seat day fighter

Crew: 1

Powerplant: one 440kW (330hp) Bristol Jupiter VIIF radial piston engine

Performance: max speed 280km/h (174mph); service ceiling 8930m (29,300ft); range 563km (350 miles)

Dimensions: wing span 10.31m (33ft 10in); length 7.62m (25ft); height 2.99m (9ft 10in)

Weight: 1601kg (3530lb) loaded

Armament: two 7.7mm (0.303in) Vickers machine guns

NO. 23 SQUADRON, ROYAL AIR FORCE FIGHTER COMMAND, RAF BIGGIN HILL, KENT, 1932

No. 23 Squadron was one of 10 frontline units that operated the Bulldog between 1929 and 1937. No. 23's Bulldog era in fact only lasted from 1931 to 1933. This aircraft, K1678, served with the squadron throughout this period, before going to No. 2 Aircraft Servicing Unit (ASU) until it was struck off charge in August 1938. The squadron flew multi-place fighters into the 1960s when it received the single-seat Lightning. Returning to two-seaters with the Phantom and Tornado F.3, No. 23 Squadron exists today as the operator of some of the RAF's Sentry AEW.1 AWACS aircraft at RAF Waddington.

Polikarpov I-16

The Polikarpov I-16, which first flew on 31 December 1933, was the first production monoplane in the world to feature a retractable undercarriage. The type saw considerable action during its career, starting with the Spanish Civil War.

The I-16 – nicknamed 'Mosca' ('Fly') by the Republicans and 'Rata' ('Rat') by the Nationalists – proved markedly superior to the Heinkel He 51. It was also faster than its most numerous Nationalist opponent, the Fiat CR.32, although the Italian fighter was slightly more manoeuvrable and provided a better gun platform.

In 1937–39 the I-16 also saw action during the Sino-Japanese conflict and over the disputed Khalkhin-Gol area on the Soviet-Manchurian border. I-16s also took part in the Russo-Finnish 'Winter War' of 1939–40, specializing mainly in low-level attacks on Finnish airfields by flights of three or four aircraft.

The I-16 still equipped the majority of the Red Air Force's first-line fighter units at the time of the German invasion in June 1941. The I-16 continued to operate as a first-line combat aircraft on the Leningrad front and in the Crimea until 1942. Altogether, 6555 examples of the I-16 were built before production ended in 1940.

POLIKARPOV I-16

Specification
Type: fighter
Crew: 1
Powerplant: one 820kW (1100hp) Shvetsov M-63 nine-cylinder
radial engine
Performance: 489km/h (304mph); service ceiling 9000m (29,530ft);
range 700km (435 miles)
Dimensions: 9.00m (29ft 6in); length 6.13m (20ft 1in); height 2.57m
(8ft 5in)
Weight: 2095kg (4619lb) loaded
Armament: four 7.62mm (0.30in) machine guns or two 7.62mm
(0.30in) machine guns and two 20mm (0.79in) cannon; external
bomb and rocket load of 500kg (1102lb)

4TH ESCUADRILLA DE MOSCAS, SPANISH REPUBLICAN AIR ARM, 1938
The first machines to arrive in Spain went into battle on 15 November 1936, providing air cover for a Republican offensive against Nationalist forces advancing on Valdemoro, Sesena and Equivias. The distinctive 'Popeye' marking on the tail of this I-16 signifies that it is an aircraft of the 4th Escuadrilla. This particular aircraft, coded CM-125, was lost on 13 September 1938.

BRISTOL BULLDOG VS POLIKARPOV I-16

ALTHOUGH OBSOLETE by 1939, the Bristol Bulldog performed creditably in action with the Finnish Air Force against far superior Russian equipment during the so-called 'Winter War' of 1939–40.

The first contact between Finnish Bulldogs and Russian aircraft occurred in the morning of 1 December, when two Bulldogs of LLv 26 were attacked by six Polikarpov I-16 fighters. In the ensuing melée the two Bulldogs became separated, leaving one pilot, Flight Sergeant Toivo Uuttu, to face the enemy alone. He scored some hits on an I-16, which subsequently crashed to become the first aerial victim of the Winter War. Uuttu himself was also forced to make a crash-landing, in which he was injured.

It was clear that the Bulldog was completely outclassed by this nimble Russian aircraft – the first monoplane fighter in the world to feature a retractable undercarriage.

Before the end of the month more Russian aircraft – two SB-2 bombers and an I-16 – were also shot down by the Bulldog pilots, and a further SB-2 was destroyed in January, but it was clear that the

BELOW: The Bristol Bulldog served valiantly with Finland during the Winter War of 1939–1940, despite its obvious shortcomings.

Bulldog was completely outclassed by this nimble Russian aircraft – the first monoplane fighter in the world to feature a retractable undercarriage.

Export Success

When the Bristol Bulldog entered service with the Royal Air Force in the early 1930s, it represented a considerable advance over earlier fighter types, particularly in terms of speed, and attracted a healthy export market. The seventeen aircraft supplied to Finland had a number of refinements, including an uprated Bristol Mercury VIS2 engine, and some were fitted with skis.

Towards the end of the Winter War, I-16s were used increasingly for ground-attack work. Several of the Russian I-16 units became adept in hit-and-run intruder tactics, ranging deep inside Finnish territory in flights of three or four aircraft. On several occasions Finnish aircraft were caught by marauding I-16s just as they were landing or taking off, a number being lost in this way.

Bristol Bulldogs also fought in the Spanish Civil War, as did I-16s. In this case both types were on the Republican side, some of the Bulldogs being flown by English pilots and the I-16s by Russian

ABOVE: The I-16 was used to attack German ground forces during the defence of Moscow in 1941, and continued in front line service until late 1943.

'volunteers' as well as Spanish Republicans. The Russians tended to be squadron and flight commanders. In the later stages of the conflict in Spain, obsolete types like the Bulldog were concentrated into a single unit known as the 'Krone Circus' after its commander, which was employed in the defence of Santander.

> **Apart from the obvious differences in design and performance, the main difference was in the armament of the two types. Whereas the Bulldog had only two machine guns, the I-16 had four, or alternatively two machine guns and two cannon.**

In Spain, I-16s were used extensively for ground-attack work. Some of their most successful missions were flown in March 1937, when five Italian divisions numbering some 30,000 men, fighting on the side of the Spanish Nationalists, advanced along the Barcelona highway from the village of Algora. Within 48 hours the Italians had advanced 32km (20 miles), the Republican forces falling back ahead of them in good order. In fact, the Republicans had known about the attack several days before it happened, and the reason for their orderly withdrawal soon became apparent. On 10 March, over 100 Republican aircraft, including many I-16s, swept down on the congested highway and cut the Italians to pieces. The road quickly became clogged with burning transports as the Italians fought to get out of the bottleneck, only to get bogged down in clinging mud caused by heavy rainfall the day before.

Armament Differences

Thanks to the proximity of their airfields, the Republican fighter-bombers were able to mount incessant attacks throughout that day. The two Italian fighter wings and three bomber squadrons which had been meant to cover the advance, however, were operating from Soria, in the north, and there was high ground between their base and the combat area. Consequently, when bad weather clamped down, only small numbers of Italian aircraft managed to find their way through the fogbound hills to oppose the deluge of Republican aircraft. The Republicans counter-attacked in strength and rolled the Italians back 16km (10 miles). The Italians lost over 4000 dead and wounded, and large quantities of their equipment was either destroyed during the strafing attacks or had to be abandoned in the mud.

It would perhaps be unfair to make a searching comparison between the Bristol Bulldog and the Polikarpov I-16, because the Bulldog was already obsolete by the time the Russian fighter made its appearance. Apart from the obvious differences in design and performance, the main difference was in the armament of the two types. Whereas the Bulldog had only two machine guns, the I-16 had four, or alternatively two machine guns and two cannon.

Messerschmitt Bf 109

The prototype Messerschmitt Bf 109V-1 flew for the first time in September 1935, and by the time World War II began in September 1939, 1060 Bf 109s of various subspecies were in service with the Luftwaffe's fighter units. These included the Bf 109C and Bf 109D, which were already being replaced by the Bf 109E series; this model was to be the mainstay of the Luftwaffe's fighter units throughout 1940. The series extended to the E-9, including models built as fighters, fighter-bombers and reconnaissance aircraft. Ten Bf 109Es were converted for

operations from Germany's planned aircraft carrier, the *Graf Zeppelin*, under the designation Bf 109T.

The Bf 109E-3, the Royal Air Force's principal fighter opponent in the Battle of France, featured four MG17 machine guns, two mounted in the nose and two in the wings, and an engine-mounted FF cannon firing through the propeller boss; however, complaints about this arrangement led to the deletion of the nose-mounted cannon, two Oerlikons being installed in the wings of the Bf 109E-4 variant, which equipped most German fighter units during the Battle of Britain.

MESSERSCHMITT BF 109E-4

Specification
Type: fighter
Crew: 1
Powerplant: one 876kW (1175hp) Daimler-Benz DB 601Aa
  12-cylinder inverted-Vee engine
Performance: max speed 560km/h (348mph); service ceiling
  10,500m (34,450ft); range 660km (410 miles)
Dimensions: wing span 9.87m (32ft 4.5in); length 8.64m (28ft 4.5in);
  height 2.50m (8ft 2.33in)
Weight: 2665kg (5875lb) loaded
Armament: two 20mm (0.79in) cannon and two 7.92mm (0.31in)
  machine guns

I GRUPPE, JAGDGESCHWADER 3, LUFTWAFFE, GRANDVILLIER, FRANCE, AUGUST 1940
The Bf 109E-4 seen here was the personal aircraft of *Gruppenkommandeur* Hans von Hahn, and displays the emblem of I *Gruppe*, *Jagdgeschwader* (I/JG 3), a *Tatzelwurm* (serpent with claws), on its nose. The emblem was applied in green to *Stab* (staff flight) aircraft, in white to aircraft of 1. *Staffel*, in red to aircraft of 2. *Staffel*, and in yellow to aircraft of 3. *Staffel*. Hans von Hahn ended the war with 34 kills.

Hawker Hurricane

Built to essentially the same specification as the Spitfire and fitted with the same Merlin engine, the Hawker Hurricane was slower and less manoeuvrable, but was a more stable gun platform and was often available where and when Spitfires were not. The Hurricane prototype flew in November 1935 and was the most numerous and effective fighter in Royal Air Force (RAF) service during the Battle of Britain.

Although thereafter quickly replaced on home defence duties, the Hurricane was issued to units in the Mediterranean, North Africa and Far East, where it was often the best Allied fighter available. Hurricanes distinguished themselves in the defence of Malta, in North Africa and on the Burma front.

The Hurricane Mk II had a Merlin XX with two-stage supercharger and spawned many subvariants, differing mainly in their armament. The IID was a dedicated ground-attack version, armed with two heavy cannon for the tank-busting role and fitted with additional armour on the undersides. Success with the Mk IID led to the Hurricane Mk IV, which possessed the same gun armament as the Mk IID, but was capable of exchanging the cannon pods for rockets or bombs.

HAWKER HURRICANE MK IID

Specification

Type: single-seat ground-attack fighter

Crew: 1

Powerplant: one 955kW (1280hp) Rolls-Royce Merlin XX V-12 piston engine

Performance: max speed 460km/h (286mph); service ceiling 10,365m (34,000ft); range 740km (460 miles)

Dimensions: wing span 12.19m (40ft 0in); length 9.81m (32ft 2in); height 3.95m (12ft 11.5in)

Weight: 3719kg (8200lb) loaded

Armament: two 40mm (1.5in) Vickers S guns in underwing pods and two 7.7mm (0.303in) Browning machine guns in wings

No. 6 Squadron, Desert Air Force, Royal Air Force, Tunisia, 1943

HV663 was built in late 1943 and shipped to North Africa, where it was initially used at No. 71 Operational Training Unit (OTU) at Carthago, Sudan. It was then assigned to No. 6 Squadron, nicknamed the 'Flying Can-Openers', which had operated the Hurricane Mk IID from June 1942. The squadron moved from Egypt into the combat zone in February 1943, and supported the Eighth Army all the way to Tunisia, taking a large toll of Afrika Korps vehicles with their powerful 40mm (1.5in) cannon.

MESSERSCHMITT BF 109 VS HAWKER HURRICANE

THE HAWKER HURRICANE was the workhorse fighter for the RAF throughout World War II, although it met a formidable opponent in the Messerschmitt Bf 109E.

One RAF Fighter Pilot, Wing Commander (then Flying Officer) Jack Rose of No. 32 Squadron, recalled the virtues of the Hawker Hurricane during the Battle of France. 'During this period I became more and more impressed by the robust qualities of the Hurricane. I think that some of the emergency repairs that were carried out by the maintenance crews during those few days in France would have made Sydney Camm's hair stand on end, but they worked.'

Hurricane Attack

'On 19 May, after a few hectic days, I was flying one of a formation of six Hurricanes which had been ordered to patrol between Tournai and Oudenarde, about midway between Lille and Brussels, where we had been told to expect German bombers by ground control. We soon spotted twelve or so Heinkel 111s flying in close formation roughly

BELOW: The Messerschmitt Bf 109 was an excellent fighter in skilled hands, but it could be very tricky to land. Far more were destroyed in accidents than in actual combat.

level with us at 12,000 feet [3600m], and after a quick check of the sky for enemy fighters we attacked the German aircraft from astern.

'I suddenly saw tracer fly past and felt strikes on the Hurricane.'

'I was positioned to attack the Heinkel on the port flank of the enemy formation and closed very rapidly, firing for a few seconds up to very close range, and as I was about to break away the Heinkel's port engine erupted oil which covered my windscreen, almost completely blocking off my forward vision and making the reflector sight useless... I pulled a handkerchief from my right trouser pocket but I couldn't reach far enough to wipe the front of the windscreen clear without releasing my seat harness, so I had to do that and then set about cleaning the windscreen.

'As I was doing a speed of somewhere between stalling and cruising, my seat harness undone, more or less standing on the rudder stirrups and half out of the aircraft, concentrating on clearing the windscreen and with no armour plate behind, I suddenly saw tracer fly past and

ABOVE: A section of Hawker Hurricanes taking off on a sortie during the Western Desert campaign in 1942. The Hurricane played a key role in North Africa.

felt strikes on the Hurricane. I was being attacked from the rear by a 109 which had not been in sight a few seconds earlier – probably no German fighter pilot has ever had a more exciting target.

'At my low speed, immediate evasive action resulted in a spin, and from my point of view this was probably the best thing that could have happened. As I was spinning down I left a long trail of glycol and petrol which must have satisfied my German opponent that he need not waste any further rounds on me. I switched off the engine as soon as I became aware of the glycol and petrol spewing out, but carried on with the spin until the immediate danger of a second attack seemed over. After I had checked the spin and adjusted the Hurricane to a glide I had to decide whether to leave the aircraft in a hurry or try a landing without engine. Then, slightly to the west and 6–7000 feet [1800–2100m] below, I spotted the airfield of Seclin, just south of Lille... After a long zig-zag glide approach, still with the tell-tale stream behind, I used the hand pump to lock the undercarriage down and lowered the flaps in the last few seconds before touching down.'

German Adversary

The German air ace Adolf Galland, who flew Bf 109E-4s in the Battle of Britain, also noted the Hurricane's robustness.

'...she was on fire and ought to have been a dead loss.'

'Any encounter with British fighters called for maximum effort. One day on my way back from London I spotted a squadron of twelve Hurricanes north of Rochester. Attacking from 2500 feet [760m] above them and behind, I shot like an arrow between the flights and from ramming distance fired on one of the aircraft in the real line of the formation, tearing large pieces of metal out of the plane. At the last moment I pulled my nose up and leaped over her, then flew right through the centre of the enemy's formation. It was not a pleasant sensation... Luckily, the British had had a similar or even bigger fright than I. No one attacked.

'It was not as simple as this with another Hurricane I shot down west of Dungeness. I had damaged her so badly that she was on fire and ought to have been a dead loss. Yet she did not crash, but glided down in gentle curves. My flight companions and I attacked her three times without a final result. As I flew close alongside the flying wreck, by now thoroughly riddled, with smoke belching from her, from a distance of a few yards [metres] I saw the dead pilot sitting in his shattered cockpit, while his aircraft spiralled slowly to the ground as though piloted by a ghostly hand. I can only express the highest admiration for the British fighter pilots who, although technically at a disadvantage, fought bravely and indefatigably.'

Messerschmitt Bf 110

The first of three Bf 110 long-range escort fighter prototypes flew on 12 May 1936, with deliveries of the production Bf 110C-1 being made in 1938. The Bf 110C-2 differed from the C-1 only in its radio equipment. The C-2 and C-3 had modified 20mm (0.79in) cannon. A fighter-bomber version, the Bf 110C-4/B, carried two 250kg (550lb) bombs under the centre section. This variant was first issued to *Zerstörergeschwader* (ZG) I, and then to *Erprobungsgruppe* (EG) 210, formed to carry out attacks on Britain's coastal radar stations and other precision targets. The Bf 110C-5 was a special reconnaissance version.

Numerous other variants appeared, including the Bf 110C-6, with additional firepower, and the Bf 110C-7 specialized bomber, which could carry two 500kg (1100lb) bombs, making it necessary to strengthen the undercarriage. The Bf 110D and E could be used in either the fighter or bomber roles. The Bf 110F-1 (bomber), F-2 (heavy fighter), F-3 (long-range reconnaissance aircraft) and F-4 (night-fighter) had 970kW (1300hp) DB 601F engines; however, the final major production aircraft, the Bf 110G, produced in larger numbers than any other variant, adopted the 1007kW (1350hp) DB 605 engine. It was as a night-fighter, equipped with Lichtenstein AI radar, that the Bf 110 truly excelled.

MESSERSCHMITT BF 110C-4/B

Specification

Type: fast fighter-bomber

Crew: 2

Powerplant: two 1099 kW (1475hp) Daimler-Benz DB 605B-1 12-cylinder inverted-Vee type engines

Performance: Max speed 550km/h (342mph); service ceiling 8000m (26,245ft); range 1300km (808 miles)

Dimensions: wing span 16.25m (53ft 3in); length 13.05m (42ft 9in) including SN-2 radar antenna; height 4.18m (13ft 8in)

Weight: 9888kg (21,799lb) loaded

Armament: two 20mm (0.79in) cannon and four 7.92mm (0.31in) machine guns in the nose and one 7.92mm (0.31in) machine gun in the rear cockpit; two 250kg (550lb) bombs

II GRUPPE, ERPROBUNGSGRUPPE 210, LUFTWAFFE, SUMMER 1940

The Messerschmitt Bf 110C-4/B seen here carries the *Wespe* (Wasp) insignia of ZG I, the 1. *Staffel* of which formed the nucleus of II/EG 210. The distinctive wasp marking was retained when the surviving aircraft were returned to their original unit in 1942.

Bristol Blenheim

A privately funded prototype of the aircraft which was to evolve into the Bristol Blenheim, named 'Spirit of Britain', was first flown in 1935. The aircraft proved 80km/h (50mph) faster than the fighters of the day and was adopted by the Royal Air Force (RAF) as the basis of a new light bomber. The first Blenheim I flew in September 1936 and was ordered by several European nations in addition to Britain.

A number of the exported aircraft fell into Axis hands in the early years of World War II. By the time the production Blenheim was equipped with guns, armour plate and other military equipment, it had lost the edge it once had over fighters, which in turn had become faster. The snub-nosed Blenheim I was the first production model, some of which were built as Mk IF fighters. The Mk IV with an elongated nose was the most numerous version, with more than 3000 produced. Used in small numbers on daylight raids in 1939–41, the Mk IV bombers were easy prey for German flak and Messerschmitts. The last examples in regular RAF Bomber Command squadrons were retired in October 1942. They proved adequate with other commands in the night-fighter and anti-shipping roles, and later provided useful trainers for new bomber crews.

BRISTOL BLENHEIM MK IV

Specification

Type: twin-engined light bomber

Crew: 3

Powerplant: two 742kW (995hp) Bristol Mercury XV radial piston engines

Performance: max speed 428km/h (266mph); service ceiling 8300m (27,280ft); range 1810km (1215 miles)

Dimensions: wing span 17.22m (56ft 6in); length 12.98m (42ft 7in); height 2.99m (9ft 10in)

Weight: 6532kg (14,400lb) loaded

Armament: one 7.7mm (0.303in) machine gun in port wing and one in rear turret; up to 601kg (1325lb) of bombs

NO. 88 SQUADRON, ROYAL AIR FORCE BOMBER COMMAND, RAF ATTLEBRIDGE, 1941
Blenheim Z7427 is illustrated here in the colours of No. 88 Squadron at Attlebridge in Norfolk, where they were based from August 1941 to September 1942. It served with No. 105 Squadron before and after its time with No. 88. After that the aircraft went to No. 21 Squadron, and ended its days with an Operational Training Unit (OTU) in Scotland before being struck off charge as surplus in December 1943.

MESSERSCHMITT BF 110 VS BRISTOL BLENHEIM

THE BATTLE OF BRITAIN showed that the Messerschmitt Bf 110 was hopelessly miscast in the fighter-bomber role, just as it was in the role of long-range escort fighter.

On the morning of 12 August 1940, 24 hours before the main air offensive against England was due to begin, 21 Messerschmitt 109s and 110s of *Erprobungsgruppe* (EG) 210 took off from Calais-Marck airfield and set course at low level over the English Channel. As they approached the English coast they climbed and split up, heading for their individual targets. The 1. *Staffel*, comprising six Bf 110s led by *Oberleutnant* Martin Lutz, attacked the radar station at Pevensey, near Eastbourne, each aircraft dropping two 454kg (1000lb) bombs and causing damage to installations, while the Bf 109s of *Oberleutnant* Otto Hintze's 3. *Staffel* swept down on Dover, with similar results. Despite the damage, however, all the stations were operational again within three hours.

BELOW: The Messerschmitt Bf 110 was a failure in its intended role of long-range 'destroyer', but it went on to enjoy enormous success as a night fighter.

In the afternoon of 12 August, EG 210 attacked the forward airfield of Manston with 20 Messerschmitts. Manston was temporarily disabled. All the Messerschmitts returned to Calais-Marck with the exception of one, which crash-landed near Calais and was written off after an engagement with RAF fighters over the Channel.

Disastrous Raid

EG 210 was back in action on Wednesday 14 August, a day in which air operations were hampered by bad weather. Once again, Manston was the target. The attack was carried out by the Bf 110s of 1. *Staffel*, and on this occasion two 110s fell victim to Manston's anti-aircraft defences, three of the four crew members being killed.

The next day, 15 August, was disastrous for EG 210. In the early evening, 15 Bf 110s and eight Bf 109s set course over the Channel to attack Kenley, south of London, but they made a navigational error and bombed Croydon by mistake, destroying 40 training aircraft. One

ABOVE: *The Bristol Blenheim was faster than contemporary fighters when it first appeared, but suffered terrible losses in the early years of World War II.*

of the 110s was attacked by a Hurricane and crash-landed, its crew surviving to be taken prisoner.

The commander of EG 210, *Hauptmann* Walter Rubensdörffer, was an early casualty, his aircraft crashing in flames at 7pm after being attacked by Spitfires. Also at this time, a Bf 110C of II. *Staffel* was attacked and shot down by Squadron leader Worrall and Flight Lieutenant Crossley of No. 32 Squadron, its pilot being wounded and taken prisoner and the observer/gunner killed. Three more Bf 110s and a Bf 109 fell to the guns of the British fighters.

Blenheim Losses

The Bf 110 units suffered horrendous losses in the Battle of Britain; but the losses suffered by the Blenheim bomber squadrons of No. 2 Group, RAF Bomber Command, were even more tragic, as they had to be endured for a much longer period. Many of the Blenheims' operations were directed against targets in enemy-occupied Norway, involving a long over-water flight. In one attack directed against Stavanger airfield, 12 Blenheims of No. 107 Squadron set out, but six of them either failed to find the target or had to return because of appalling weather conditions.

'Soon after leaving the Scottish coast [one pilot told in his report] we ran into rain that was literally tropical in its fury. After some time we climbed and then the rain turned into snow. At 13,000 feet [4000m] the engines of two of the Blenheims became iced up and

stopped. One of the aircraft dropped more or less out of control until only 600 feet [180m] above the sea, when the engines started again.'

'The Focke-Wulf 190s always got through, and they made mincemeat out of us.'

Despite its growing obsolescence, the Blenheim continued to operate over Europe in daylight well into 1942. As one pilot recalled:

'I can remember flying a lot of sorties without seeing anything, but when the Luftwaffe did come up all hell was let loose. Our Spitfire escort could usually cope with Messerschmitt 109s, but the Focke-Wulf 190s always got through, and they made mincemeat out of us. One thing sticks in my mind very vividly. We had had a very hectic week, with almost continual operations in the Pas de Calais area and heavy losses... Then, on the last mission, half our escort didn't show up on time and we lost three out of six aircraft. As we turned back towards the coast, I remember thinking that if I'd had an Air Marshal in front of my nose gun I'd have shot him without a moment's hesitation. It was totally irrational, looking back, but a lot of us felt like that at the time...'

Lockheed Hudson

A conversion of Lockheed's Model 14 Super Electra design was ordered by the Royal Air Force (RAF) to fulfil its needs for a modern patrol bomber and navigation trainer in 1938. The prototype Hudson Mk I flew in December that year, and the initial order of 250 was completed by October 1939. The Hudson had a bomb bay instead of a freight hold and a Boulton-Paul defensive turret. There was also a ventral gun position, and two more forward-firing guns operated by the pilot. The airliner-type windows were retained and Hudsons saw much service as transports, as well as patrol aircraft with RAF Coastal Command and other users such as the Royal Australian Air Force and Royal New Zealand Air Force.

Development continued, and aircraft powered by both Wright Cyclone and Pratt & Whitney Twin Wasp engines rolled off the production lines with the designations A-28 and A-29. The Hudson VI was the A-28A. A total of 410 Hudson VIs went to the RAF and others to Canada.

LOCKHEED HUDSON

Specification

Type: twin-engined maritime patrol bomber

Crew: 4

Powerplant: two 895kW (1200hp) Pratt & Whitney R-1830-67
air-cooled radial engines

Performance: max speed 420km/h (261mph); service ceiling 8,220m
(27,000ft); range 3476km (2160 miles)

Dimensions: wing span 19.96m (65ft 6in); length 19.96m (44ft 4in);
height 3.63m (11ft 10in)

Weight: 8399kg (18,500lb) loaded

Armament: two forward-firing 7.62mm (0.30in) machine guns, two
in dorsal turret and one in ventral position; up to 726kg (1600lb)
bombs or depth charges

No. 48 Squadron, RAF Coastal Command, Royal Air Force, Gibraltar, 1943

FK395 was delivered to No. 48 Squadron of Coastal Command, then used for a time by the Air Transport Auxiliary. It was returned to No. 48 Squadron and finally ended up with the Airborne Forces Experimental Establishment at Ringway, Manchester. It was struck off charge in June 1946. No. 48 itself was based at North Front airfield on Gibraltar from December 1942 to February 1944, when it was reassigned to Transport Command and swapped its Hudsons for Dakotas. Equipped with ASV sea-search radar and armed with bombs and depth charges, the Gibraltar-based Hudsons hunted German U-boats in the Mediterranean. On 28 March 1943, a No. 48 Squadron Hudson attacked and damaged U-77 with depth charges east of Cartagena, Spain. The U-boat was finished off by another Hudson from No. 233 Squadron.

Focke-Wulf Fw 200 Kondor

Initially designed and flown as an airliner, the Focke-Wulf Kondor first flew in July 1937, after a remarkably quick development. The Japanese were impressed by the Kondor, and ordered several airliner versions. Additionally, the tenth development aircraft was completed as a prototype maritime patrol aircraft for the Imperial Japanese Navy. Japan's Kondors were never delivered.

On Hitler's orders, in the spring of 1939 the Luftwaffe Chief of Staff directed a young officer, *Oberstleutnant* Edgar Petersen, to establish a new unit to attack ships in the Bay of Biscay. To fulfil this role, the Kondor was adapted as the Fw 200C-0, and entered service with the I *Gruppe* of *Kampfgeschwader* 40 (I/KG 40) in 1940, initially with limited armament. The first true production model was the Fw 200C-1, armed with one cannon and four machine guns, and racks for bombs and mines under the wings and central fuselage. The Kondor was not stressed for all this extra weight, and many suffered structural failure on landing. Later versions had more guns and could even carry guided anti-ship missiles. Until the Allies introduced long-range patrol aircraft of their own and were able to base fighters in Iceland, the Kondor was the 'scourge of the Atlantic' and took a heavy toll of Allied shipping.

FOCKE-WULF FW 200C-1 KONDOR

Specification
Type: four-engined maritime patrol bomber
Crew: 5
Powerplant: four 619kW (830hp) BMW 132H radial piston engines
Performance: max speed 360km/h (224mph); service ceiling 6000m
  (19,685ft); range 4440km (2795 miles)
Dimensions: wing span 32.82m (107ft 8in); length 23.46m (76ft
  11.5in); height 6.3m (20ft 8in)
Weight: 22,700kg (50,045lb) loaded
Armament: three 7.92mm (0.31in) MG 15 machine guns and
  one 20-mm MG FF cannon; bomb load of up to four 250kg
  (551lb) bombs or two 1000kg (2205lb) mines

I/KG 40 IV FLIEGERKORPS, LUFTFLOTTE 3, BORDEAUX-MÉRIGNAC, FRANCE, 1940
Fw 200C-1 F8+AH was normally flown by *Gruppe* commander Edgar Petersen and his crew, who were quite successful judging by the ship kill markings on the aircraft's tailfin. On 5 February 1941, while flown by another pilot, this aircraft's luck ran out. Attacking a British convoy to the west of Ireland, it was hit and damaged by return fire. The aircraft then encountered dense fog and flew into Cashelfeane Hill, in County Cork. Five of the six crew aboard were killed; the sixth was badly burnt.

LOCKHEED HUDSON VS FOCKE-WULF FW 200 KONDOR

THE HUDSON WAS a tough bird, as more than one crew lived to testify. One Hudson captain, Pilot Officer Leslie Bennett, described what happened when his aircraft was pounced on by seven Messerschmitt 109s as it was attacking an enemy ship off the Norwegian coast in 1940.

'We were just making a second attack on the supply ship when they appeared. They were like a swarm of angry bees looking for trouble. They closed on us, and the fun began. My crew went to action stations. I opened up the engines, and we skimmed low over the waves. The Mes came up four on one side and three on the other. They kept on coming in, delivering beam attacks in turn. The guns were blazing away and I remember looking behind me into the smoke-filled cabin to see how things were going.'

Then the enemy fighters changed their tactics, attacking from ahead and astern.

Desperate Battle

'I watched them approaching over my shoulders, and every time one approached us head on I pulled the stick back and we jumped out of the line of fire. It was a sort of game of leapfrog. I could see the cannon shells and bullets zipping into the sea and churning it up into steam. Four holes suddenly appeared in the window beside my head, and shrapnel and bullets were coming into the back of the machine pretty steadily. I was flying in my shirt-sleeves and had hung my tunic in the back of the cabin.

'When I took it down again there were four neat bullet-holes...'

'Later in the fight I looked back again and saw blood on the floor. The wireless operator – he was a veteran of the last war – had been hit in the arm, but was carrying on with his gun. We were now going up towards some scattered cloud. Even there the fighters hung on for a while, playing hide-and-seek with us, but eventually we shook them off. The gunner asked permission to leave his turret. I found that he had been wounded in the leg, and he also had carried on without

BELOW: Developed from the Lockheed 14 airliner, the Hudson provided the RAF with a vital anti-submarine and patrol aircraft in the early part of World War II.

ABOVE: *In the early months of the war the Fw 200 was literally the scourge of the Atlantic, sinking more ships than the German U-boats.*

saying anything about it. While the navigator was bandaging him I asked him if he had had any luck. He held up one finger and grinned, then pointed down to the drink. Then he held up another, and pointed down slantingly. We had got one for certain and sent another gliding down apparently out of control.'

Long-range Killers

In the first half of 1941, German aircraft presented the main threat to British Atlantic and North Sea traffic. *Oberstleutnant* Edgar Petersen, an experienced long-range pilot, was given the task of forming the first long-range anti-shipping unit, KG 40, which was equipped with Focke-Wulf Fw 200 Kondors. He recalled that 'The Kondor had all the requirements of range, but it was by no means ideal. Its structure was much too weak for a military aircraft, especially in the area of the rear fuselage, and there were frequent structural failures, especially on landing.

'The range, however, was phenomenal. Operating from Bordeaux in France, we could fly out over the Atlantic to the west of Ireland and then go on to land in Norway.'

> **'Its structure was much too weak for a military aircraft, especially in the area of the rear fuselage, and there were frequent structural failures, especially on landing.'**

From 1 January 1941, KG 40 came under the control of the *Fliegerführer Atlantik*, a naval command. The Fw 200 threat began to diminish with the establishment of No. 252 Squadron RAF at Aldergrove, in Northern Ireland, in the spring of 1941. Equipped with long-range, heavily armed Bristol Beaufighters, the squadron and its successors formed a barrier of sorts between the German bombers and the convoys they were threatening.

Hudsons were occasionally encountered, but the Kondors' main adversary remained the Beaufighter, joined later by Grumman Martlets operating from escort carriers. Another solution from the Admiralty was for the convoys to take their own defensive aircraft with them. As a stop-gap measure until escort carriers became available, a makeshift system was devised whereby merchant ships were fitted with catapults from which a single fighter – a Hawker Hurricane or Fairey Fulmar – could be launched with rocket assistance, the pilot either ditching or bailing out after making his interception. Thirty-five merchant vessels were so equipped, and the first success was registered on 3 August 1941, when a Hurricane flown by Lieutenant Everett, RN, of No. 804 Squadron from the SS *Maplin* destroyed a Fw 200 644km (400 miles) from land. Five Kondors in all were shot down by the catapult fighters. But it was the escort carriers that spelled the end for the Kondors. In December 1942, Martlets from the first such carrier, HMS *Audacity*, shot down four Fw 200s before the carrier was sunk by a U-boat.

Savoia-Marchetti SM.79 Sparviero

The prototype SM.79 was a fast eight-seater airliner which flew for the first time in October 1934. Production of the military SM.79 Sparviero (Sparrowhawk) began in October 1936 and was to have an uninterrupted run until June 1943, by which time 1217 aircraft had been built.

The *Regia Aeronautica* lost no time in testing the SM.79 operationally in Spain, where the type was used with considerable success. When Italy entered World War II in June 1940, SM.79s accounted for well over half the Italian air force's total bomber strength. From June 1940 onwards, SM.79s saw continual action in the air campaign against Malta and in North Africa, becoming renowned for their high-level precision bombing, while the torpedo-bomber version was active against British shipping.

After the Italian surrender in September 1943, SM.79s continued to fly with both sides. The SM.79B, first flown in 1936, was a twin-engined export model, the middle engine being replaced by an extensively glazed nose.

SAVOIA-MARCHETTI SM.79 SPARVIERO

Specification

Type: torpedo bomber

Crew: 5

Powerplant: three 746kW (1000hp) Piaggio P.XI RC 40 radial engines

Performance: max speed 435km/h (270mph); service ceiling 6500m (21,325ft); range 1900km (1181 miles)

Dimensions: wing span 21.20m (69ft 2in); length 15.62m (51ft 3in); height 4.40m (14ft 5in)

Weight: 11,300kg (24,912lb) loaded

Armament: three 12.7mm (0.5in) and one 7.7mm (0.303in) machine guns; two 450mm (17.7in) torpedoes or 1250kg (2756lb) of bombs

283 Squadriglia, 130 Gruppo, Autonomo Aerosiluranti, Regia Aeronautica, Gerbini, Sicily, 1942

The 130 *Gruppo Autonomo Aerosiluranti* (Specialist Torpedo-Bomber Group), comprising the 280 and 283 *Squadriglie*, concentrated on attacking convoys to the besieged island of Malta, inflicting heavy damage on the convoy code-named 'Harpoon' which sailed from Gibraltar in June 1942. The SM.79 seen here features the standard 'sand-and-spinach' camouflage scheme, consisting of a sand-coloured base with mottles of two tones of green. In common with Luftwaffe aircraft operating in the Mediterranean, white theatre bands were worn around the rear fuselage and engine cowlings.

Vickers Wellington

The Vickers Wellington was designed by Barnes Wallis, who was later to conceive the mines that destroyed the Ruhr Dams. The prototype flew on 15 June 1936 and was lost on 19 April 1937, when it broke up during an involuntary high-speed dive, the cause being determined as elevator imbalance. As a result, the production Wellington Mk I and subsequent aircraft were fitted with a revised fin, rudder and elevator. The first Mk I, L4212, flew on 23 December 1937, and the first Bomber Command squadron to rearm, No. 9, began receiving its aircraft in December 1938.

The most numerous early model was the Mk IC, but the principal version in service with Bomber Command was the Mk III

(1519 built), with two 1119kW (1500hp) Bristol Hercules engines replacing the much less reliable Pegasus. The Wellington III entered service with the experienced No. 9 Squadron on 22 June 1941, and was to be the backbone of Bomber Command's night offensive against Germany until such time as the Command's four-engined heavy bombers became available in numbers. The last bomber version of the Wellington was the Mk X, of which 3803 were built, accounting for more than 30 per cent of all Wellington production. The Wellington was also used extensively by Royal Air Force (RAF) Coastal Command.

VICKERS WELLINGTON

Specification
Type: bomber
Crew: 6
Powerplant: two 1119kW (1500hp) Bristol Hercules XI radial
  engines
Performance: max speed 411km/h (255mph); service ceiling 5790m
  (19,000ft); range 2478km (1540 miles)
Dimensions: wing span 26.26m (86ft 2in); length 19.68m (64ft 7in);
  height 5.0m (17ft 5in)
Weight: 15,422kg (34,000lb) loaded
Armament: eight 7.7mm (0.303) machine guns; up to 2041kg
  (4500lb) of bombs

No. 115 Squadron, Royal Air Force, RAF Marham, Norfolk, 1942
No. 115 Squadron received its first Wellington Mk Is in April 1939 and was the first RAF unit to attack a mainland target in World War II, bombing the German-occupied airfield of Stavanger-Sola in Norway in April 1940. It used Wellington Mk IIIs from November 1941 until March 1943, when it received Lancasters.

SAVOIA-MARCHETTI SM.79 VS VICKERS WELLINGTON

ALTHOUGH THEY SHARED SIMILAR roles, there was one big difference between Italy's SM.79 and Britain's Wellington: the latter could survive heavy battle damage, while its Italian counterpart could not.

From the earliest days of the Axis campaign in North Africa, the SM.79 suffered serious losses at the hands of the RAF's Hawker Hurricanes, and when the British launched a counter-offensive in December 1940 many of the Italian bombers had to be abandoned on their airfields, having been rendered unserviceable through battle damage. The SM.79s escaped relatively unscathed in their early attacks on Malta, which was defended initially by only three Sea Gladiators, but when Hurricanes began to arrive in some numbers losses rose here, too.

Bombing Run

The British learned at a very early stage in the war that the Wellington was capable of surviving tremendous damage. On 18 December 1939, 24 Wellingtons of Nos 9, 37 and 149 Squadrons under the leadership of Wing Commander R. Kellett set out to attack units of the German Fleet. The aircraft were loaded with 227kg (500lb) semi-armour-piercing bombs and the crews were

BELOW: The SM.79 Sparviero was a very versatile aircraft. In its role as a torpedo bomber, it presented a significant threat to British convoys in the Mediterranean.

ordered to attack any shipping located in the Schillig Roads, Wilhelmshaven, or the Jade Estuary. The bombing level was to be at least 3048m (10,000ft). The bombers climbed to 4267m (14,000ft) in four flights of six aircraft. Less than an hour after leaving the English coast they were flying in a cloudless sky, with visibility more than 48km (30 miles). About two-thirds of the way across the North Sea, two aircraft dropped out with engine trouble and returned to base.

At 10.50 the bombers were detected by two experimental radar stations on Heligoland and Wangerooge, both equipped with the new 'Freya' detection apparatus. The officer in charge on Wangerooge immediately alerted the fighter operations room at Jever, only to be told that something must be wrong with his set; the British would never be foolhardy enough to mount an attack in a cloudless sky with brilliant sunshine.

Meanwhile, the 22 Wellingtons had made a detour round Heligoland to avoid the anti-aircraft batteries there and were now turning in towards Wilhelmshaven from the north. After a delay of several minutes the first German fighters, six Messerschmitt Bf 109s of X/JG 26, led by *Oberleutnant* Johannes Steinhoff, took off from Jever to intercept. None of the other fighter units at Jever or the

ABOVE: *RAF aircrew heading for their Wellington 1A bombers prior to a sortie. These Wellingtons belong to No. 149 Squadron, as indicated by their 'OJ' code markings.*

adjacent airfield of Wangerooge was on readiness, and there was a further delay before these were able to take off.

Steinhoff's 109s met the Wellingtons on the approach to Wilhelmshaven and scored their first two kills almost immediately. The fighters then sheered away as the bombers flew at 3962m (13,000ft) through heavy flak over the naval base. The Wellingtons crossed Wilhelmshaven without dropping any bombs, then turned and crossed it again, still without bombing, before heading away to the north-west. By this time, the Bf 109s of X/JG 26 had been joined by the twin-engined Messerschmitt 110s of ZG 76 and the Bf 109s of JG 77, and the combined force of fighters now fell on the Wellington formation as it passed to the north of Wangerooge.

Wellington Massacre

Another bomber went down, the victim of a Bf 110, and crash-landed on the island of Borkum. Only one crew member survived. Other Bf 110s accounted for five more Wellingtons in an area some 24km (15 miles) north-west of Borkum, and a sixth bomber was destroyed 48km (30 miles) north of the Dutch island of Ameland.

Manning the nose gun position of one of the Wellingtons, Aircraftman Charles Driver had the bottom and side of his turret blown away by cannon shells. 'The first thing I knew,' he said

afterwards, 'was that I felt pretty cold around my feet and legs. I looked down and saw water below me. The next thing I knew was that my guns refused to fire. I looked to see what was the matter and saw they'd been blown in halves at the barrels.'

> **'As I looked out I saw all the fabric flapping on the wings…. The nose of the aircraft was sheared away. The engines themselves looked as though someone had used a sledge hammer and chisel on them, the metal was all ripped away.'**

The Wellington's pilot, Sergeant Ramshaw, ordered Driver to step up to the astrodome and look out for more fighters. He was horrified by what he saw. 'As I looked out I saw all the fabric flapping on the wings. The insides were all exposed and you could see the way they were built up. It was as though someone had taken a great knife and carved all along the leading edge of the wings. The nose of the aircraft was sheared away, but I had closed the bulkhead doors to exlude the blast from the other part of the fuselage. The engines themselves looked as though someone had used a sledge hammer and chisel on them, the metal was all ripped away.'

Ramshaw managed to nurse the crippled aircraft almost to within sight of England before being forced to ditch in the sea. All the crew survived except Sergeant Lilley, the rear gunner, who had been killed during the fighter attacks. The airmen were picked up by a trawler and landed at Grimsby.

Macchi MC.202 Folgore

The Macchi MC.202 Folgore (Thunderbolt) was a direct descendant of the MC.200 Saetta (Lightning), the second of Italy's monoplane fighters, which was powered by a Fiat A74 radial engine and which first flew on 24 December 1937. Deliveries to the *Regia Aeronautica* began in October 1939, and about 150 aircraft were in service by June 1940.

Attempts to improve the performance of the MC.200 began in 1938, but it was not until early in 1940 that a suitable engine became available in the shape of the German Daimler-Benz DB 601A-1 liquid cooled in-line engine. This was installed in a standard Saetta airframe and flown on 10 August 1940. The subsequent flight tests produced excellent results, and the aircraft, designated MC.202 Folgore, was ordered into production fitted with the licence-built DB 601, the engine being produced by Alfa Romeo as the RA.1000 RC.411.

The type entered service with 1 *Stormo* at Udine in the summer of 1941, moving to Sicily to take part in operations over Malta in November. The Folgore remained in production until the Italian armistice of September 1943, although the rate of production was always influenced by the availability of engines. Macchi built 392 MC.202s, and around 1100 more were produced by other companies, mainly Breda.

MACCHI MC.202

Specification

Type: fighter

Crew: 1

Powerplant: one 802kW (1075hp) Alfa Romeo RA 1000 RC.411 12-cylinder inverted V-type

Performance: max speed 600km/h (373mph); service ceiling 11,500m (37,730ft); range 610km (379 miles)

Dimensions: wing span 10.58m (34ft 8|in); length 8.85m (29ft); height 3.50m (11ft 6in)

Weight: 2930kg (5490lb) loaded

Armament: two 12.7mm (0.5in) Breda-SAFAT and two 7.7mm (0.303in) machine guns; late-production aircraft, two 20mm (0.79in) cannon in wings

151 Squadriglia, 20 Gruppo, 51 Stormo, Regia Aeronautica, Sicily, 1942

The Macchi MC.202 Serie VII illustrated here was flown by Sergeant Ennio Tarantola of 151 *Squadriglia*, 20 *Gruppo*, 51 *Stormo* of the *Regia Aeronautica*. One of Italy's air aces, Tarantola had eight victories to his credit. His aircraft was named '*Dai Banana*' ('Go, Banana!'), Tarantola having been a banana importer before the outbreak of World War II.

Supermarine Spitfire

Converted from Mk I airframes, the Spitfire Mk V was the major Spitfire production version, with 6479 examples completed. The first examples entered service with Royal Air Force (RAF) Fighter Command in March 1941.

The majority of Spitfire Vs were armed with two 20mm (0.79in) cannon and four machine guns, affording a greater chance of success against armour plating. The Mk V was powered by a Rolls-Royce Merlin 45 engine, developing 1055kW (1415hp) at 5000m (19,000ft) against the 858kW (1150hp) of the Merlin XII fitted in the Mk II. Nevertheless, the Mk V was essentially a compromise aircraft, rushed into service to meet an urgent Air Staff requirement for a fighter with a performance superior to that of the latest model of Messerschmitt.

The debut of the Spitfire V came just in time, for in May 1941 the Luftwaffe fighter units began to receive the Messerschmitt Bf 109F; it had suffered from technical problems in its development phase, but these had now been resolved. The Spitfire V, however, failed to provide the overall superiority Fighter Command needed so badly. At high altitude, where many combats took place, it was found to be inferior to the Bf 109F on most counts, and several squadrons equipped with the Mk V took a severe mauling during that summer. The type gave good service, however, in North Africa, Sicily and Italy.

SUPERMARINE SPITFIRE V

Specification
Type: fighter/fighter-bomber
Crew: 1
Powerplant: one 1074kW (1440hp) Rolls-Royce Merlin 45/46/50 V-12 engine
Performance: max speed 602km/h (374mph); service ceiling 11,280m (37,000ft); range 756km (470 miles)
Dimensions: wing span 11.23m (36ft 10in); length 9.11m (29ft 11in); height 3.48m (11ft 5in)
Weight: 3078kg (6785lb) loaded
Armament: two 20mm (0.79in) cannon and four 7.7mm (0.303in) machine guns

No. 2 Squadron, South African Air Force, Sicily, 1943
No. 2 Squadron of the South African Air Force (SAAF), which was part of the Desert Air Force's No. 7 Wing, became operational in Sicily on 23 August 1943, subsequently moving to new bases on the Italian mainland.

MACCHI MC.202 FOLGORE VS SUPERMARINE SPITFIRE

IT WAS OVER THE embattled island of Malta that frequent encounters occurred between Spitfires and Macchi 202s.

One replacement RAF pilot who reached Malta on 3 June 1942, and who subsequently fought with the Italian fighters, was Flight Sergeant George Beurling, a Canadian who was to become Malta's best-known and top-scoring ace.

Beurling's arrival on Malta was dramatic. Seconds after he taxied his Spitfire clear of the runway at Luqa, a big enemy raid developed and he was bundled unceremoniously into a slit trench while waves of Junkers 88s and Italian bombers pounded the airfield. Beurling watched the action unfolding all around him, and craved to be part of it. The craving was satisfied sooner than he expected. At 15.30 he was strapped into the cockpit of a Spitfire at immediate readiness, with 11 other Spitfires of No. 249 Squadron ready to taxi from their dispersals. The pilots, even though they wore only shorts and shirts, were dizzy with the heat as the sun beat down mercilessly; although the temperature would be as low as –30ºC (–22ºF) at 6000m

(20,000ft), to don heavier flying clothing would be to risk sunstroke on the island's baked surface.

Interception

It came as a relief when the Squadron was ordered to scramble to intercept an incoming raid over Gozo, Malta's neighbouring island. The Spitfires climbed in sections of four, their pilots searching the sky to the north. Suddenly they saw the enemy: 20 Ju 88s, escorted by 40 Messerschmitt Bf 109s and Macchi MC.202s. Beurling's section went for the fighter escort while the remaining Spitfires tackled the bombers.

'My adversary shot past me; it was a Macchi C.202, and now it hung in my sights...'

There was no time for manoeuvre; the opposing sides met head-on at 5486m (18,000ft) over the sea. George loosed off an ineffectual burst at a Messerschmitt that flashed across his nose; a moment later he got another enemy fighter in his sights, but at the last instant the

BELOW: The Macchi MC.202 was one of the best fighters produced by Italy during World War II, and continued to fight on both sides after the armistice of September 1943.

Messerschmitt skidded out of the line of fire and dived away. 'The next moment,' Buerling said later, 'I myself came under fire and pulled my Spitfire round in a maximum-rate turn. My adversary shot past me; it was a Macchi C.202, and now it hung in my sights as I turned in behind it.

'I saw it shudder as my cannon shells struck home and then it went down in a fast spin. There was no time to see whether the Macchi had crashed; the sky was still full of aircraft and I went after a section of Ju 88s which was diving in the direction of Valletta harbour. Closing to within fifty yards of the nearest bomber I opened fire; it burst into flames and the crew baled out.'

During the remainder of June there was a comparative lull in the air fighting over Malta. The Germans and Italians had suffered considerably during their air offensive of April and May, and were now gathering their strength for a renewed offensive. In July, however, the fighting flared up again, and on the 11th Beurling destroyed three Macchi 202s in the course of a single afternoon, an exploit that earned him the award of the Distinguished Flying Medal.

New Allies

Later in the war, Spitfires and Macchi MC.202s fought on the same side with the Italian Co-Belligerent Air Force, which joined the Allies after the Italian Armistice in September 1943. Other MC.202s continued to fight with the Republican Air Force, which joined the Germans in northern Italy.

Sergeant Emilio Tarantola, who flew the MC.202 against most Allied types in the Mediterranean theatre, later said that:

'It was always the Spitfires that caused us trouble. We could easily out-turn most other fighter types, and could get the better of the P-51 Mustang, which came along later in the war.'

His words were borne out by the combat report of one Mustang pilot, Lieutenant John J. Voll of the 31st Fighter Group, an ace with 21 victories. According to Voll, the Macchi 202 was one of the most formidable aircraft he encountered:

'On our way home I saw a Macchi 202 through a break in the clouds and went after him. Going in and out of the cloud I was chasing his vapour trail rather than actually seeing him all the time and when I finally got into position to fire I glanced behind me and there was another Macchi on my tail. I started firing and although I only used up twenty rounds per gun on the Macchi in front of me, it seemed as though I had used a hundred before my hits blew the cockpit apart and the pilot bailed out. I started to attack the other plane, but by this time another had joined the fight. Since the Macchi can turn a shade sharper than a Mustang, they soon had me boxed. I got into a cloud and headed home.'

Hawker Typhoon

The Hawker Typhoon was designed in response to a 1937 Air Staff requirement for an aircraft capable of taking on heavily armed and armoured escort fighters such as the Messerschmitt Bf 110. The first of two prototypes flew for the first time on 24 February 1940. The first production aircraft, however, did not fly until May 1941.

Delays in production were blamed on the unreliability of the massive Sabre engine, but there were other problems, including structural failures of the rear fuselage. These had still not been cured when the Royal Air Force's No. 56 Squadron at Duxford was issued with the Typhoon in September 1941, and several pilots were lost in accidents. Moreover, although the aircraft was fast and handled well at medium and low altitudes, its performance at high altitude was inferior to that of both the Focke-Wulf 190 and the Messerschmitt Bf 109F, and its rate of climb was poor. In fact, only its success at intercepting German low-level intruders saved its from being cancelled.

By the end of 1943, with the aircraft's technical problems cured and a growing number of Typhoon squadrons striking hard at the enemy's communications, shipping and airfields, the Typhoon was heading for its place in history as the most potent Allied fighter-bomber of all. In all, 3330 Typhoons were built.

HAWKER TYPHOON MK IB

Specification

Type: low-level interceptor and ground-attack aircraft

Crew: 1

Powerplant: one 1566kW (2100hp) Napier Sabre 24-cylinder in-line
  engine

Performance: max speed 663km/h (412mph); service ceiling
  10,730m (35,200ft); range 1577km (980 miles)

Dimensions: wing span 12.67m (41ft 7in); length 9.73m (31ft 11in);
  height 4.67m (15ft 4in)

Weight: 5171kg (11,400lb) loaded

Armament: four 20mm (0.79in) cannon in wing; external bomb load
  of up to 907kg (2000lb) or eight 27kg (60lb) rocket projectiles

No. 175 Squadron, 2nd Tactical Air Force, Royal Air Force, Normandy, 1944

After the Allied landings in Normandy, the name of the rocket-armed Typhoon became synonymous with the destruction of enemy armour, especially in the Falaise Gap during the German retreat from Normandy, where this aircraft was based.

Republic P-47 Thunderbolt 🇺🇸

One of the truly great fighters of World War II, the Republic XP-47B Thunderbolt prototype flew for the first time on 6 May 1941, with the first production P-47B coming off the assembly line in March 1942 after many teething troubles had been rectified.

In June 1942, the 56th Fighter Group began to rearm with the P-47, and in December 1942 – January 1943 it deployed to England, flying its first combat mission on 13 April 1943. During the next two years, it was to destroy more enemy aircraft than any other fighter group of the US Army Air Force (USAAF) Eighth Fighter Command. From that first operational sortie over Europe until the end of the fighting in the Pacific in August 1945, Thunderbolts flew 546,000 combat sorties. By the time the 56th Fighter Wing flew its first operational sortie in the spring of 1943, huge orders had been placed for the P-47D, the most numerous Thunderbolt variant. Considerable numbers of Thunderbolts were used by the Royal Air Force (RAF) in Burma. Overall P-47 production was 15,660 aircraft, many of which found their way into foreign air forces post-war. During World War II, the Soviet Union received 195 P-47s out of the 203 allocated, some having been lost en route.

REPUBLIC P-47D Thunderbolt

Specification
Type: fighter
Crew: 1
Powerplant: one 1715kW (2300hp) Pratt & Whitney R-2800-59
  radial engine
Performance: max speed 689km/h (428mph); service ceiling
  12,800m (42,000ft); range 2028km (1260 miles)
Dimensions: wing span 12.43m (40ft 9in); length 11.01m (36ft 1in);
  height 4.32m (14ft 2in)
Weight: 8800kg (19,400lb) loaded
Armament: six or eight 12.7mm (0.5in) machine guns; two 454kg
  (1000lb) bombs or ten rocket projectiles

56TH FIGHTER GROUP, UNITED STATES EIGHTH FIGHTER COMMAND, UNITED STATES ARMY AIR FORCES, BOXTED, ENGLAND, 1944
The P-47D illustrated here was the personal mount of Colonel David C. Schilling, who took over as commander of the 56th Fighter Group from Colonel Hubert 'Hub' Zemke in August 1944. Schilling flew 132 combat missions with the 56th Fighter Group, recording 22.5 victories. He died in 1956, and Schilling Air Force Base, Kansas, is named in his honour.

HAWKER TYPHOON VS REPUBLIC P-47 THUNDERBOLT

THE TYPHOON AND THE P-47 were both designed as medium-altitude fighters, but whereas the P-47 was a success in this role, the Typhoon was a failure. Threatened with cancellation at one point, Typhoon survived to join the P-47 as a superlative ground-attack aircraft.

Wing Commander Roland Beamont, whose role in operationally testing the Typhoon was crucial to its ultimate success, flew the aircraft – a Mk 1A with twelve machine guns – for the first time on 8 March 1942, and had this to say about the aircraft:

'Once it was established that the noise, vibration and general commotion caused by the big Sabre engine and enhanced by the draughty cockpit with rattling 'wind-up' side windows were not actually breaking or stopping anything, it was soon apparent that the aeroplane was pleasantly stable and responsive to controls in all axes, very manoeuvrable (and exceptionally so for that period at speeds above 400mph [640km/h]) and it had a tremendous turn of speed. A 75-percent-power low-level cruise at over 300mph [480km/h] was fast for those days, as was a maximum power "level" of 385mph [620km/h]; and at the advertised dive limit of 500mph [800km/h] there was adequate control remaining, though with heavy control forces and a most impressive noise level.

'A look at low speed handling and the stall confirmed the briefing that controllability was excellent down to 100mph [160km/h], but it became sluggish near the stall at 68mph [109km/h] in landing configuration. Approaches, overshoots and landings showed that this big aeroplane handled much like a Hurricane (and more docilely than a Spitfire), although it had less tendency to "float" than either. A major bonus was its very wide undercarriage which made it surprisingly stable on rough ground and much less sensitive to crosswinds than a Spitfire.

'It began to look as if this heavy and noisy aeroplane could meet a number of operating roles other than those specified for it, while being pleasant to fly in the process.'

'So, as the flight ended, it became clear that this big ugly fighter was actually pleasant to fly – if only the pilot could stick his fingers in his ears and could see properly out of it.'

ABOVE: *Hawker Typhoon 1b of No. 183 Squadron. A failure in its intended role of interceptor, the Typhoon went on to excel as a ground attack aircraft in the Normandy campaign.*

ABOVE: *A formation of P-47Bs from the 56th Fighter Group in October 1942. The lead aircraft is flown by P-47 ace Hubert Zemke.*

In the summer of 1942 the first three Typhoon squadrons, Nos 56, 266 and 609, were sent into action against German fighter-bombers, whose low-level hit and run attacks on coastal targets on the English coast were becoming increasingly troublesome. There was no longer any doubt about the aircraft's effectiveness at low level, and 609 Squadron's performance effectively killed a last-ditch attempt by the Engineering Branch of RAF Fighter Command, early in 1943, to have the fighter axed in favour of the American P-47 Thunderbolt. By the end of the year, with the aircraft's technical problems cured and a growing number of Typhoon squadrons – now carrying a pair of 226kg (500lb) bombs on their aircraft in addition to the built-in armament of four 20-mm (0.78in) cannon – striking hard at the enemy's communications, shipping and airfields, the Typhoon was heading for its place in history as the most potent Allied fighter-bomber of them all.

P-47 Tactics

The leading exponent of the P-47 Thunderbolt in the USAAF was Colonel Robert S. Johnson, who arrived in England as a young lieutenant with the 56th Fighter Group in January 1943. He soon formulated sound fighting tactics which were to pay dividends. His advice to fellow pilots was simple:

'Never let a Jerry get his sights on you. No matter whether he is at 100 yards [91m] or at 1000 yards [910m] away, a 20mm [0.78in] will carry easily that far and will knock down a plane at 1000 yards [910m].

It is better to stay at 20,000 feet [6100m] with a good speed with a Jerry at 20,000 feet [6100m] than it is to pull up to his vicinity at a stalling speed. If he comes down on you, pull up into him, and nine times out of ten, if you are nearly head-on with him he'll roll away to his right. Then you have him. Roll on his tail and go get him.'

Armed with rockets, like the Typhoon, the P-47 proved devastating in the ground-attack role.

Johnson described how he put his theory into practice.

'It was a clear day. We were over the coast, the line of breakers curving white against the shore. ..I looked round and saw a Hun on my tail. As he came in on my tail, shooting, I did a tight climbing turn. The Jerry had the position – and I had that belly tank, which I hadn't been able to release. He kept inside me, trying for a deflection burst. I held the turn until his nose dropped a bit. Then I slipped down and hit him.

'Then he was on me again and we went through the same thing. On this turn my belly tank finally dropped. When his nose dipped I came over and hit him again. We went through this four times, and it took ten minutes, which is an awful long time in a dogfight. Then his cockpit flew into the air and the plane flew under it. He was coming apart, and I gave him another burst just to make sure of it.'

As bomber escort duty was progressively taken over by the P-51 Mustang, the P-47 was increasingly assigned to ground attack, ranging over Northwest Europe and seeking targets of opportunity. Armed with rockets, like the Typhoon, the P-47 proved devastating in this role.

Junkers Ju 88

One of the most versatile and effective combat aircraft ever produced, the Junkers Ju 88 remained of vital importance to the Luftwaffe throughout World War II, serving as a bomber, dive-bomber, night-fighter, close support aircraft, long-range heavy fighter, reconnaissance aircraft and torpedo bomber. A pre-series batch of Ju 88A-0s was completed during the summer of 1939, the first production Ju 88A-1s being delivered to a test unit, *Erprobungskommando 88*.

The Ju 88A was built in 17 different variants up to the Ju 88A-17, with progressively uprated engines, enhanced defensive armament and improved defensive capability. The most widely used variant was the Ju 88A-4, which served in both Europe and North Africa. Twenty Ju 88A-4s were supplied to Finland, and some were supplied to Italy, Romania and Hungary. Some 7000 examples of the Ju 88A series were delivered.

The Ju 88As saw considerable action in the Balkans and the Mediterranean, and on the Eastern Front. They operated intensively during the German invasion of Crete, and were the principal threat to the island of Malta and its supply convoys. Some of their most outstanding service, however, was in the Arctic, where aircraft of KG 26 and KG 30, based in northern Norway, carried out devastating attacks on Allied convoys to Russia.

JUNKERS JU 88A-4

Specification

Type: bomber

Crew: 4

Powerplant: two 999kW (1340hp) Junkers Jumo 211J inverted V-12 engines

Performance: max speed 450km/h (280mph); service ceiling 8200m (26,900ft); range 2730km (1696 miles)

Dimensions: wing span 20.00m (65ft 7in); length 14.40m (47ft 3in); height 4.85m (15ft 11in)

Weight: 14,000kg (30,865lb) loaded

Armament: up to seven 7.92mm (0.31in) MG15 or MG81 machine guns; maximum internal and external bomb load of 3600kg (7935lb)

I Gruppe, Kampfgeschwader 30, Luftwaffe, Netherlands, 1940

In August 1939, *Erprobungskommando 88* was redesignated I *Gruppe, Kampfgeschwader* 25 (I/KG 25), and soon afterwards it became I/KG 30, carrying out its first operational mission – an attack on British warships in the Firth of Forth – in September, making it the first unit to use the type in action. The same target was attacked on 16 October, when two Ju 88s were shot down by Spitfires.

Bristol Beaufighter

In the remarkably quick time of six months from concept to completion of the prototype, Bristol created the Type 156 Beaufighter, a powerful fighter with twin Hercules engines and a narrow fuselage housing the pilot at the front and the crewman in the mid-fuselage under a Perspex dome. Rapid development was aided by using the general layout of the Type 152 Beaufort torpedo bomber and many parts from it, namely the wings, tail group and undercarriage. The Type 156 prototype first flew in July 1939, and the Mk IF night-fighter entered service in September 1940. The Beaufighter TF.10 was developed as a long-range strike fighter, armed with rockets, torpedoes or bombs, as well as cannon and machine guns. Used mainly by RAF Coastal Command, the TF.10 wreaked havoc on German shipping in Norway and against enemy patrol aircraft in World War II.

The Australian Department of Aircraft Production (DAP) produced 364 Beaufighter Mk 21s, based on the TF.10, from 1944. Originally intended to have Wright R-2600 engines, they were actually produced with the standard Hercules. The Australian 'Beaus' were distinguished by a prominent hump in front of the windscreen intended to house a Sperry Autopilot, which was never fitted, and by use of 12.7mm (0.50in) rather than 7.7mm (0.303in) machine guns.

BRISTOL BEAUFIGHTER MK 21

Specification

Type: twin-engined attack aircraft

Crew: 2

Powerplant: two 1294kW (1735hp) Bristol Hercules XVII radial engines

Performance: max speed 514km/h (320mph); service ceiling 8839m (29,000ft); range 2400km (1500 miles)

Dimensions: wing span 17.64m (57ft 10in); length 12.59m (41ft 4in); height 4.84m (15ft 10in)

Weight: 11,521kg (25,400lb) loaded

Armament: four 12.7mm (0.5in) machine guns in wings, four 20-mm Hispano cannon in forward fuselage; eight rocket projectiles under wings

NO. 22 SQUADRON, NO. 77 (ATTACK) WING, ROYAL AUSTRALIAN AIR FORCE, MOROTAI, MOLUCCAN ISLANDS, 1945
A8-186 was delivered in early 1945 and joined No. 22 Squadron in New Guinea in July, flying several operations including the last flown by the squadron. It became an instructional airframe in 1947, and in 1950 was sold to a farmer as a children's plaything. Recovered in 1965, it was restored by the private Camden Museum of Aviation at Camden, New South Wales.

JUNKERS JU 88 VS BRISTOL BEAUFIGHTER

THE LUFTWAFFE'S JU 88S were in action against the British Isles from the earliest weeks of the war. The first attack, aimed at warships of the Royal Navy in the Firth of Forth, was mounted on 16 October 1939 by nine Ju 88s of KG 30, based at Westerland on the island of Sylt.

The raid leader was *Hauptmann* Helmut Pohle. Arriving over the anchorage, Pohle selected a target and began his dive. Flak was coming up thick and fast, rocking the aircraft with near misses.

'Suddenly there was a loud bang,' Pohle said, 'and a gale of cold air roared into the cockpit. The transparent hatch in the cockpit roof had gone, taking the upper rearward-firing machine gun with it. I forced my attention back to the target, which now filled my sights. A second later, the bombs fell away and we were rocketing skywards again.' One of the bombs exploded in the water; the other hit the cruiser HMS *Southampton* starboard amidships, smashed through three decks, emerged from the side of the hull and reduced the admiral's barge to matchwood. It failed to explode. The rear gunner's voice came over the intercom, warning Pohle that enemy fighters were approaching from astern. They were the Spitfires of No. 602 Squadron.

BELOW: A true multi-role aircraft, the Junkers Ju 88 is seen here armed with two Henschel Hs 293 anti-shipping missiles. The Ju 88/Hs 293 combination was not used operationally.

The leading fighter was flown by Flight Lieutenant Pinkerton. He fired and saw bullet strikes dance and sparkle on the Junkers' dark-green camouflage. There was a flicker of fire from one engine and the bomber started to go down. The Junkers was losing height steadily. Struggling to keep the aircraft flying on one engine, Pohle sighted a trawler. He said later:

'I thought it might be Norwegian (Norway was then a neutral country) and turned towards it. I was just able to clear the trawler before ditching the Junkers, although the sea was running at strength 4. The crew of the trawler did not rescue me; instead I was picked up by a Navy destroyer, as well as my badly injured fourth crew member. However, I collapsed on the deck with concussion and facial injuries. My crewman died from his injuries the next day.'

Its high speed made the Ju 88 a very difficult aircraft to intercept.

Pohle woke up five days later in Port Edward Hospital, Edinburgh. The bodies of his other two crew members were recovered from the sea.

When the Ju 88 began night operations over the British Isles after the Battle of Britain, only the heavily armed, twin-engined Bristol Beaufighter had enough speed to pursue and destroy it. But there were many problems to be overcome by the Allies in facing the Ju 88.

> **'The Beaufighter was a very toughly built, rather brutal looking aircraft. It was a jolly good war machine, but its airborne radar was extremely unreliable in the early days.'**

Night Clash

Wing Commander Guy Gibson of 'Dam Busters' fame flew a tour with No. 29 (Beaufighter) Squadron, and described some of his night-fighting experiences.

'Once we were put on to an 88... I quickly swung round to the left, as I was told he would be slightly on my left, but on looking the other way we were flying practically alongside him, and he saw us first and disappeared. Another night we got so close that the operator said that we would collide any minute, but I couldn't see a thing. In desperation I fired all four cannons into space to try to make him fire back at me, and immediately back came the tracer from his rear gunner from far below; something again was wrong with our airborne apparatus. This time the rear gunner paid for his folly though, and I saw a lot of cannon shells pump into him before he managed to escape.'

ABOVE: *The Beaufighter was operated in the South-West Pacific theatre by No 30 Squadron Royal Australian Air Force, one of whose aircraft is seen here being refuelled.*

Gibson's radar operator had experienced a phenomenon known as 'squint', described here by Group Captain John Cunningham, the RAF's leading night-fighter ace.

'We had to rely on external aerials on the aircraft and we had endless trouble with "squint". Because these planes lived out in the open, when they got wet, water got into the radar system and the signal that came in from the wing aerials could not be balanced up. We learned early on to send the planes up in daylight to test their radar. Your target would sit in front of you and your radar operator would sit in the back of the Beaufighter looking towards the tail. As you came up to your "target aircraft" you'd ask him to sing out its range and elevation. You'd position the target dead ahead and ask him, "Where is it now?" He'd look at the radar and say, "It's about thirty degrees left and above you." So you'd tell him to come off his seat and look forward and he'd see that the aircraft which he thought was in one place was somewhere else. That was "squint."'

Once the problems had been resolved, however, the Beaufighter proved to be a killer, and an aircraft that became much feared by German pilots on night raids over Britain. On the night of 10 May 1941, for example, Beaufighters destroyed a total of 14 German bombers attacking London – the highest loss sustained by the Luftwaffe on any one night since the Blitz offensive began.

Junkers Ju 87 Stuka

Although the word Stuka – an abbreviation of *Sturzkampfflugzeug*, which literally translates as 'diving combat aircraft' – was applied to all German bomber aircraft with a dive-bombing capability during World War II, it will forever be associated with the Junkers Ju 87. The first prototype Ju 87V1 was flown for the first time in the late spring of 1935, powered by a 477kW (640hp) Rolls-Royce Kestrel engine. In December 1937, three production Ju 87A-1s were sent to Spain for operational trials with the *Kondor* Legion, the German units flying in support of the Spanish Nationalists.

The Ju 87A-2 subseries, the next to appear, was succeeded on the production line in 1938 by an extensively modified version, the Ju 87B. By the outbreak of World War II, first-line Stuka units had

standardized on the Ju 87B-1, which was fitted with the more powerful 820kW (1100hp) Junkers Jumo 211A 12-cylinder engine with fuel injection. The most important external change was the replacement of the A model's 'trousered' undercarriage by a 'spatted' one, with close-fitting streamlined oleo covers and streamlined wheel spats. The Ju 87B-2 was similar, but was powered by a 895kW (1200hp) Junkers Jumo 211D engine with moveable radiator flaps. An anti-shipping version of the Ju 87B-2 was known as the Ju 87R. The next production model was the Ju 87D, several subseries of which were produced in some quantity. The last Stuka variant was the Ju 87G, a standard Ju 87D-5 converted to carry two BK37 cannon (37mm Flak 18 guns) under the wing.

JUNKERS JU 87B-2 STUKA

Specification

Type: dive-bomber

Crew: 2

Powerplant: one 895kW (1200hp) Junkers Jumo 211D inverted-Vee engine

Performance: max speed 380km/h (237mph); service ceiling 8000m (26,248ft); range 600km (372 miles)

Dimensions: wing span 13.80m (45ft 3.33in); length 11.00m (37ft 1in); height 3.88m (12ft 9in)

Weight: 4250kg (9321lb) loaded

Armament: three 7.92mm (0.31in) machine guns; external bomb load of up to 1000kg (2205lb)

I Gruppe, Stukageschwader 76, Luftwaffe, France, July 1940
The aircraft pictured is a Junkers Ju 87B-2 Stuka of I *Gruppe*, Stukageschwader 76, France, July 1940, flown by *Hauptmann* Walter Siegel.

Douglas SBD-1 Dauntless

The Douglas Dauntless was developed from the Northrop BT-1 light bomber. At the time Northrop was a subsidiary of Douglas, and, when the parent company absorbed it in 1939, Ed Heinemann revised the design to meet a US Navy requirement for a carrier-based dive-bomber. The prototype XSBD-1 was a conversion from a BT-1 and flew in early 1939. In April, the US Marine Corps (USMC) and US Navy placed orders for the SBD-1 and SBD-2, respectively, the latter having increased fuel capacity and twin rear guns, rather than the single weapon of the USMC version.

There were 57 examples of the SBD-1 built, and they entered service with Marine dive-bomber squadron VMB-2 in late 1940. The first SBD-2s joined the US Navy in early 1941. Sometimes called the 'Barge' or the 'Clunk', or the 'Speedy One' (an ironic reading of SBD-1), the nickname that stuck was 'Slow but Deadly'. Using its swinging bomb cradle to make high-angle dive attacks, the Dauntless was a very accurate bomber and could defend itself well with its fixed and flexible armament.

DOUGLAS SBD-1 DAUNTLESS

Specification

Type: carrier-based dive-bomber

Crew: 2

Powerplant: one 746kW (1000hp) Wright R-1820-32 Cyclone radial piston engine

Performance: max speed 427km/h (266mph); service ceiling 9175m (31,000ft); range 972km (604 miles)

Dimensions: wing span 12.65m (41ft 6in); length 9.68m (31ft 9in); height 3.91m (12ft 10in)

Weight: 3183kg (7018lb) loaded

Armament: two 12.7mm (0.50in) Browning machine guns in the nose and one 7.62mm (0.30in) in the rear cockpit; bomb load of one 454kg (1000lb) bomb under centre fuselage and two 45kg (100lb) bombs under wings

VMB-2, MARINE AIR GROUP 11, US MARINE CORPS QUANTICO, VIRGINIA, 1941
In the colour-coded US Navy and USMC of the 1930s, the full red cowling, red bands and code letters on the SBD-1 illustrated all indicated the first aircraft of the first section, which was flown by the squadron commander. This in fact is the second production Dauntless, Bureau Number 1597. Its fate is unknown, but is not believed to have been lost in an accident or to enemy action. Most of the SBD-1s were used for training, but the later SBD-3 was vital in the Battle of Midway in June 1942 and played an important role at Guadalcanal and in other island campaigns in the early Pacific war.

JUNKERS JU 87 STUKA VS DOUGLAS SBD DAUNTLESS

THE JU 87 STUKA and the Douglas Dauntless were both designed as dedicated dive-bombers, the Stuka being intended for land-based, and the Dauntless for naval, operations.

One Stuka *Gruppe* was formed to operate from the German aircraft carrier *Graf Zeppelin*. She was never completed, and so the opportunity to compare the Stuka and the Dauntless in a naval role never arose.

Many Allied pilots had an opportunity to fly captured Stukas, especially in the Western Desert, where the rapid Allied advance after El Alamein forced the Germans to abandon hundreds of aircraft. One such pilot was Squadron Leader D.H. Clarke, DFC, AFC, who lost no chance of flying as many different aircraft as possible while serving as an instructor with an operational training unit in Egypt in 1944. His recollection of the Stuka was far from favourable, although in fairness the example he flew had been much abused both before and after its capture.

Stuka Test Flight

'The rumble of the Jumo 211J engine, when I started up, retained a little of its ferocity as though it could remember past victories; but the husky growl of old age can never imitate the snarl of aggression, and the fuselage rattled and shook from the rough running. The cockpit was roomy and the visibility all round was excellent – there was even a Perspex panel in the floor so that the pilot could view the target between his legs. I failed to see the point of this refinement.

'The rumble of the Jumo 211J engine, when I started up, retained a little of its ferocity, but … the fuselage rattled and shook from the rough running.'

After many dive-bombing experiences in Skuas and Kittyhawks, the only method I knew of going down was to put the target under one wing and then peel over and aim directly at it. Fancy contoured lines

BELOW: Junkers Ju 87 Stukas operating over the Russian Front were distinguished by a yellow or white band around the rear fuselage.

ABOVE: *The Douglas Dauntless dive-bomber played a crucial part in the Pacific war, being largely responsible for the destruction of the Japanese carrier task force in the Battle of Midway.*

were painted around the inside of the windscreen and the hood and marked in degrees. Obviously they were for the pilot to line against the horizon and thereby know the angle of his dive – but what good did that do him? Usually you had enough worries trying to keep the nose pointed at the target, without bothering about judging the angle!

'I taxied out. The take-off was longer than I thought it would be, and it seemed strange not to have an undercarriage to retract. The climb was laborious. A Kittyhawk, pre-arranged, darted out of the sun and I turned to meet it, clawing for height and aiming just under its belly as I had done so many times against 109s. But the Stuka could not hold the angle, shuddered, stalled, and fell into a dive. It was like flying a brick. I was shot down a dozen times that morning. My opponent was only a clapped-out P-40, so against a Spitfire or a Hurricane there would only be one answer!

'The dive brakes were unserviceable but I tried a shallow dive without them, aiming for the Anzac Memorial overlooking Lake Timsah. When the ASI was indicating 400 kilometres per hour the aircraft was disliking it so much that I pulled out cautiously … I was very glad that I never had to fly the Stuka on ops. I returned to Ballah and eased the creaking carcass into a gentle landing.'

Destructive Dauntless

In 1942, while the Ju 87 Stuka was experiencing its final glory days in North Africa and Russia, another dive bomber was literally turning the course of the war on the other side of the world. On 4 June, 1942,

Douglas SBD Dauntless aircraft from the US aircraft carriers *Enterprise* and *Yorktown* sank the Japanese carriers *Akagi*, *Kaga* and *Soryu*, at one stroke depriving the Imperial Japanese Navy of its principal striking force. The devastating attack was described by Mitsuo Fuchida, the Japanese air commander aboard the carrier *Akagi*.

'Visibility was good. Clouds were gathering at about three thousand metres, however, and though there were occasional breaks, they afforded good concealment for approaching enemy planes. At 10.24 the order to start launching came from the bridge via loudspeaker. The Air Officer flapped a white flag, and the first Zero fighter gathered speed and whizzed off the deck. At that instant a lookout screamed: "Hell-Divers!" I looked up to see three black enemy planes plummeting towards our ship. Some of our machine guns managed to fire a few frantic bursts at them, but it was too late. The plump silhouettes of the American Dauntless dive-bombers quickly grew larger, and then a number of black objects suddenly floated eerily from their wings. Bombs! Down they came straight towards me! I fell intuitively to the deck …

'The terrifying scream of the dive-bombers reached me first, followed by the crashing explosion of a direct hit. There was a blinding flash and then a second explosion, much louder than the first. I was shaken by a weird blast of warm air. There was still another shock, but less severe, apparently a near-miss. There then followed a startling quiet as the barking of guns suddenly ceased. The enemy planes had already gone from sight….Looking about, I was horrified at the destruction that had been wrought in a matter of seconds… I could see that *Kaga* and *Soryu* had also been hit and were giving off heavy columns of black smoke. The scene was horrible to behold.'

COMBAT TYPES OF THE DECISIVE YEARS 1943–45

Between 1939 and 1943, huge advances were made in the capability of combat aircraft. From Britain and the United States came the heavy bombers that would take the war to the heart of Germany: the Lancaster and Halifax, the B-17 Flying Fortress and the B-24 Liberator. Between them, they would pound the Third Reich around the clock, the RAF by night and the USAAF by day.

In North Africa, decisive battles were being fought, culminating in the last stand of the Axis forces in Tunisia early in 1943. This marked the swansong of the Luftwaffe's transport fleet, as the aircraft that had sustained it through Germany's early war campaigns, the Junkers Ju 52, was battered to destruction in frantic attempts to supply the German forces making their vain last stand on the shores of the Mediterranean, The Ju 52's contemporary, the Douglas C-47, proved a more rugged and long-lasting design, and the type remains in cargo service in some parts of the world today.

LEFT: *The North American P-51 Mustang, once it was fitted with Packard-built Rolls-Royce Merlin 61 engines, had one of the best performances of any WWII fighter.*

BELOW: *The Mitsubishi A6M Zero was a capable fighter, but it was very vulnerable to battle damage – a single strike of gunfire could lead to mid-air disintegration.*

Elsewhere, on the great plains of Russia, a combination of winter weather and bitter Soviet resistance had brought the triumphant German offensives to a standstill. The Soviet aviation industry was now beginning to produce excellent combat aircraft in huge numbers; types like the Lavochkin La-5, in which Ivan Kozhedub, who was to become the leading Allied air ace with 62 victories, gained his successes. Aircraft such as this, at last, could counter Germany's formidable Focke-Wulf Fw 190, the 'Butcher Bird' that was at least the equal of Allied fighter types in the West, and better than most.

But it was in the West that the decisive air battles were fought. Now, at last, the Allies had a fighter, the North American P-51 Mustang, that could escort the bombers of the USAAF all the way to Berlin and back, and face the sternest challenge of the last months of the war – the Messerschmitt Me 262 jet fighter, deployed in increasing numbers from the autumn of 1944. The Me 262 was the shape of future conflict in the air, and its aerodynamic design would be reflected in the jet-powered combat aircraft of East and West that would appear in the early post-war years. There were other radical innovations, too: amazing aircraft like the rocket-powered Me 163, as much a danger to its pilots as to the enemy, which laid the foundation for much rocket research after the war.

Finally, on the other side of the world, the aircraft that had helped to forge many of Japan's early victories, the Mitsubishi Zero, had at last met its match in the shape of the nimble Grumman Hellcat naval fighter, which destroyed more enemy aircraft than any other in World War II, and played an enormous part in securing final victory for the Allies.

Douglas A-20 Havoc

A 1938 US Army requirement for a twin-engined light bomber was met by Douglas with its Model 7, or DB-7, design, a high-winged single-tail aircraft which first flew in October that year. The French initially showed more interest in the DB-7 than the United States, ordering nearly 200. About half of these reached France before June 1940, and the rest were delivered to the United Kingdom as the Boston, as were a further 200 examples, some of which became Havoc night-fighters.

The first United States Army Air Forces (USAAF) version was the A-20, with a glazed nose like the French and British aircraft, but a strengthened airframe. The next important version and the first with a solid nose rather than a glazed bomb-aimer's position was the A-20G. The flexible gun mount in an open position was replaced with a powered Martin gun turret during A-20G production. The wings were strengthened to allow up to four 227kg (500lb) bombs under the wings. The Royal Air Force's Bostons were reasonably effective as low-level bombers, but the USAAF used them either at medium altitude or as low-level strafers, particularly in the Pacific. To this end, some had additional 'package' guns on the fuselage sides, like the nose guns fired by the single pilot.

DOUGLAS A-20G HAVOC

Specification

Type: twin-engined attack bomber

Crew: 2

Powerplant: two 1193kW (1600hp) Wright R-2600-23 Cyclone supercharged 14-cylinder radial piston engines

Performance: max speed 510km/h (317mph); service ceiling 7225m (23,700ft); range 1603km (996 miles)

Dimensions: wing span 18.67m (61ft 3in); length 14.32m (47ft); height 4.83m (15ft 10in)

Weight: 10,964kg (24,127lb) loaded

Armament: six 12.7mm (0.50in) Browning machine guns in nose, two in mid-upper turret and one in ventral position; bomb load of up to 2722kg (6000lb)

647TH BOMB SQUADRON, 410TH BOMB GROUP, 97TH BOMB WING (LIGHT), NINTH AIR FORCE, USAAF, UK, 1944

'Joker' was an A-20G-35-DO of the 647th Bomb Squadron, known as 'Beaty's Raiders'. The squadron and its parent group, the 410th Bomb Group (Light), were formed in July 1943 and entered combat in May 1944 as part of the Ninth Air Force, which was mainly used on tactical missions to support the advancing troops. In September 1944, the group moved to forward airfields in France. Just at the end of the European war, the 410th made the transition to the A-26 Invader, Douglas's successor to the A-20.

North American B-25 Mitchell

One of the most important US tactical warplanes of World War II, the North American B-25 Mitchell flew for the first time in January 1939. US Army Air Forces (USAAF) B-25B Mitchells operated effectively against Japanese forces in New Guinea, carrying out low-level strafing attacks in the wake of Allied bombing operations. The B-25B was followed into service by the virtually identical B-25C and B-25D. The dedicated anti-shipping version of the Mitchell was the B-25G, 405 of which were produced.

Developed for use in the Pacific theatre, the B-25G had a four-man crew and was fitted with a 75mm (2.95in) M4 gun in the nose, adding to its already powerful nose armament of four 12.7mm (0.50in) guns. The follow-on variant, the B-25H (1000 built), had a lighter 75mm (2.95in)

gun. The 4318 examples of the next variant, the B-25J, featured either a glazed B-25D nose or, in later aircraft, a 'solid' nose with eight 12.7mm (0.50in) machine guns. The Royal Air Force (RAF) took delivery of 869 Mitchells, and 458 B-25Js were transferred to the US Navy from 1943, these aircraft being designated PBJ-1H. The Soviet Union also took delivery of 862 Mitchells under Lend-Lease, and surplus B-25s were widely exported after World War II.

On 16 April 1942, the Mitchell leapt into the headlines when the aircraft carrier USS *Hornet*, from a position at sea 1075km (668 miles) from Tokyo, launched 16 B-25Bs of the 17th AAF Air Group, led by Lieutenant Colonel J.H. Doolittle, for the first attack on the Japanese homeland.

NORTH AMERICAN B-25H MITCHELL

Specification

Type: medium bomber

Crew: 5

Powerplant: two 1268kW (1700hp) Wright R-2600-13 18-cylinder two-row radial engines

Performance: max speed 457km/h (284mph); service ceiling 6460m (21,200ft); range 2454km (1525 miles)

Dimensions: wing span 20.60m (67ft 7in); length 16.12m (67ft 7in); height 4.82m (15ft 10in)

Weight: 18,960kg (41,800lb) loaded

Armament: six 12.7mm (0.50in) machine guns; internal and external bomb/torpedo load of 1361kg (3000lb)

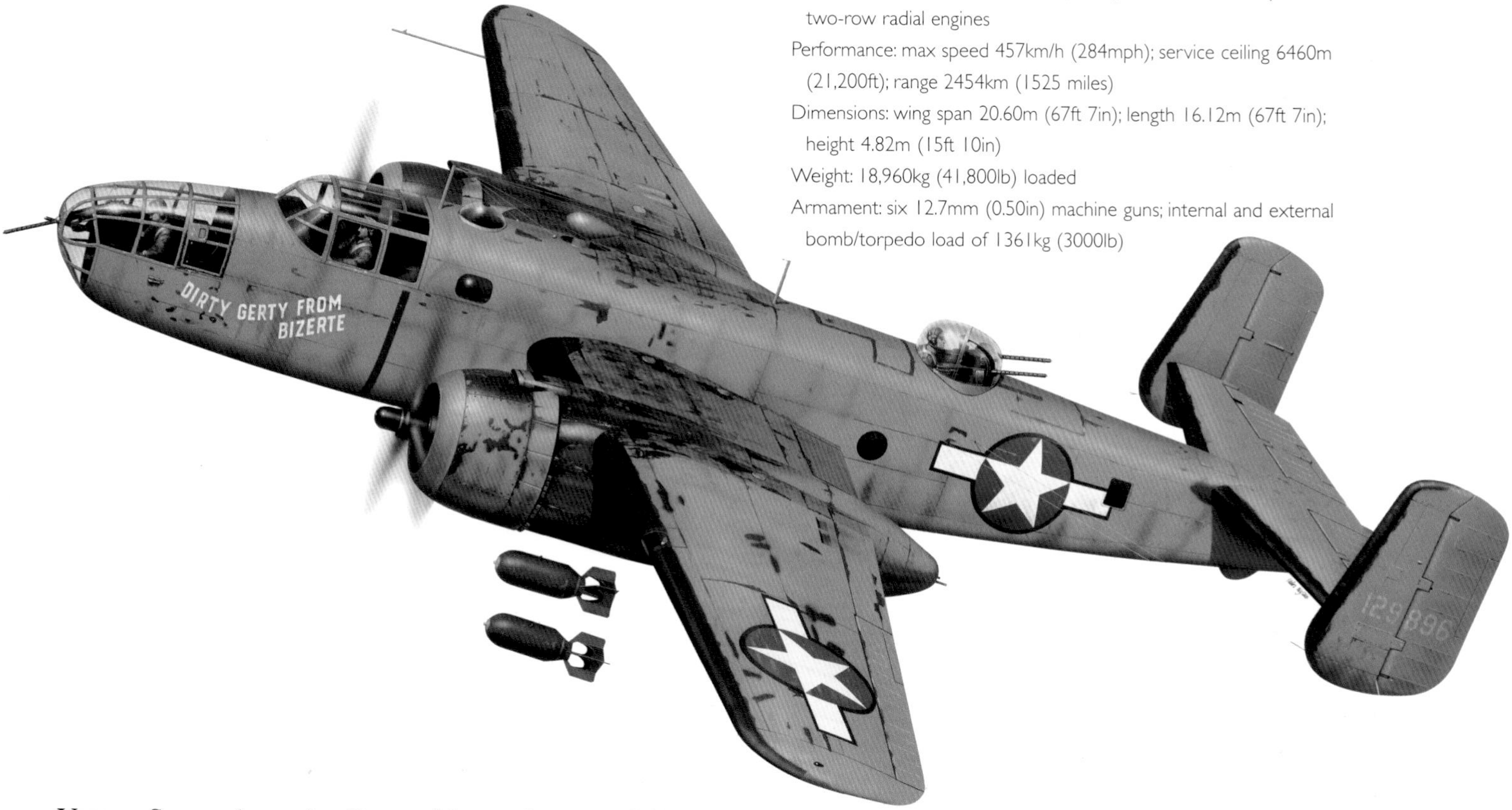

UNITED STATES ARMY AIR FORCES NORTH AFRICA, 1943
The example of a B-25H Mitchell illustrated here bore the serial number 41-29896.

A-20 Havoc vs B-25 Mitchell

ACHIEVING NOTABLE SUCCESSES in every theatre during World War II, both the Douglas A-20 Havoc and the North American B-25 Mitchell were extremely rugged, versatile and dependable twin-engined attack bombers.

Early in 1944, three US bombardment groups, the 3rd, 312th and 417th, were operational with A-20s in the New Guinea theatre, where they performed excellent service.

The 312th and 417th Bombardment Groups began their combat operations with the A-20G from the start and the 3rd BG converted to the A-20G at about the same time. In September 1944, 370 Havocs were deployed with the Fifth Air Force in the South West Pacific Area. Most sorties were flown at low level, since Japanese flak was not nearly as intense as German flak in Europe. During these low-level bombing operations, it was found that there was little need for a bomb aimer. Consequently, the

BELOW: The Douglas A-20 Havoc was fast and well-armed. It provided valuable service with the Allied air forces in every theatre, including the Russian Front.

bomb aimer was often replaced by additional forward-firing machine guns mounted in a faired-over nose.

The A-20's heavy firepower, manoeuvrability, speed and bomb load made it an ideal weapon for pinpoint strikes against aircraft, hangers and supply dumps.

In shipping attacks, made by a formation of three A-20s attacking in line abreast, the heavy forward firepower of the attackers could overwhelm shipboard defences, and at low level the A-20s could skip their bombs into the sides of transports and destroyers with deadly effect. These tactics were initially worked out by Army Captain Paul I. 'Pappy' Gunn, who also adapted the same tactics to the B-25 Mitchell. The spectacularly successful results of these field adaptations led to increases in the forward

ABOVE: The B-25 Mitchell was an excellent medium bomber, and in the Pacific Theatre proved deadly in the anti-shipping role.

firepower of production A-20s which were introduced on the production line with the A-20G model.

Devastating Fire

Some Fifth Air Force A-20s had their heavy forward-firing armament supplemented by clusters of three Bazooka-type rocket tubes underneath each wing. These tubes each held an M8, T-30 114mm (4.5in) spin-stabilized rocket. These rocket launcher tubes proved to be heavy and complicated, and were generally more trouble than they were worth and were not often used.

The A-20 groups turned their attention to the Philippines following the end of the New Guinea campaign. By mid-April 1944, three full four-squadron A-20 groups of the Fifth Air Force were active in the island hopping campaign that led to the invasion of Luzon on January 7, 1945. After the Philippines were secured, A-20 units turned their attention to Japanese targets on Formosa in early 1945. The 312th BG replaced its A-20s with A-26s, while the 417th BG traded in its A-20s for B-32 Dominators and became a Very Heavy Bombardment Group. The old 3rd BG retained its A-20s until the end of the war, becoming the last operational Army A-20 unit, and was preparing to move to Okinawa in readiness for the invasion of the Japanese home islands when Japan surrendered.

Tokyo Raid

Effective in combat though the A-20 was, it was the North American B-25 Mitchell, one of the best tactical bombers of World War II, that captured the public imagination through its daring attack on Tokyo in April 1942, when the American people were in dire need of a morale-booster. The following narrative of the attack on Tokyo is based on an eye-witness account.

'The B-25 jumped, lightened of its 2000lb load...'

'They stayed low, as low as two hundred feet [60m] above the sea… At 1.30pm, Jimmy Doolittle sighted the enemy coast. Potter (his navigator) told him that they would make landfall thirty miles [48km] north of Tokyo, and he turned out to be dead right. As they crossed the coast, Doolittle picked out a large lake over on the left, and a quick check with the map confirmed his navigator's accuracy. He turned south, skimming low over a patchwork of fields. Peasants looked up and waved, mistaking the speeding B-25 for one of their own aircraft. Once, Doolittle looked up and saw five Japanese fighters, cruising a couple of thousand feet [600m] above, but they made no move to attack and eventually turned away…

'The bombers thundered on, skirting the slopes of hills, leap-frogging high tension cables. There was no flak; it was just like one of those many training flights back home. Suddenly, dead ahead, was the great sprawling complex of the Japanese capital city, and Doolittle took the B-25 up to 1500 feet [450m].

'In the glazed nose, bombardier Fred Braemer peered ahead, searching for the munitions factory that was their target. He found it and steered Doolittle towards it, the pilot holding the aircraft rock-steady in response to the bombardier's instructions. On Doolittle's instrument panel a red light blinked four times, each blink denoting the release of an incendiary cluster. The B-25 jumped, lightened of its 2000lb [900 kg] load, and Doolittle opened the throttles, anxious to get clear of the target area.

'The flight across Tokyo lasted thirty seconds… There was no time to observe the results of the attack; it was full throttle all the way to the coast…'

Handley Page Halifax

Like the Avro Lancaster, the Halifax began as a twin-engined design, although it was revised to take four Merlins before the first example flew in October 1939. The Mk I and Mk II versions with various armament layouts had Merlins, while the Mk III introduced the Bristol Hercules radial. The Mk VII was essentially similar, but was fitted with lower powered versions of the Hercules and a glazed dome in place of the rotating front turret. Subvariants were used to drop agents and commandos, and as troop transports, glider tugs and freighters. The Halifax had lesser performance than the Lancaster and usually flew at a lower altitude. The Canadian squadrons in No. 6 Group of Bomber Command were largely equipped with the Halifax for much of the war.

HANDLEY PAGE HALIFAX B.MK VII

Specification

Type: four-engined heavy bomber

Crew: 7

Powerplant: four 1231kW (1650hp) Bristol Hercules XVI air-cooled 14-cylinder radial engines

Performance: max speed 460km/h (285mph); service ceiling 5669m (18,600ft); range 1657km (1030 miles)

Dimensions: wing span 31.76m (104ft 2in); length 21.82 m (71ft 7in); height 6.32m (20ft 9in)

Weight: 29,448kg (65,000lb) loaded

Armament: two 12.7mm (0.50in) Browning machine guns in tail turret, four 7.7mm (0.303in) Browning machine guns in mid upper turret and one in nose; bomb load of up to 5895kg (13,000lb)

NO. 408 'GOOSE' SQUADRON, NO. 6 GROUP, ROYAL CANADIAN AIR FORCE, LINTON-ON-OUSE, YORKSHIRE, 1944

'Vicky the Vicious Virgin' is a rare example of a Royal Air Force (RAF) bomber with large and vivid nose art. The Canadian squadrons were less restrained than their British colleagues in this respect. PN230 was one of a batch of 150 B.IIIs and B.VIIs built under contract by Fairey Aviation at Stockport. Its only operational unit was No. 408 'Goose' Squadron, and it survived the war, being sold for scrap in 1949.

No. 408 Squadron received Halifaxes in September 1942, flying the Mk V and then the Mk II until October 1943. From then until September 1944 the squadron flew the radial-engined Lancaster Mk II, but reverted to the Halifax Mks III and VII in September 1944.

Avro Lancaster

The Avro Lancaster is the most famous of the Royal Air Force's 'heavies' of World War II, being able to carry a greater load at higher altitude than its contemporaries, the Halifax and Stirling. The Lancaster was derived from the unsuccessful Manchester, which had two Rolls-Royce Vulture engines and a three-fin tail section. The Manchester was redesigned to take four Merlins, and the central fin was removed. The first Lancaster was originally known as the Manchester III and flew in January 1941.

Making its first (daylight) raids in April 1942, the Lancaster went on to become the backbone of RAF Bomber Command's night-bomber force. The Lancaster also proved adaptable to carry various weapons for special operations, the most famous of which was the Dams Raid carried out by No. 617 Squadron in May 1943. The 'Dambusters' squadron was often partnered by No. 9 Squadron, which also conducted precision attacks with modified aircraft.

AVRO LANCASTER B.MK I

Specification

Type: four-engined heavy bomber
Crew: 7
Powerplant: four 1233kW (1640hp) Rolls-Royce Merlin 24 V-12
  piston engines
Performance: max speed 462km/h (287mph); service ceiling 7467m
  (24,500ft); range 2675km (1660 miles)
Dimensions: wing span 31.1m (102ft); length 21.1m (69ft 4in);
  height 5.97m (19ft 7in)
Weight: 31,750kg (71,000lb) loaded
Armament: eight 7.7mm (0.303in) Browning machine guns, up to
  6350kg (14,000lb) of conventional bombs or one 5443kg
  (12,000lb) 'Tallboy' or one 10,000-kg (22,000lb) 'Grand Slam' bomb

NO. 9 SQUADRON, ROYAL AIR FORCE, RAF BARDNEY, LINCOLNSHIRE, 1945
'Getting Younger Every Day' was normally flown by Flight Lieutenant Douglas Tweddle and crew of No. 9 Squadron. The aircraft was an Armstrong Whitworth–built Lancaster B.I (Special), which was modified to carry the 5443kg (12,000lb) Tallboy bomb designed by Barnes Wallis, who had also invented the 'bouncing bomb' used against the Ruhr dams. It is depicted dropping a Tallboy on the U-boat pens at Bergen, Norway, during a raid on 11/12 January 1945. Thirty-two Lancasters of Nos. 9 and 617 Squadrons were despatched and three, including one from No. 9 Squadron, lost. The U-boat pens were damaged, but not destroyed. A minesweeper in the harbour was sunk by a Tallboy while trying to escape. No. 9 Squadron went on to fly the Canberra and Vulcan bombers, and today flies the Tornado GR.4 from Lossiemouth, Scotland.

HANDLEY PAGE HALIFAX VS AVRO LANCASTER

ALTHOUGH THE HANDLEY PAGE Halifax was slower than the newer Lancaster, had a lower ceiling and could not carry as large a bomb load, it was much loved by its crews. Both bomber types could absorb a huge amount of battle damage and still get home.

The two incidents recounted here serve to illustrate the robustness of the two famous RAF night bombers, as well as the courage and tenacity of their crews. Each pilot was awarded the Victoria Cross. This is Flight Lieutenant Bill Reid's citation:

'On the night of 3 November, 1943, Flight Lieutenant William Reid was pilot and captain of a Lancaster aircraft detailed to attack Düsseldorf. Shortly after crossing the Dutch coast, the pilot's windscreen was shattered by fire from a Messerschmitt 110. Owing to a failure in the heating circuit, the rear gunner's hands were too cold for him to open fire immediately or to operate his microphone and so give warning of danger; but after a brief delay he managed to return the Messerschmitt's fire and it was driven off.

'During the fight with the Messerschmitt Flight Lieutenant Reid was wounded in the head, shoulders and hands. The elevator trimming tabs of the aircraft were damaged and it became difficult to control. The rear turret, too, was badly damaged and the communications system and compasses were put out of action. Flight Lieutenant Reid ascertained that his crew were unscathed, and saying nothing about his own injuries, he continued his mission.

'Soon afterwards, the Lancaster was attacked by a Focke-Wulf 190. This time, the enemy's fire raked the bomber from stem to stern. The rear gunner replied with his only serviceable gun, but the state of his turret made accurate aiming impossible. The navigator was killed and the wireless operator fatally injured. The mid-upper turret was hit and the oxygen system put out of action. Flight Lieutenant Reid was again wounded and the flight engineer, although hit in the forearm, supplied him with oxygen from a portable supply.

'Flight Lieutenant Reid refused to be turned from his objective and Düsseldorf was reached some 50 minutes later. He had memorized his course to the target and had continued in such a normal manner that the bomb-aimer, who was cut off by the failure of the communications system, knew nothing of his captain's injuries or of the casualties to his comrades. Photographs show that, when the bombs were released, the aircraft was right over the centre of the target.

'Steering by the pole star and the moon, Flight Lieutenant Reid then set course for home. He was growing weak from loss of blood. The

BELOW: A Halifax II of No. 10 Squadron RAF. In addition to its primary bombing role, the Halifax was used extensively for special duties, dropping agents and supplies into occupied Europe.

The Battle of Britain memorial flight Lancaster in the codes ('KM-B') of an aircraft of No.44 (Rhodesia) Sqn which took part in the Augsburg raids of April 1942.

emergency oxygen supply had given out. With the windscreen shattered, the cold was intense. He lapsed into semi-consciousness. The flight engineer, with some help from the bomb-aimer, kept the Lancaster in the air despite heavy anti-aircraft fire over the Dutch coast.

'The North Sea crossing was accomplished. An airfield was sighted. The captain revived, resumed control and made ready to land. Ground mist partially obscured the runway lights. The captain was also much bothered by blood from his head wound getting into his eyes, but he made a safe landing although one leg of the damaged undercarriage collapsed when the load came on.

'Wounded in two attacks, without oxygen, suffering severely from cold, his navigator dead, his aircraft crippled and defenceless, Flight Lieutenant Reid showed superb courage and leadership in penetrating a further 200 miles [320km] into enemy territory to attack one of the most strongly defended targets in Germany, every additional mile increasing the hazards of the long and perilous journey home. His tenacity and devotion to duty were beyond praise.'

Halifax Homecoming

On the night of 30/31 March 1944, Bomber Command despatched 572 Lancasters and 214 Halifaxes to Nuremberg, on what proved to be its most disastrous night raid of the war. The bomber stream came under constant attack from the moment it crossed the enemy coast.

One Halifax of No 578 Squadron, flown by Pilot Officer Cyril Barton, was attacked by a Junkers 88 some 70 miles [110km] from Nuremberg, and the night fighter's first burst of fire shattered the intercom system. A Messerschmitt 210 then joined in the battle, putting the Halifax's machine guns out of action. The attacks continued almost without pause as the bomber struggled on, and in the confusion at the height of the battle the navigator, bombardier and wireless operator, misinterpreting a hand signal from the pilot and believing the aircraft was about to crash, took to their parachutes.

Barton was now faced with an impossible situation. His aircraft was badly damaged, his navigator was gone and he was unable to communicate with the rest of the crew. If he continued the mission his defenceless aircraft would be completely at the mercy of hostile fighters when silhouetted against the fires of the target area, and if he survived he would have to make a four-and-a-half-hour journey home on three engines across heavily defended territory. Despite everything Barton decided to press on. The aircraft reached Nuremberg without further incident, and the pilot released the bomb load himself.

As Barton turned for home the propeller of the damaged engine, which was vibrating badly, flew off. To make matters worse, it was found that two of the fuel tanks had suffered battle damage and were leaking. He nevertheless stuck to his course and, in spite of strong headwinds, successfully avoided the most dangerous defensive areas along his route. He eventually crossed the English coast only ninety miles [145km] north of his base at Burn, in Yorkshire.

By this time the fuel supply was almost exhausted, and before a suitable landing place could be found the remaining port engine stopped. With two dead engines on the same wing the damaged aircraft was almost uncontrollable, and it was too low to be abandoned successfully. As Barton ordered the three remaining crew members to take up crash stations the starboard outer engine also stopped. With only one engine working the pilot made a desperate attempt to avoid some houses. The Halifax crashed on open ground and broke up. Barton was killed, but the three members of his crew survived to tell the full story of his gallantry. Barton was awarded a posthumous Victoria Cross.

For Bomber Command, the cost of the Nuremberg raid was stupendous; 96 bombers failed to return and 71 were damaged. It was the greatest victory achieved by the German night fighters. It was also their last.

Focke-Wulf Fw 190

The Focke-Wulf Fw 190 arose from a 1937 German Air Ministry requirement for a new single-seat fighter. Designer Kurt Tank produced a compact fighter around the most powerful engine available. The prototype Fw 190V1 first flew in June 1939, powered by a BMW 139 air-cooled radial. Production aircraft had the 1193kW (1600hp) BMW 801 14-cylinder engine. The first Fw 190As saw combat over the Channel front in September 1941, completely surprising Allied intelligence, who until then had no inkling of the new fighter's development. The early 190s were superior to the Spitfire V, setting in train a seesaw of development that lasted throughout the war.

The Fw 190F was a dedicated fighter-bomber with provision for a 500kg (1102lb) bomb under the fuselage and two 250kg (551lb) bombs under the wings. The F-2 subtype was based on the A-8 and introduced a new blown canopy. On the Eastern Front, the ground-attack units (*Schlachtgeschwadern*, literally 'slaughter wings') equipped with the Fw 190 were mainly used against Soviet armour, vehicles, outposts and troops, using a wide variety of anti-personnel and anti-armour weapons. Russian fighters were often encountered and a number of *Schlacht* pilots scored over 20 aerial victories.

FOCKE-WULF FW 190F-2

Specification
Type: single-engined ground-attack fighter
Crew: 1
Powerplant: one 1567kW (2100hp) BMW 801D-2 14-cylinder
 radial piston engine
Performance: max speed 634km/h (394mph); service ceiling
 13,410m (44,000ft); range 750km (466 miles)
Dimensions: wing span 10.51m (34ft 5.5 in); length 8.95m (29ft
 4.25in); height 3.95m (12ft 11.5in)
Weight: 4400kg (9700lb) loaded
Armament: two 7.9mm (0.31in) MG 17 machine guns in upper
 fuselage, with 1000 rounds each and two 20mm MG151/20 cannon
 with 200 rounds each in wings; bomb load of up to 350kg (802lb)

5. STAFFEL, II GRUPPE, SCHLACHTGESCHWADER 1, LUFTWAFFE KHARKOV, SOVIET UNION, 1943
The second *Gruppe* of *Schlachtgeschwader* 1 (II/SG 1) converted from the Ju 87 Stuka to the Fw 190F-2 at Deblin-Irena, Poland in March 1943. The 5. *Staffel* (squadron) used red spinners and code letters with white trim, but it was thought that red could be mistaken for Soviet markings, and these were changed to black before the unit entered combat.

Lavochkin La-5

The Lavochkin La-5 was a radial-engined development of the earlier LaGG-3. The first combat formation to equip with the new fighter was the 287th Fighter Air Division, commanded by Colonel S.P. Danilin, which was assigned to the 8th Air Army on the Volga Front, in the defence of Stalingrad.

Early combats showed that the La-5 was a better all-round performer than the Messerschmitt 109G, although its rate of climb was inferior. Lavochkin therefore undertook some redesign work to reduce the fighter's weight and re-engined it with the 1126kW (1510hp) M-82FN direct-injection engine, which endowed the La-5

with better climbing characteristics and manoeuvrability than either the Bf 109G or the Focke-Wulf FW 190A-4.

In addition to Soviet Air Force units, the La-5FN also equipped the 1st Czech Fighter Regiment, the pilots of which scored some notable successes. A variant of the La-5, the La-7, had a similar engine to the La-5 and differed only in minor design detail. A two-seat trainer version, the La-5UTI, was also produced, bringing total production of the La-5/La-7 series to 21,975 examples by the end of the war. Although the primary role of the La-5/La-7 series was that of low- and medium-level fighter, it was occasionally assigned ground-attack missions.

LAVOCHKIN LA-5FN

Specification
Type: fighter
Crew: 1
Powerplant: one 1230kW (1650hp) Ash-82FN radial engine
Performance: max speed 647km/h (402mph); service ceiling 11,000m (36,090ft); range 765km (475 miles)
Dimensions: wing span 9.80m (32ft 1in); length 8.67m (28ft 6in); height 2.54m (8ft 4in)
Weight: 3402kg (7500lb) loaded
Armament: two 20mm (0.79in) or 23mm (0.91in) cannon, plus provision for four 82mm (3.23in) RS-82 rockets or 150kg (330lb) of bombs or anti-tank mines

159TH FIGHTER AVIATION REGIMENT, SOVIET AIR FORCE, 1944
This Lavochkin La-5FN was flown by Kapitan Petr Yakovlevich Likholetov of the 159th Fighter Aviation regiment. Petr Likholetov's final score was 30 enemy aircraft destroyed. Seriously injured in a car crash at the end of 1944, he died of his injuries on 13 July 1945.

FOCKE-WULF FW 190 VS LAVOCHKIN LA-5

THIS SNAPSHOT OF a dogfight between the Fw 190 and the La-5 on the Eastern Front comes from a report by Feldwebel Schmidt of I/JG 51.

'In February 1943 we had to fly another escort sortie for the Stukas, for an attack on targets near Mzensk. The Chief and "Pepi" (Lt Jennewein), together with two other pilots, first start to clear the sky over Mzensk. Today it is the Day of the Red Army; we get pamphlets from the Russians in which they announce a new surprise. I am allotted to Karl as wingman. Karl has become my best friend – we understand each other better than brothers, but this action is to be our last flight together. Soon after take-off I realise that all is not well with my Fw 190, for the propeller blade control goes to negative by itself. I must control the regulation by hand to maintain my speed; a great problem for me. I am practically only an extra because I cannot share in any fighting under these conditions. I tell Karl what has happened and ask if I am allowed to return to base, but Karl says no, and he will give the necessary protection to the escorted Stukas.'

Into Combat

'Shortly before reaching the target I see the sky is full of Fw 190s, which are doing turning dogfights amongst themselves. I ask Karl if they have gone crazy. But Karl's sharp eyes have recognised that of about 40 planes only four are Fw 190s. The others are the announced surprise of the day – La-5s, which we meet here for the first time. Viewed in flight the only difference between them and our birds are the rounded wing-tips.

'After Karl's first burst one La-5 is immediately a fireball...'

BELOW: *One of the first 190A-3s being rolled off the production line at Bremen. The aircraft came as a nasty surprise to the Allies when it first appeared.*

ABOVE: *The Lavochkin La-5 at last gave the Soviet Air Force an aircraft that could meet the Fw 190 on equal terms. It was flown by the leading Allied air ace, Ivan Kozhedub.*

'The Stukas have realised the situation and dive down and disappear homewards as quickly as possible. Thank God! As soon as they are away I feel lighter in heart, and Karl and I turn for home when, suddenly, two La-5s come towards us at the same altitude. "Emmes, try to keep my speed," shouts Karl. I will try as best as possible, for without him I am lost with my lame bird. When we are just in front of the La-5s, Karl turns; the Russians do the same. Now I am really worried, but Karl is one of the best pilots I know. He begins the fight with a right turn. Most people like a left turn better; every cyclist will acknowledge this. Whoever can now do the right turn best has the advantage, and this, undoubtedly, is us. After Karl's first burst one La-5 is immediately a fireball, burning remarkably brightly. It dives down, and crashes in a cloud of black smoke.'

Eastern Front Ace

One of the most remarkable Soviet La-5 pilots was Alexei Maresyev, who despite losing both legs in a crash returned to fly combat aircraft in the summer of 1943, fitted with artificial limbs. During the battle of Kursk, in July 1943, Maresyev's fighter regiment was on patrol over the front with a squadron of Yakovlev Yak-9s flying top cover when a

shoal of blunt-nosed fighters slid by to starboard, at a lower altitude. They were quickly identified as Fw 190s.

'It was a 190, cannon twinkling, heading straight for him.'

The sky became filled with individual dogfights. A Yak-9 shot past with a 190 in hot pursuit, and Maresyev went after them, getting off a solid burst that tore off the German's tail unit. The 190 went over on its back and disappeared. Maresyev looked round and saw another Focke-Wulf, flying along straight and level. A short burst from Maresyev's guns and the German went into a spin, streaming a long ribbon of flame.

As the Russian pilot turned away steeply, a black dot on the centre of his windscreen grew rapidly larger. It was a 190, cannon twinkling, heading straight for him. Maresyev levelled out and doggedly held the La-5 steady. Tracer flashed over his cockpit. One of them would have to break, or there would be a collision. At the last instant, the German pulled up and Maresyev fired a burst into the 190's belly. The Russian hauled back the stick, pulled his fighter up into a loop and half-rolled off the top, looking down as he did so. The Focke-Wulf had vanished. Then he saw it, spinning down into the ground. It was his fifth kill in two days; he would finish the war with a score of 15.

Junkers Ju 52

The story of the Junkers Ju 52/3m, one of the most famous transport aircraft in history, began on 13 October 1930, with the maiden flight of the single-engined Ju 52/1m commercial transport. Eighteen months later, a new variant of the basic design appeared: this was the Ju 52/3m, fitted with three 429kW (575hp) BMW 132A radial engines (licence-built Pratt & Whitney Hornets). In 1934, a military version of the civil Ju 52/3m airliner was produced for use by the still-secret Luftwaffe. Designated Ju 52/3mg3e, the aircraft was designed as a heavy bomber. In 1934–35, no fewer than 450 Ju 52/3ms were delivered to the Luftwaffe. The type featured prominently in the Spanish Civil War, flying 5400 sorties for the loss of eight aircraft.

In April 1940, the Ju 52 was at the forefront of the invasions of Denmark and Norway. About 475 Ju 52s were available for the invasion of the Netherlands, and 493 took part in the invasion of Crete in May 1941. By the end of the year, around 300 Ju 52s were operating in the Mediterranean theatre. Between 5 and 22 April 1943, no fewer than 432 German transport aircraft, mostly Ju 52s, were destroyed as they tried to fly in supplies to Axis forces trapped in Tunisia. On the Russian front, five Ju 52 *Gruppen* took part in the Stalingrad airlift. Total production of the Ju 52/3m between 1939 and 1944, including civil models, was 4845 aircraft.

JUNKERS JU 52/3M

Specification

Type: transport aircraft

Crew: 2/3, plus 18 troops or 12 stretcher cases

Powerplant: three 544kW (730hp) BMW 132T-2 nine-cylinder radial engines

Performance: max speed 286km/h (178mph); service ceiling 5900m (19,360ft); range 1305km (811 miles)

Dimensions: wing span: 29.20m (95ft 10in); length 19.90m (62ft); height 4.52m (14ft 10in)

Weight: 11,030kg (24,317lb) loaded

Armament: four 7.92mm (0.31in) machine guns

GRUPPE, KAMPFGESCHWADER ZBV (TRANSPORT WING) 172, LUFTWAFFE, ITALY, 1943

The example illustrated here is a Junkers Ju 52/3mg5e of KGzbV 172. On its nose and tailfin, the aircraft carries a badge depicting Iolanthe, a flying cartoon pig popular in Germany.

Douglas C-47 Skytrain

The immortal C-47 first flew as the Douglas DST in December 1935 and, as the DC-3, was the most numerous airliner in US commercial service before World War II. From 1938, the US military took the first of many thousands of DC-3s with many different designations. The C-47 Skytrain was the main military transport version, which entered service in 1942. During and after the war, almost every Western air force acquired C-47s (often known by the British name Dakota), and a small number remain in service today, mainly in Africa and South America. The C-47 has had a new lease of life in recent years with the Basler Company at Oshkosh converting many to BT-67 Turbo Dakotas with PT6A-67R turboprops, lengthened fuselages and new instrumentation. Following the example of the AC-47 'Spooky' in Vietnam, several nations have converted some of their basic transports to gunships, with three 7.62mm (.30in) miniguns firing through the port-side windows.

DOUGLAS C-47 SKYTRAIN

Specification

Type: twin-engined transport aircraft

Crew: three plus up to 28 fully equipped troops

Powerplant: two 895kW (1200hp) Pratt & Whitney R-1830-92 Twin
  Wasp radial engines

Performance: max speed 370km/h (230mph); service ceiling 7315m
  (24,000ft); range 2340km (1510 miles)

Dimensions: wing span 28.96m (95ft 0in); length 19.66m (64ft 6in);
  height 5.16m (16ft 11.5in)

Weight: 12,701kg (28,000lb) loaded

COMANDO AÉREO DE TRANSPORTE MILITAR, FUERZA AÉREA COLOMBIANA, COLOMBIA, 1990S

This aircraft was built at Douglas's Oklahoma City plant in 1944 and delivered to the US Army Air Forces (USAAF) as 44-76916. After many years as a standard transport, FAC 681 was converted to BT-67 configuration circa 1987, then equipped as a gunship. It received the new serial FAC 1681.

JUNKERS JU 52 VS DOUGLAS C-47

Although there was a gap of only five years between the respective first flights of these iconic transport aircraft, there was a huge difference between Germany's Ju 52 and America's C-47.

Both were developed from civil airliners, but compared to the sleek, streamlined C-47, with its retractable undercarriage, the Ju 52 appeared lumbering and obsolescent. Nevertheless, the 'Tante Ju' (Auntie Ju) as it was known to its crews, played an enormous part in Germany's early victories – but at heavy cost.

During the invasion of Holland in May 1940, for example, Ju 52 units lost a total of 167 aircraft to enemy action, and a further 98 had been so badly damaged that they were irreparable. The transport unit responsible for landing airborne forces at the Hague, KGrzbV9, lost 39 of its 55 aircraft, while in the same sector KGrzb12 lost 40 machines and

BELOW: The Ju 52/3m, pictured here in the snow of Russia, was easy prey for Allied fighters. Hundreds were sacrificed in attempts to supply German forces.

was disbanded on the spot. Nevertheless, the assault on Holland, despite the losses incurred by the Germans, provided a shattering example of the effectiveness of airborne forces.

Ground fire accounted for most of the Ju 52 losses sustained during the invasion of Holland, and the same was true a year later, when German airborne forces invaded Crete. Initially, the airborne assault went well, only seven of the 493 Ju 52s being lost to enemy action. It was a different story later in the day, however, when the Ju 52s attempted to land troops of the 100th Mountain Regiment on Maleme airfield. Allied gunfire destroyed one third of the transport force as the aircraft landed to disgorge their troops, until the airfield was littered with the wrecks of 80 Ju 52s. 'Maleme was like the gates of hell,' reported the German divisional commander, Lieutenant-General Ringel.

ABOVE: *Built in huge numbers and still in service in many parts of the world today, the Douglas C-47 has a history unlike that of any other military aircraft.*

Allied C-47s usually had the benefit of far more fighter cover and ground attack support than did the luckless German Ju 52 units.

The Ju 52 transport units suffered further martyrdom in the winter of 1942–43, as they tried to supply the doomed German Sixth Army at Stalingrad; 266 Ju 52s were lost in that operation, and further disastrous losses were suffered in North Africa a few months later. In one combat alone, American P-40 Tomahawks and RAF Spitfires shot down 77 Ju 52s off the African coast.

Allied C-47s usually had the benefit of far more fighter cover and ground attack support than did the luckless German Ju 52 units. Sometimes, however, they had to penetrate areas lacking such support. During the British airborne operation at Arnhem in September 1944, although an Allied fighter screen kept the Luftwaffe at bay, fighter-bomber support was absent and transport aircraft were subjected to murderous fire. One such mission resulted in the posthumous award of the Victoria Cross to a Dakota pilot, Flight Lieutenant David Lord. The citation tells the story.

'Flight Lieutenant David Lord was pilot and captain of a Dakota aircraft detailed to drop supplies at Arnhem on the afternoon of the 19th September 1944. Our airborne troops had been surrounded and were being pressed into a small area defended by a large number of anti-aircraft guns. Aircrews were warned that intense opposition would be met… To ensure accuracy they were ordered to fly at 900 feet [275m] when dropping their containers.

Concentrated Fire

'While flying at 1500 feet [450m] near Arnhem the starboard wing of Flight Lieutenant Lord's aircraft was twice hit by anti-aircraft fire. The starboard engine was set on fire. He would have been justified in leaving the main stream of supply aircraft and continuing at the same height or even abandoning his aircraft. But on learning that his crew were uninjured and that the dropping zone would be reached in three minutes he said he would complete his mission, as the troops were in dire need of supplies.

'By now the starboard engine was burning furiously. Flight Lieutenant Lord came down to 900 feet [275m], where he was singled out for concentrated fire of all the anti-aircraft guns. On reaching the dropping zone he kept the aircraft on a straight and level course while supplies were dropped. At the end of the run, he was told that two containers remained.

'Although he must have known that the collapse of the starboard wing could not long be delayed, Flight Lieutenant Lord circled, rejoined the stream of aircraft and made a second run to drop the remaining supplies. These manoeuvres took eight minutes in all, the aircraft being continuously under heavy anti-aircraft fire.

'His task completed, Flight Lieutenant Lord ordered his crew to abandon the Dakota, making no attempt himself to leave the aircraft, which was down to 500 feet [150m]. A few seconds later the starboard wing collapsed and the aircraft fell in flames. There was only one survivor, who was flung out while assisting other members of the crew to put on their parachutes…'

David Lord's gallant exploit speaks for the bravery of all the transport aircraft crews, of whatever nationality, who risked everything to 'deliver the goods' in World War II.

Mitsubishi A6M Reisen

One of the finest aircraft of all time, the Mitsubishi A6M Reisen (Zero fighter) first flew on 1 April 1939, powered by a 582kW (780hp) Zuisei 13 radial engine; after 15 aircraft had been evaluated under combat conditions in China, the type was accepted for service with the Japanese Naval Air Force in July 1940, entering full production in November that year as the A6M2 Model 11. Sixty-four Model 11s were completed, these being powered by the more powerful Sakae 12 engine, and were followed by the Model 21 with folding wingtips. This was the major production version at the time of the attack on Pearl Harbor in December 1941.

The A6M2 soon showed itself to be clearly superior to any fighter the Allies could put into the air in the early stages of the Pacific war. In 1942, the Americans allocated the code name 'Zeke' to the A6M, but as time went by the name 'Zero' came into general use. During the first months of the conflict, the Zeros carved out an impressive combat record. In the battle for Java, which ended on 8 March 1942, they destroyed 550 Allied aircraft. These remarkable victories earned enormous prestige for the Japanese Navy pilots and tended to overshadow the achievements of their Army colleagues.

MITSUBISHI A6M2 REISEN

Specification
Type: carrier-borne fighter
Crew: 1
Powerplant: one 708kW (950hp) Nakajima NK1C Sakae 12
   14-cylinder radial engine
Performance: max speed 534km/h (332mph); service ceiling
   10,000m (32,810ft); range 3104km (1929 miles)
Dimensions: wing span 12.00m (39ft 4in); length 9.06m (29ft 8in);
   height 3.05m (10ft)
Weight: 2796kg (6164lb) loaded
Armament: two 20mm (0.79in) cannon and two fixed 7.7mm
   (0.303in) machine guns; external bomb load of 120kg (265lb)

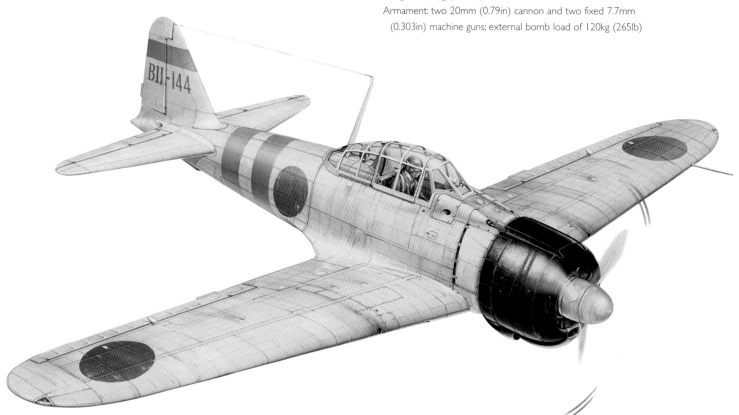

2ND SENTAI, 1ST KOKU KENTAI (AIR FLEET), *HIRYU* CARRIER AIR WING, IMPERIAL JAPANESE NAVY, MAY 1942
The Zero depicted here is in the colours of an aircraft that fought at the crucial Battle of Midway in June 1942, when the sinking of four Japanese aircraft carriers, including the *Hiryu*, effectively turned the tide of the Pacific war.

Grumman F6F Hellcat

In 1938, the airframe of the XF4F-2, predecessor of the Wildcat, was to be modified with the 1492kW (2000hp) R-2600 radial, but it was soon realized that this was impractical, not least because the necessarily larger propeller would not clear the ground. A complete redesign was begun, but this was put on hold as development of the Wildcat progressed. It was dusted off to produce a new fighter to replace the Wildcat in US Navy and US Marine Corps (USMC) service.

The XF6F-1 first flew in October 1942 and was broadly similar to the F4F, but was much larger (with the largest wing area of any US single-seat fighter), and its undercarriage retracted into the rearwards-folding wing. The armament was six machine guns. Deliveries of the production F6F-3 started in early 1943, and the Hellcat first saw combat on the Marcus Island raid, site of a Japanese naval base, which took place in August 1943.

The F6F-5 appeared from 1944 with relatively few changes to the F6F-3. The canopy glazing was altered and provision for bombs and rockets was added. This was the main production version, with more than half the 12,275 Hellcats being F6F-5s. A subvariant was the F6F-5P, which could carry cameras for the tactical reconnaissance role.

GRUMMAN F6F-5P HELLCAT

Specification
Type: single-seat carrier-based fighter
Crew: 1
Powerplant: one 1492kW (2000hp) Pratt & Whitney R-2800-10W
   18-cylinder radial piston engine
Performance: 612km/h (380mph); service ceiling 11370m (37,300
   ft); range 1674km (1040 miles)
Dimensions: 13.05m (42ft 10in); length 10.23m (33ft 7in); height
   3.99m (13ft 1in)
Weight: 6991kg (15,413lb)
Armament: six 12.7mm (0.50in) Browning machine guns in wings
   and up to two 454kg (1000lb) bombs or six 127mm (6in) rockets

VF-84, CVG-84, United States Navy, USS *Bunker Hill*, 1945
This F6F-5P was based aboard the USS *Bunker Hill* in February 1945 during a series of raids over Tokyo alongside two Marine Corsair units. VF-84 also flew some of the F6F-5N night-fighter model. The unit lost many aircraft and pilots when the *Bunker Hill* was hit by a Kamikaze attack on 11 May 1945. The squadron was disestablished on 8 October 1945. Later its nickname ('Jolly Rogers') and traditions were adopted by a new VF-84 and carried through to the modern era with the F-14 Tomcat.

A6M Reisen 'Zero' vs F6F Hellcat

By the summer of 1944 the Hellcat ruled the Pacific skies, and the best of Japan's pilots were dead. An account of one of the last air battles fought by Japanese air ace Saburo Sakai gives a clear idea of the odds the Japanese fighter pilots were facing at this period of the Pacific War.

'The formation of Japanese Navy aircraft droned steadily on over the featureless waters of the Pacific. There were seventeen of them: eight twin-engined Mitsubishi G4M 'Betty' bombers escorted by nine A6M Zero fighters. An hour earlier, the aircraft had taken off in a cloud of volcanic dust from the bomb-shattered airstrip on the island of Iwo Jima. For two days, American carrier aircraft had struck at the island with overwhelming force, destroying installations and virtually wiping out the Japanese combat squadrons based there. At the end of those two days, the Imperial Japanese Navy's original complement of 80 Zero fighters had been reduced to nine, while the eight G4Ms were all that remained of the original wing of 50 machines.

'The crews of fighters and bombers alike knew that in a very short time they were likely to die.'

'What was left of the Japanese Naval Air on Iwo was being pitted against impossible odds. Somewhere ahead of the formation, detected

BELOW: Japanese Zeros, in the foreground, assembled with other types at the start of the Pacific War.

by a reconnaissance aircraft the previous day, lay a large American task force, and Japanese Intelligence guessed that its destination was Iwo Jima. Intelligence, in fact, was only partly correct; although part of the task force had been detailed to bomb Iwo, the bulk of it was destined for the Philippines.'

Suicide Mission

'Japanese Naval Air Command had ordered every available aircraft on Iwo Jima to launch an immediate attack on the enemy. When the order first came through there had been plenty of machines to do the job, but then the US carrier aircraft had launched three massive strikes on the island. In the last raid alone, 40 Zeros had been destroyed, either in the air or on the ground, leaving the few survivors to carry out this hopeless mission.

'The crews of fighters and bombers alike knew that in a very short time they were likely to die. Once in the target area they were each to select an enemy ship and dive into it. The formation passed the black, bare rock that was Pagan Island, the first sight of land since leaving Iwo. Forty minutes later, a line of towering storm clouds rose above the horizon; somewhere beneath them lay the American warships. The

ABOVE: *The Grumman Hellcat was the fighter that turned the tide of the air war in the Pacific. At last, the Americans had a fighter that was more than a match for the Zero.*

Japanese began a gradual descent from 16,000 to 13,000 feet [5000 to 4000m]. The pilots would begin their last dives as soon as the warships were sighted, building up speed in the faint hope of evading the fighters that were sure to be there, alerted by radar.

'A Hellcat flashed through Sakai's sights and he fired...'

'A minute later, the glitter of sunlight on a wing surface ahead and above caught Sakai's eye. More flashes, and an avalanche of American fighters came tumbling down on the Japanese. They were Hellcats, and there were at least twenty of them. In line astern they ripped through the Japanese formation, firing as they went. The two leading Bettys disintegrated in a cloud of flame and smoke as the torpedoes they were carrying exploded.

'Two more Hellcat formations, more than fifty fighters, converged on the Japanese. A Hellcat flashed through Sakai's sights and he fired; the American fighter went into a series of flick rolls and plunged down, trailing smoke. The Zero pilots were soon fighting isolated

battles for their lives as the Bettys were hacked out of the sky. In under a minute, seven of the bombers were destroyed, their charred remains fluttering down towards the ocean beneath spreading clouds of black smoke. Two Zeros went down, balls of brilliant flame.

Escape from Death

'Sakai realised that it was pointless to fight on; the odds were too overwhelming. Gradually, in the middle of a whirling mass of Hellcats, his two wingmen sticking to him like glue, he edged his way towards a large storm cloud. Seizing their chance the three Zeros dived between two groups of Hellcats and plunged into the sheltering cloud. For endless minutes they went through the swirling darkness, eventually dropping from the cloud base a few hundred feet over a sea lashed by torrential rain.

'...Sakai decided to abandon the mission. The three Zeros turned and set course for Iwo Jima. Three hours later, they landed in darkness on the island's airstrip. One other Zero pilot had also found his way back, together with the sole surviving Betty bomber. The latter's pilot had found the ships, released his torpedo and run for it...

'The following day, 16 American warships appeared off Iwo Jima. They were unopposed. Their first salvo blasted the airstrip and wiped out the four Zeros that had fought their way back only a few hours earlier.'

Heinkel He 111

The most fascinating of all the varied operations carried out by the versatile Heinkel He 111H bomber were those undertaken by the Luftwaffe's *Kampfgeschwader* (G) 3, which was equipped with the Heinkel He 111H-22 variant. Following experiments at Peenemünde, the German secret weapons research establishment, in 1943, several He 111H-6s, H-16s and H-21s were modified to carry a Fieseler Fi 103 (V-1)

missile under the starboard wing and given the new designation He 111H-22. Despite the development of special night-attack techniques by the Germans, the lumbering combination of He 111 and the V-1 proved easy prey for the Royal Air Force's Mosquito night fighters, which patrolled constantly over the sea on the bombers' approach routes, often directed to their targets by radar picket ships.

HEINKEL HE 111H-22
AND FIESELER FI 103

Specification

Type: bomber and missile combination

Crew: 5

Powerplant: two 1007kW (1350hp) Junkers Jumo 211F inverted V-12 engines

Performance: max speed 436km/h (271mph); service ceiling 6700m (21,980ft); range 1950km (1212 miles)

Dimensions: wing span: 22.60m (74ft 1in); length 16.40m (53ft 9|in); height 3.40m (13ft 1in)

Weight: 14,000kg (30,865lb) loaded

Armament: one 20mm (0.79in) MG FF cannon in nose, one 13mm (0.51in) MG131 gun in dorsal position, two 7.92mm (0.31in) MG15 guns in rear of ventral gondola and two 7.92mm (0.31in) MG81 guns in each of two beam positions; one Fieseler Fi 103 flying bomb

III Gruppe, Kampfgeschwader 3, Luftwaffe Venlo, The Netherlands, 1944
The type was assigned to the newly formed III/Kampfgeschwader (KG) 3, which became operational at Venlo and Gilze-Rijn in the Netherlands in July 1944.

De Havilland Mosquito

Although designed as an unarmed, high-speed day bomber, the de Havilland Mosquito branched into two distinct paths of development, including a very successful series of night-fighters and fighter-bombers. The glazed-nosed bombers spawned a series of photo-reconnaissance models, which used their speed and high-altitude capability to avoid interception. They were largely built of wood, which reduced weight and the need for strategic materials. Subassemblies were constructed by such enterprises as furniture makers and piano factories.

The later reconnaissance Mosquitoes featured pressurized cockpits, lightened airframes and longer wings for high-altitude performance. The P.R.34 was built from late 1944 for use in the Far East, with a range of over 5633km (3500 miles), helped by its 1818-litre (400-gallon) slipper tanks, which were usually carried on the wings. The PR.34 was fitted with four F.52 vertical cameras and one F.24 oblique camera. The vertical camera was sighted by the observer in the nose, but the oblique cameras were aimed by lining up markings on the wing with the subject. The PR.34A differed mainly in having different marks of Merlin engine.

DE HAVILLAND MOSQUITO PR.34A

Specification
Type: twin-engined reconnaissance aircraft
Crew: 2
Powerplant: two 1261kW (1690hp) Rolls-Royce Merlin 113/114 V-12 piston engines
Performance: max speed 684km/h (425mph); service ceiling 12,120m (40,000ft); range 5630km (3500 miles)
Dimensions: wing span 16.5m (54ft 2in); length 12.7m (41ft 9in); height 4.66m (15ft 3.5in)
Weight: 11,340kg (25,000lb) loaded
Armament: none

NO. 81 SQUADRON, FAR EAST AIR FORCE, ROYAL AIR FORCE, RAF SELETAR, SINGAPORE, 1955
The Royal Air Force's No. 81 Squadron flew a mix of photo-reconnaissance Spitfires and Mosquitoes from Seletar, Singapore, into the 1950s. The squadron flew the last operational flight by an RAF Spitfire in 1954. No. 81 Squadron played an important role in the Malayan campaign, mapping the jungle in a search for terrorist camps.

HEINKEL HE 111 VS DE HAVILLAND MOSQUITO

ONE ROLE in which the de Havilland Mosquito particularly excelled was that of night-fighter, and it was the Mosquito that formed the first line of defence against the air-launched V-1.

In fact, by the time KG 53's Heinkels began operating as the world's first cruise missile carriers, Mosquito night-fighter crews had already amassed a great deal of experience in intercepting the elusive missiles when they were launched from their ramps in the Pas de Calais.

It was a Mosquito crew of No. 605 Squadron, Flight Lieutenant J.G. Musgrave and Flight Sergeant Sanewell, who became the first to shoot down a V-1. Soon after midnight on 15 June 1944 they were on alert at Manston in Kent when they received a warning of incoming V-1s and took off to intercept. Musgrave reported that 'It was like chasing a ball of fire across the sky. It flashed by our starboard side a few thousand feet away at the same height as we were flying. I quickly turned to port and gave chase. It was going pretty fast, but I caught up with it and opened fire from astern. At

BELOW: More than 7300 He 111s were produced between 1942 and 1945, the vast majority being -H models. This is an He 111H-16.

first, there was no effect so I closed in another hundred yards [91m] and gave it another burst. Then I went closer still and pressed the button again. This time, there was a terrific flash and explosion and the thing fell down in a vertical dive into the sea. The whole show was over in about three minutes.'

The first confirmed destruction of an He 111 carrier was achieved by a Mosquito of No. 409 Squadron.

Air-launched Missiles

The air-launched V-1 phase began on the night of 8/9 July 1944, when a missile came in from somewhere over the North Sea. In the early hours of 5 September a batch of air-launched bombs was launched at London. During this initial phase, which saw the launch of about 130 V-1s, the Heinkel crews operated with caution, choosing Portsmouth and Southampton as their primary targets. A few bombs were launched towards Gloucester, and those

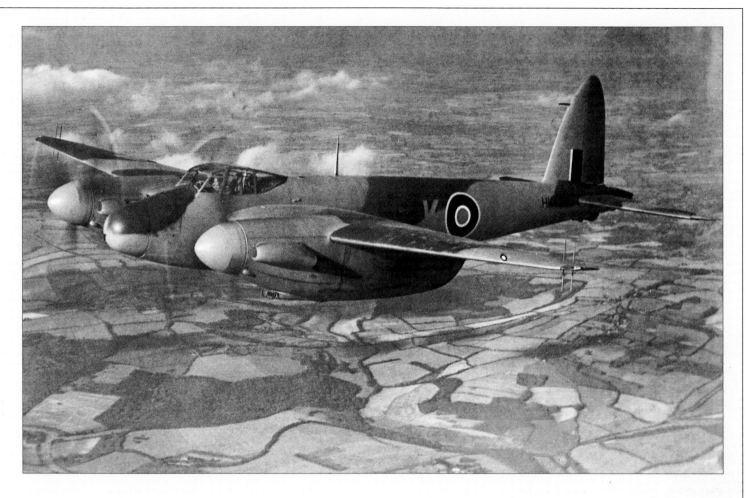

ABOVE: *Mosquito night-fighters inflicted serious losses on the Heinkel V-1 launchers. This photograph shows a B.XVI of No 571 Squadron, Light Night Striking Force.*

intended for London were released well out over the North Sea. The first confirmed destruction of an He 111 carrier was achieved by a Mosquito of No. 409 Squadron, on 25 September 1944. The main phase of the air-launched V-1 campaign lasted from 16 September 1944 to 14 January 1945, and the principal defence against it was provided by the Mosquito night-fighter squadrons based at Castle Camps, Coltishall and Manston. During this period the Mosquito crews certainly destroyed 14 Heinkels, six of them by the end of October 1944.

Hazardous low-level flights

Catching the Heinkels was difficult, for they flew low and slowly. Patrols were generally flown at 1219m (4000ft) between Britain and Holland, and since it was hard to locate the Heinkels by radar because of their low operating altitude, the Mosquito crews learned to look out for the flash as the V-1's pulse jet engine ignited when the weapon was launched.

As soon as the launch was completed, the Heinkel would turn hard through 180 degrees and head for its base at very low level. To improve interception rates a radar equipped frigate, HMS *Caicos*, and later a radar-equipped Wellington bomber, were used.

One of the most successful Mosquito squadrons was No. 25, which began anti-V-1 patrols from Coltishall on 24 September 1944. Its pilots damaged four Heinkels on the first night, and two were destroyed by the squadron commander, Wing Commander L.J. Mitchell, five nights later. By the time No. 25 Squadron moved from Coltishall to Castle Camps in October its crews had shot down at least three Heinkels and 22 V-1s. Another of the Mosquito squadrons involved was No. 68. One of its busiest nights was on 25 October, when the crews engaged nine V-1s, and on 5 November Sergeant Neal destroyed a Heinkel just after it had released its missile.

The Heinkels operated only on dark nights. To set up his attack, a Mosquito pilot had to fly at about 32m (100ft) above the sea at close to stalling speed, a hazardous manoeuvre that cost some crews their lives.

On one night in October, No. 125 Squadron scrambled three Mosquitoes from Coltishall. One crew made contact with an enemy bomber at a range of 7km (4.5 miles) and closed in to 609m (2000ft), at which point a V-1 was released. Closing right in to 274m (900ft), the Mosquito pilot, Sergeant Beal, reduced his speed to 193km/h (120mph) and opened fire, obtaining hits on the Heinkel's fuselage. He finished off the bomber with a two-second burst from only 25m (82ft).

Messerschmitt Me 163 Komet

The Me 163 Komet was based on the experimental DFS 194, designed in 1938 by Professor Alexander Lippisch and transferred, together with its design staff, to the Messerschmitt company for further development. The first two Me 163 prototypes were flown in the spring of 1941 as unpowered gliders, with the Me 163V-1 being transferred to Peenemünde later in the year to be fitted with its 750kg (1653lb) thrust Walter HWK R.II rocket motor. The fuel used was a highly volatile mixture of T-Stoff (80 per cent hydrogen peroxide; 20 per cent water) and C-Stoff (hydrazine hydrate, methyl alcohol and water).

The first rocket-powered flight was made in August 1941. During subsequent trials the Me 163 broke all existing world air speed records, reaching speeds of up to 1000km/h (620mph).

In May 1944, an operational Komet unit, *Jagdgeschwader* (JG) 400, began forming at Wittmundhaven and Venlo. Many Me 163s were lost in landing accidents. About 300 Komets were built, but JG 400 remained the only operational unit. The rocket fighter recorded only nine kills during its brief career, while at the same time losing 14 of its own aircraft in combat. All the victories were credited to I/JG 400, which ended the war at Nordholz in northern Germany and continued operating until the cessation of hostilities.

MESSERSCHMITT ME 163

Specification
Type: rocket-powered interceptor
Crew: 1
Powerplant: one 1700kg (3748lb) thrust Walter 109-509A-2 rocket motor
Performance: max speed 955km/h (593mph); service ceiling 12,000m (39,370ft); range 35.5km (22 miles)
Dimensions: wing span 9.33m (30ft 7in); length 5.85m (19ft 2in); height 2.76m (9ft)
Weight: 4310kg (9502lb) loaded
Armament: two 30mm (1.18in) Mk 108 cannon in wing roots

I Gruppe, Jagdgeschwader 400, Luftwaffe, Brandis, near Leipzig, Autumn 1944
This Me 163 displays the emblem of I *Gruppe, Jagdgeschwader* 400 (I/JG 400), depicting the notorious liar Baron Münchausen riding a cannonball. I/JG 400 was formed at Bad Zwischenahn in February 1944, II *Gruppe* being formed later at Wittmundhaven.

Boeing B-17 Flying Fortress

The Flying Fortress was the best-known US bomber of World War II and symbolized American air power for a decade from the late 1930s. The Boeing Model 299 flew in July 1935 and was followed by 13 pre-production Y1B-17s and then the B-17B, C and D. All of these had limited defensive armament, slim rear fuselages and a 'shark' fin. None of these versions was particularly successful in combat, having many troubles with superchargers and oxygen systems at altitude.

The B-17E introduced the familiar outline of the majority of Flying Fortresses, over 12,000 of which were eventually built by several contractors. The B-17F and the B-17G were the main versions used in Europe by the Eighth Air Force from 1942 to 1945. The chin turret was introduced on late-model B-17Fs and was fitted to all production Gs. Enclosed waist windows made life less uncomfortable for the gunners, and a new tail turret, not fitted to the aircraft illustrated, provided better visibility.

BOEING B-17G FLYING FORTRESS

Specification
Type: four-engined heavy bomber
Crew: usually 10
Powerplant: four 895kW (1200hp) Wright R-1820-97 Cyclone
  nine-cylinder radial piston engines
Performance: max speed 475km/h (295mph); service ceiling
  10,850m (35,600ft); range 5085km (3160 miles)
Dimensions: wing span 31.62m (103ft 9in); length 22.80m (74 ft
  9in); height 5.85m (19ft 2in)
Weight: 29,710kg (65,500lb) loaded
Armament: 13 x 12.7mm (0.50in) machine guns; bomb load of
  up to 6169kg (13,600lb)

322ND BOMBARDMENT SQUADRON, 91ST BOMBER GROUP, UNITED STATES EIGHTH AIR FORCE, RAF BASSINGBOURN, ENGLAND, 1944
B-17G serial No 42-31367 was built by the parent factory in Washington State, ferried to England and assigned to Lieutenant Jerry Newquist and crew, who christened it 'Chow-Hound'. The aircraft flew over 30 missions. The original crew flew their assigned missions and returned to the United States in mid-1944. Lieutenant Jack Thompson and crew took over 'Chow Hound', flying an additional dozen missions in the aircraft. On their thirteenth mission, a raid on Caen supporting the Normandy campaign carried out on 8 August 1944, the aircraft was shot down over France by a direct flak hit. Thompson was the only survivor and became a POW.

ME 163 KOMET VS B-17 FLYING FORTRESS

ON 28 JULY, 1944, P-51 Mustangs of the US Eighth Army Air Force's 359th Fighter Group, led by Colonel Avalin P. Tacon, Jr., were escorting B-17s at 7620m (25,000ft) over Merseburg when the pilots sighted two condensation trails at six o'clock.

The Mustang leader's combat report described the ensuing action: 'I identified them immediately as the new jet-propelled aircraft. Their contrails could not be mistaken and looked very dense and white, somewhat like an elongated cumulus cloud some three-quarters of a mile [1200m] in length.

'**Their speed, I estimated, was 500 to 600mph [800–950km/h].**'

BELOW: *The Me 163 was powered by a lethal fuel mixture that often turned it into a death trap.*

My section turned 180 degrees back towards the enemy, which included two with jets turned on and three in a glide without jets operating at the moment. The two I had spotted made a diving turn to the left in close formation and feinted towards the bombers at six o'clock, cutting off their jets as they turned. Our flight turned for a head-on pass to get between them and the rear of the bomber formation. While still 3000 yards [2750m] from the bombers, they turned into us and left the bombers alone. In this turn they banked about 80 degrees but their course changed only about 20 degrees. Their turn radius was very large but their rate of roll appeared excellent. Their speed, I estimated, was 500 to 600mph

ABOVE: *A Boeing B-17G Flying Fortress. The chin turret, also installed retrospectively in the B-17F, was to counter head-on attacks by enemy fighters.*

[800–850km/h]. Both planes passed under us 1000 feet [300m] below while still in a close formation glide. In an attempt to follow them, I split-S'd. One continued down in a 45-degree dive, the other climbed up into the sun very steeply and I lost him. Then I looked back at the one in the dive and saw he was five miles [8km] away at 10,000 feet [3000m].'

In fact, the attackers were not jet-propelled aircraft at all, but early operational examples of the rocket-powered Me 163.

Rocket Flight

What it was like to fly this remarkable aircraft was graphically described by Luftwaffe pilot *Leutnant* Mano Ziegler. 'During the first two hundred yards [180m] of my take-off run I was preoccupied with the pressure indicator. The pressure in the rocket's chamber had to be 340lb/sq in [2350kPa], and it was vitally necessary that it did not drop below 256 lb/sq in [1765kPa]. In such an eventuality I had to switch off the engine immediately and just hope for the best. Simultaneously, I had to ensure that my take-off run was perfectly straight, but this was not difficult once the Komet reached speed.

'The needle of the airspeed indicator flickered to the 190mph [300 km/h] mark and I felt the wheels leave the runway. I threw the switch jettisoning the undercarriage and the Komet lurched forward, pushing me back into my seat. A hurried glance at the airspeed indicator – 435 mph [700 km/h] – and I gently pulled on the stick, flashing upwards in a near vertical climb, the earth receding at a startling speed.'

Fast Climb

'The exhilaration of that first climb is indescribable. For the first time I felt at one with this remarkable aircraft. The Walter rocket thundered away behind me, but its deafening roar did not reach my consciousness, and I gave no thought to those lethal T-Stoff tanks on either side of my seat, which could turn me into a ball of fire without a second's warning.

> ## 'I was completely lost in the ecstasy of that seemingly endless climb.'

'I was completely lost in the ecstasy of that seemingly endless climb. Above me stretched the wide violet canopy of the sky, and I felt completely detached from the earth below…

'My Komet shuddered slightly and the rocket motor cut out. My fuel was exhausted and the drag was straining my body against the seat straps. I eased the throttle back to zero, levelled off, and reported to the control tower. I pushed the nose down slightly and now had some ten minutes of gliding flight available to examine the fighter's behaviour.

'I trimmed the plane carefully and then pulled the stick back slowly to discover what would happen in a stall. Virtually nothing happened. The airflow broke away, but the plane remained horizontal, dropping gently like an elevator. I pushed the stick forward, and immediately the speed began to build up. Port wing down, and I was in a steep dive… by now the altimeter indicated some 25,000 feet [7600m], and at the speed of 560mph [900km/h] that I had attained, my Mach number was 0.82, not much below the Komet's limiting Mach number, so I pulled back on the stick.. I had soon regained most of the altitude that I had lost in my dive.'

Messerschmitt Me 262

Delays in the development of satisfactory engines, the massive damage caused by Allied air attacks and Hitler's later obsession with using the aircraft as a bomber rather than a fighter all meant that six years elapsed between the Me 262 taking shape on Messerschmitt's drawing board and its entry into Luftwaffe service. The jet fighter presented a serious threat to Allied air superiority during the closing weeks of 1944.

Two versions were developed in parallel: the Me 262A-2a Sturmvogel (Stormbird) bomber variant and the Me 262A-1a fighter. The Sturmvogel was issued to *Kampfgeschwader* (KG) 51 'Edelweiss' in September 1944; other bomber units that armed with the type at a later date were KG 6, 27 and 54. Problems encountered during operational training delayed the aircraft's combat debut, but in the autumn of 1944 the 262s began to appear in growing numbers,

carrying out low-level attacks on Allied targets, mainly moving columns. There were also two reconnaissance versions, the Me 262A-1a/U3 and Me 262A-5a.

Towards the end of 1944, a new Me 262 fighter unit, *Jagdgeschwader* (JG) 7 'Hindenburg' was formed under the command of Johannes Steinhoff. Later, authority was also given for the formation of a second Me 262 jet-fighter unit, known as Jagdverband 44 and commanded by Adolf Galland. It comprised 45 highly experienced pilots, many of them Germany's top-scoring aces. Its principal operating base was München-Riem.

Sixteen German pilots became history's first jet-fighter aces. Foremost among them was *Oberst* Heinz Bär, who claimed 16 of his 220 victories while flying the Messerschmitt Me 262.

MESSERSCHMITT ME 262

Specification

Type: jet fighter

Crew: 1

Powerplant: two 900kg (1984lb) thrust Junkers Jumo 109-004B turbojets

Performance: max speed: 870km/h (541mph); service ceiling 11,450m (37,565ft); range 1050km (652 miles)

Dimensions: wing span 12.51m (41ft); length 10.60m (34ft 9in); height 73.83m (11ft 6in)

Weight: 7130kg (15,720lb) loaded

Armament: four 30mm (1.18in) MK108 cannon in nose; 24 R4M unguided air-to-air missiles on underwing racks

III GRUPPE, 9. STAFFEL, JAGDGESCHWADER 3, LUFTWAFFE PARCHIM, NORTHEAST GERMANY, APRIL 1945

North American P-51 Mustang

The North American P-51 Mustang was initially produced in response to a 1940 Royal Air Force (RAF) requirement for a fast, heavily armed fighter able to operate effectively at altitudes in excess of 6100m (20,000ft), the prototype flying on 26 October 1940. The first of 320 production Mustang Is for the RAF flew on 1 May 1941, powered by an 820kW (1100hp) Allison V-1710-39 engine. RAF test pilots soon found that with this powerplant the aircraft did not perform well at high altitude, but that its low-level performance was excellent. It was therefore decided to use the type as a high-speed ground attack and tactical reconnaissance fighter.

The RAF suggested that the aircraft would perform better at high altitude if it were fitted with the Rolls-Royce Merlin engine, and this arrangement produced the P-51B Mustang, along with a dramatic improvement in performance. The P-51B/C Mustang was followed by the P-51D, which featured a one-piece sliding canopy. In this guise, the aircraft became the P-51D.

The first production P-51Ds began to arrive in England in the late spring of 1944 and quickly became the standard equipment of the US Army Air Forces (USAAF) Eighth Fighter Command. There is no doubt at all that the Mustang, with its ability to escort bombers all the way to their targets and back, won the daylight battle over Germany.

NORTH AMERICAN P-51D MUSTANG

Specification

Type: long-range fighter

Crew: 1

Powerplant: one 1111kW (1490hp) Packard Rolls-Royce Merlin V-1650-7 V-type engine

Performance: max speed 704km/h (437mph); service ceiling 12,770m (41,900ft); range 3347km (2080 miles)

Dimensions: wing span 11.28m (37ft); length 9.85m (32ft 3in); height 3.71m (12ft 2in)

Weight: 5493kg (12,100lb) loaded

Armament: six 12.7mm (0.50in) machine guns, plus provision for up to two 454kg (1000lb) bombs or six 127mm (5in) rockets

47TH FIGHTER SQUADRON, 15TH FIGHTER GROUP US SEVENTH AIR FORCE, UNITED STATES ARMY AIR FORCES, IWO JIMA, 1945
P-51D Mustangs, like the 47th Fighter Squadron aircraft seen here, given the name 'Li'l Butch', arrived in the Pacific theatre early in 1945. Operating from Iwo Jima, they were able to rove over southern Japan, achieving complete air superiority for the Allies.

MESSERSCHMITT ME 262 VS P-51 MUSTANG

TOP SCORING ME 262 ace Heinz Bar, who destroyed 16 enemy aircraft while flying the fighter, had the following to say about Germany's revolutionary jet aircraft:

'Combat against American and British fighters was a highly varied thing, and pilot quality was the great imponderable factor until combat was actually joined. In general, P-38 Lightnings were not difficult at all. They were easy to outmanoeuvre and generally a sure victory. The P-47 Thunderbolt could absorb an astounding amount of lead. These aircraft had to be handled very carefully in combat because of the large number of hits they could take with no seeming impairment of their performance. The P-51 Mustang was perhaps the most difficult of all Allied fighters to meet in combat. The Mustang was fast, manoeuvrable, hard to see and difficult to identify because it resembled the Bf 109 closely in the air. These are my general impressions of Allied aircraft, and of course, the quality of the Spitfire needs no elaboration. They shot me down once and caused me at least six forced landings.

> **'The edge in performance and armament given us by the Me 262 was decisive in fighter combat.'**

'A very good pilot in any of these aircraft was tough to handle, and if he had the tactical advantage he had a good chance to win the fight. You see from my own eighteen experiences as someone else's victory, that they often did win. But when we got the Me 262 it was a different story, and they were at a tremendous disadvantage against us. The jet was just too much against a single propeller driven aircraft.

'We could accept or refuse combat with the Allied fighters. It was our choice. The edge in performance and armament given us by the Me 262 was decisive in fighter combat. This assumes, of course, that the Me 262 was functioning correctly on both engines. In the jets, we were in real trouble if we lost one engine, and it was a petrifying experience also to be low on fuel, preparing to land, and find that Allied fighters had followed you home.'

Combat Experience
That sentiment was echoed by fighter ace Adolf Galland, who commanded an elite Me 262 unit, Jagdverband 44, in the closing weeks

BELOW: The Messerschmitt Me 262 was an excellent aerodynamic design but suffered from primitive turbojet technology, its engines having a life of only 25 hours.

ABOVE: *The North American P-51D Mustang, fitted with a Rolls-Royce Merlin engine, established Allied air superiority over northwest Europe in 1944, and over Japan in 1945.*

of the war. His aircraft was damaged in an air battle and he was forced to make an emergency landing at Munch airfield just as Thunderbolts were strafing it.

'Brake! Brake! The kite would not stop, but at last I was out of it and into the nearest bomb crater. There were plenty of them on our runways. Bombs and rockets exploded all around, burst of shells from the Thunderbolts whistled and banged. A new low-level attack. Out of the fastest fighter in the world into a bomb crater – an unutterably wretched feeling!'

US Victory

February 1945 saw a great deal of Me 262 activity. The biggest day was on the 25th, when seven of the jets were destroyed by P-51s of the 55th Fighter Group during a fighter sweep in the vicinity of Giebelstadt airfield. Two of the 262s were destroyed by Captain Donald Cummings, who reported:

'The 262 then rolled to the right and went straight in from 800ft, exploding as it went.'

'I was leading Hellcat Yellow Flight on a fighter sweep in the vicinity of Giebelstadt A/D when several Me 262s were called in at nine o'clock, taking off from the field. Captain Penn, the squadron leader, ordered us to drop our tanks and engage the enemy.

'I peeled off from 11,000ft [3350m], making a 180 degree turn to the left in a seventy degree dive after a jet which was then approaching the aerodrome. I commenced firing from

approximately 1000yd [910m] in a steep, diving pass and after about three seconds observed many strikes. Since I was closing fast and approaching the airfield, which was beginning to throw up intense and accurate flak, I broke left and up, taking evasive action when about one-third of the way across the field. My wingman, who was behind me, saw the E/A touch the ground, cartwheel and burn. During the above engagement my number three and four men had become separated from the flight, so my wingman and I set out on a course of 180 degrees at 5000ft [1500m] in search of ground targets. Near Leipheim A/D we spotted an unidentified aircraft crossing the south-west corner of the field at 4000 feet [1200m]; 150 degrees. We increased our speed and closed in on the E/A which we identified as an Me 262 with dark camouflage and large crosses on its wings. As I came in range, the jet made a sharp turn to the left, losing altitude. When I followed him, closing slowly, he started to let down his nosewheel, apparently intending to land. Closing further to 400yd [365m], I commenced firing. The first burst missed, but when the jet attempted to turn to the right I gave it to him again at about ten degrees deflection and observed many strikes. Large pieces of the E/A began to fly off and the fuselage exploded below the cockpit. The 262 then rolled to the right and went straight in from 800ft [240m], exploding as it went.'

THE EARLY YEARS OF THE COLD WAR 1945–60

World War II had barely ended before a war of a different kind erupted: a Cold War in which the Western Alliance, soon to become NATO, entered into decades of confrontation with the Soviet Union and its satellites. As each side built up awesome arsenals of nuclear destruction, the need for accurate intelligence gathering became paramount. During the 20 years after 1945, it was air reconnaissance that dominated the military aviation scene, with hundreds of clandestine flights made into the air space of Soviet Russia and Communist China. Many more flights were made around the periphery of the USSR as NATO 'ferret' aircraft probed the secrets of Russia's air defences, gathering electronic information that would have meant the difference between life and death for the USAF and RAF bomber crews tasked with the nuclear annihilation of key targets in the Soviet Union.

A number of these aircraft fell victim to fighters or missiles, the facts surrounding their true fate covered up for many years after the event. There are stories of pure drama here, as the USAF took incredible risks to secure the information it needed.

This chapter examines the reconnaissance aircraft in use during the hottest part of the Cold War, including the RAF's Canberra PR.9 reconnaissance aircraft, which saw half a century of operational service, and the Boeing RB-47 Stratojet, converted from one of the earliest jet bombers. The chapter also examines the aircraft that would have fought one another had the Cold War erupted into a shooting match at the time of the Berlin blockade of 1948, aircraft like the RAF's Hawker Tempest II and Russia's Yakovlev Yak-9. It looks at the relative merits of NATO's early jet fighters, the Lockheed F-80 Shooting Star and the de Havilland Vampire, and analyzes the likely effectiveness of night-fighters like the Meteor NF. 12 against Russia's first jet bomber, the Ilyushin Il-18.

This chapter also takes a look at the aircraft developed to track and destroy the Soviet Navy's expanding submarine fleet, the Avro Shackleton and the Lockheed P-3 Orion, and the tactical transport aircraft that were to prove such an enormous asset to the Cold War ground forces, the Lockheed C-130 Hercules and the Antonov An-12. It also examines the curious instances when aircraft designed to fight on the same side against a common enemy – the North American F-86 Sabre and the Hawker Hunter – ended up fighting one another, in this case during the fierce conflict between India and Pakistan. In the same era, the state of Israel's constant confrontations with her Arab neighbours formed a deadly testing ground for the combat aircraft of East and West, as French Mystères and Mirages and Russian MiGs fought for the sky over the Middle East.

LEFT: *The North American F-86 Sabre was the first US jet fighter to enter air combat, fighting Soviet- and Chinese-built aircraft over the skies of Korea between 1950 and 1953 and shooting down 792 MiG-15s.*

BELOW: *The Dassault Mirage III was a French design that was combat tested by the Israeli air force during the 1960s, when it inflicted a heavy toll on Arab MiG fighters.*

Hawker Tempest II

The origins of the Tempest Mk II can be traced to a proposal by Hawker Aircraft for a Typhoon Mk II with a radial engine, but the prototype of the Centaurus-Typhoon Mk II was abandoned without being flown because sufficient experience had already been amassed through flight trials with the Centaurus-engined Hawker Tornado.

First flown in September 1943, the radial-engined Tempest II was intended for operations in the Far East, but the war ended before the type made its operational debut. The Tempest II entered service with No. 54 Squadron at Chilbolton, Hampshire, in November 1945, and the type subsequently equipped eight squadrons, serving in India, Malaya and with Second Tactical Air Force (TAF) in Germany.

Development of the Tempest II was delayed by problems with the powerplant, and in the event it was the Napier-engined Mk V which was the first Tempest model to enter production, seeing action in the last year of World War II. However, the fast and powerful Mk II performed a useful ground-attack function in Germany during the dangerous early years of the Cold War, and No. 33 Squadron used the type successfully against communist insurgents in Malaya from 1949–51. India and Pakistan took delivery of 89 and 24 Tempest IIs, respectively, in 1947–48.

The Tempest II was the last of the Royal Air Force's single-engined piston fighters, the squadrons that used it mostly converting to de Havilland Vampire FB.5 jet fighter-bombers in 1948. Total production of the Tempest II reached 472 examples, the first of which was completed in October 1944.

HAWKER TEMPEST F.MK II

Specification
Type: fighter-bomber
Crew: 1
Powerplant: one 1931kW (2590hp) Bristol Centaurus V 18-cylinder
    two-row radial engine
Performance: max speed 708km/h (440mph); service ceiling
    10,975m (36,000ft); range 2736km (1700 miles)
Dimensions: wing span 12.49m (41ft); length 10.49m (34ft 5in);
    height 4.42m (14ft 6in)
Weight: 6305kg (13,900lb) loaded
Armament: four 20mm (0.79in) cannon; external bomb or rocket
    load of up to 907kg (2000lb)

N<small>O</small>. 16 S<small>QUADRON</small>, S<small>ECOND</small> T<small>ACTICAL</small> A<small>IR</small> F<small>ORCE</small>, R<small>OYAL</small> A<small>IR</small> F<small>ORCE</small>, F<small>ASSBERG</small>, G<small>ERMANY</small>, 1947

Yakovlev Yak-1/9

It was not until 1939–40 that the prototypes of Soviet fighters that could really be classed as modern made their appearance. One was the Yak-1 Krasavyets (Beauty), which made its first public appearance during an air display on 7 November 1940. It was Aleksandr S. Yakovlev's first fighter design. The slow production rate of the Yak-1 in some areas following the relocation of factories led to the decision to convert a trainer variant of the Yak-1, the Yak-7V, into a single-seat fighter. In this new guise, the aircraft was designated Yak-7A. Its

development proceeded through a line of variants with heavier armament and longer range, culminating in the Yak-9, a superb fighter aircraft that did much to win air superiority over the eastern battlefront.

The Yakovlev Yak-9 was used by the Soviet and satellite air arms for some years after the war, and saw combat over Korea. A further development of the basic Yak-1 airframe was the Yak-3, which reached the front line during the early summer months of 1943 and which was probably the most manoeuvrable fighter aircraft of World War II.

YAKOVLEV YAK-1/9

Specification refers to the Yak-9

Crew: 1

Powerplant: one 1230kW (1650hp) Klimov VK-107A Vee-type
  engine

Performance: max speed 700km/h (435mph); service ceiling
  11,900m (39,040ft); range 870km (540 miles)

Dimensions: wing span 9.77m (32ft); length 8.55m (28ft); height
  2.44m (8ft)

Weight: 3068kg (6760lb) loaded

Armament: one 23mm (0.90in) cannon and two 12.7mm (0.50in)
  machine guns

303RD FIGHTER AIR DIVISION, FIRST SOVIET AIR ARMY, 3RD UKRAINIAN FRONT, 1944
The Yak-3 illustrated here was flown by Major General Georgii Nefedovich, who ended the war with a total of 23 victories. Nefedovich commanded the 303rd Fighter Air Division, one of the units of which was the Regiment Normandie, composed of Free French pilots and ground crews who had arrived in Russia from the Middle East in 1942. The air regiment was given the title 'Normandie-Niemen' in honour of its exploits.

HAWKER TEMPEST II VS YAKOVLEV YAK-9

HAD WAR ERUPTED BETWEEN the Western Allies and the Soviet Union in the late 1940s, the RAF's Hawker Tempest II fighter and the Soviet Air Force's Yakovlev Yak-9 would certainly have fought each other.

The first Tempest II squadron within the British Air Forces of Occupation in Germany was No. 33, which began to exchange its Spitfire F.Mk XVIEs for the new type at Fassberg in October 1946. This squadron in fact formed the nucleus of the Fassberg Tempest Mk II Wing, No. 135, which was eventually to comprise three squadrons. The second was No. 26, which relinquished its Spitfire F.XIVs at Chivenor in December and returned to Fassberg with new Tempest Mk IIs in January 1947; and the third was No. 16, which received Tempest IIs in April 1947.

The Tempest II remained the most potent fighter-bomber available to the Anglo-American forces in Europe.

In November 1947 No. 26 Squadron deployed to Gütersloh, where it was joined in December by the other two squadrons of No. 135 Wing. Gütersloh was to be the Wing's base for the remainder of its Tempest days. The Wing Commander (Flying) at Gütersloh during this period was the redoubtable and greatly liked Wing Commander Frank Carey, whose exploits against the Japanese in the Far East had made him an almost legendary figure.

For a long time – in fact, until the first Lockheed F-80 Shooting Stars were deployed to Germany at the time of the Berlin crisis of 1948 – the Tempest II remained the most potent fighter-bomber

BELOW: *Too late to see action in WWII, the Tempest II proved a valuable asset in the late 1940s.*

ABOVE: *The Yakovlev Yak-9 was a splendid fighter design. The inscription on these aircraft reads 'Little Theatre to the Front', indicating that they were donated by patrons of Moscow's 'Little Theatre'.*

available to the Anglo-American forces in Europe, and the Gütersloh Wing retained a high degree of efficiency in its main role of army co-operation. Its primary task was tactical reconnaissance, and the provision of close support when required. The Wing carried out frequent live practices with 227kg (500lb) and 454kg (1000lb) bombs, rocket projectiles, napalm and smoke canisters, as well as with the Tempest's built-in cannon armament.

In the months after the end of World War II, the Russians had paid much attention to repairing airfields in and around Berlin, for use by the Sixteenth Air Army's combat squadrons. It was the Sixteenth Air Army that was to form the Soviet Air Force of Occupation in their zone of Germany, and it maintained a heavy presence. For example, Tempelhof, Berlin's civil airport, was occupied by the Yak-9s of the 515th Fighter Air Regiment and later by other units of the 193rd Fighter Air Division, while the 347th and 518th Fighter Air Regiments, also with Yak-9s, moved into Schönefeld and the 265th Fighter Air Division stationed its Lavochkin La-5s at Dalgow.

Berlin Blockade

In June 1948, the Russians closed rail and road access to West Berlin through their zone, precipitating the massive year-long supply operation that became known as the Berlin Airlift. Before long, Allied transport crews began to encounter increasing numbers of Soviet aircraft in the corridors, many of them Yak-9s.

One of the favourite Russian tactics was to fly at high speed along the corridors, usually in the opposite direction to the stream of transport aircraft, either singly or in formation. The fighters would make a fast head-on pass at a transport, pulling up at the last minute. In the year from August 1948 to August 1949, American transport crews alone reported 77 'buzzing' incidents in the air corridors by Soviet aircraft, together with another 96 incidents that were loosely described as 'close flying'.

The Americans also stated that Russian fighters fired bursts of cannon and machine-gun fire in the vicinity of transport aircraft on 14 separate occasions, although no instance of a deliberate attack was recorded.

Fortunately, no actual combat comparison ever had to be made between the Tempest II and the Yak-9 (or the latter's lightweight version, the Yak-3). Commenting on this period, one senior RAF officer, Air Marshal Ian Macfadyen stated that:

'The Tempests and Spitfires of 1945 were short-lived and were replaced within two years by the Vampire FB5 – a nice aeroplane to fly and one that brought air defence in BAFO into the jet age. Both the Tempest and the Vampire retained an air/ground capability along with daylight air defence. These skills were practised on a number of ranges then in Germany, including the base at the famous beach resort of Sylt.'

Russian fighters fired bursts of cannon and machine-gun fire in the vicinity of transport aircraft...

Before the Berlin Airlift ended, two of the Gütersloh squadrons had re-equipped with Vampire FB.5s. No. 16 was the first to do so, in December 1948, followed by No. 26 in April 1949. By that time, the Yak-9 and other Soviet piston-engined fighters were also giving way to Russia's first operational jets, the Yak-15 and MiG-9.

Tupolev Tu-2

The prototype Tu-2 light bomber flew for the first time on 29 January 1941, and subsequent flight testing showed that the aircraft had an outstanding performance. Delays in engine availability, however, meant that limited production did not get under way until the beginning of 1942, and deliveries were slow because of the need to relocate many Soviet aircraft factories ahead of the rapid German advance into Russia. Pilots were particularly enthusiastic about the bomber, their reports stressing its substantial bomb load and excellent combat radius, good defensive armament, its ability to fly on one engine, and the ease with which crews were able to convert to the new type.

Series production of the Tu-2 did not start until 1943 because of the earlier problems, and combat units did not begin to rearm with the bomber until the spring of 1944, the initial major production model being the Tu-2S. The Tu-2 first saw action on a large scale in June 1944 on the Karelian (Finnish) front. In its primary bombing role, the Tu-2 carried out some extremely effective missions in the closing months of the war, particularly against fortified enemy towns.

In October 1944, a long-range variant, the Tu-2D (ANT-62), made its appearance. A torpedo-bomber variant, the Tu-2T (ANT-62T), was tested between January and March 1945, and issued to units of the Soviet Naval Aviation. The Tu-2R, also designated Tu-6, carried a battery of cameras in the bomb bay.

TUPOLEV TU-2S

Specification
Type: light bomber
Crew: 4
Powerplant: two 1380kW (1850hp) Shvetsov Ash-82FN radial
 engines
Performance: max speed 547km/h (340mph); service ceiling 9500m
 (31,170ft); range 2000km (1243 miles)
Dimensions: wing span 18.86m (61ft 10in); length 13.80m (45ft 3in);
 height 4.56m (14ft 11in)
Weight: 12,800kg (28,219lb) loaded
Armament: two 20mm (0.79in) cannon and three 12.7mm (0.50in)
 machine guns

SOVIET AIR FORCE, AUGUST 1945
Seen here is a Tupolev Tu-2S wearing a similar camouflage scheme as those aircraft which participated in the Soviet Aviation day parade over Moscow on 18 August 1945.

Northrop P-61 Black Widow 🇺🇸

Although the prototype XP-61 night fighter flew on 21 May 1942, it was another 18 months before the first production P-61A Black Widow aircraft appeared. The 421st Night Fighter Squadron (NFS) of the 18th Fighter Group was the first to rearm with the new type, operating from Mokmer in New Guinea. The 421st NFS, which was joined in the theatre at later dates by the 418th and 547th NFSs, moved to Tacloban, Leyte, on 25 October 1944.

In the European theatre, P-61As were issued to the 422nd NFS at Scorton, Yorkshire, in May 1944, followed by the 425th at Charmy Down. Their task was to provide night protection for the

American sectors of the Normandy invasion, which took place on 6 June 1944. Before departing for the continent, the two squadrons flew some sorties against V-1 flying bombs, shooting down nine of the pilotless aircraft. There were also two Black Widow squadrons, the 426th and 427th, in the China–Burma–India (CBI) theatre.

In the Central Pacific, the US Seventh Air Force had three Black Widow squadrons, the 6th, 548th and 549th. The last two arrived in the theatre on 7 and 24 March 1945, respectively, being based on Iwo Jima. The 548th NFS soon moved up to Ie Shima.

NORTHROP P-61 BLACK WIDOW

Specification
Type: night-fighter
Crew: 3
Powerplant: two 1491kW (2000hp) Pratt & Whitney R-2800-65
  18-cylinder radial engines
Performance: max speed 589km/h (366mph); service ceiling
  10,090m (33,100ft); range 4506km (2800 miles)
Dimensions: wing span 20.12m (66ft); length 15.11m (49ft 7in);
  height 4.46m (14ft 8in)
Weight: 13,472kg (29,700lb) loaded
Armament: four 20mm (0.79in) cannon and (on some aircraft) four
  12.7mm (0.50in) machine guns

548TH NIGHT FIGHTER SQUADRON, US SEVENTH AIR FORCE IE SHIMA, 1945
The P-61B seen here, dubbed 'Midnite Madness II', was crewed by Captain James W. Bradford (pilot), First Lieutenant Lawrence K. Lunt (radar operator) and Master Sergeant Reno H. Sukow (gunner). This crew destroyed a Mitsubishi G4M Betty bomber on the night of 24 June 1945.

TUPOLEV TU-2 VS NORTHROP P-61 BLACK WIDOW

THE YEARS that followed the communist victory over Chiang Kai-shek's Nationalist forces in China saw massive quantities of arms injected into the country, mostly by the Soviet Union.

Among the aircraft types delivered to the Chinese People's Liberation Air Force (CPLAF) were Tupolev Tu-2 light bombers, which had sufficient range to threaten US installations in Japan. During this period the Japan-based Black Widow night-fighter squadrons, the 68th at Itazuke and the 339th at Yokota, were on a state of constant high alert, ready to engage an attack if it should come.

Combat Tested

The Black Widow was a formidable fighting machine, as is illustrated by the following combat reports, both of which involve actions in the Pacific theatre towards the end of World War II. The first report was filed on the night of 25/26 December 1944 by Lieutenant Dale Haberman (pilot) and Lieutenant Raymond Mooney (Radar Observer).

'Scrambled from Condor Base then to Coral Base and vectored to the north of the island [Mindanao] at altitude of 15,000ft [4500m]. Coral Base ordered figure 8 orbits since they had no Bogies in the

BELOW: The Tupolev Tu-2 was the standard tactical bomber in the Soviet satellite air forces in the immediate post-war years.

vicinity but much Snow [fuzzy radar image] was in the area. Contact made with airborne radar at five miles [8km]. Control notified... reported Bogies in vicinity but could give no information. Went into starboard orbit but airborne radar kept picking up Bogie which seemed to be in orbit. Chased Bogie to the north and let down to 9000ft [2750m] when visual contact was made. Opened fire at 1500ft [450m] and closed to 700ft [210m]. Bogie made violent turns and hits observed to go into wings and fuselage. Bogie was in a slight dive indicating 300mph [480km/h]. Bogie last seen to roll to port in semblance of Split-S and nose straight down with fires observed coming from the right wing and engine. Visual lost as Bogie was at 6000ft [1800m] still going straight down, apparently out of control.

'I closed to 150ft (45m) and fired one short burst. The Tony exploded...'

'At the same time the Radar Observer called for a starboard turn as a second Bogie was out about two miles [3.2km]. Closed fast on second Bogie letting down to 4500ft [1300m] where visual was made at about 2500ft [750m]. Closed in to 700ft [210m] and opened fire with hits

ABOVE: It took the P-61 Black Widow a long time to reach operational status, but when it did it proved a very powerful weapon, its heavy armament giving its opponents little chance.

observed to spray the entire ship. Bogie exploded with its debris hitting P-61 with damage to left cowling. Bogie went down in flames and was seen to hit the water.'

The second report, by Lieutenant Bertram C. Tompkins of the 418th Fighter Interceptor Squadron, describes an action fought on 27 January 1945. The squadron was then based on Mindoro.

'Approximately one and a half hours after becoming airborne the GCI controller vectored me onto a Bogey approaching from the northwest. F/O Wertin made radar contact with Bogey at 0010 at a distance of six miles [10km] and altitude of 10,000ft [3000m] on heading of 280 degrees.

'He directed me to 2000ft [600m] directly behind and below Bogey and I obtained a visual and identified it as a Tony [Kawasaki Ki-61]. I closed to 150ft [45m] and fired one short burst. The Tony exploded and fell burning into the water approximately twenty miles [32km] west of base. No evasive action was used by enemy aircraft.

'Immediately GCI vectored me onto second Bogey, which was twenty miles [32km] southeast of me. F/O Wertin made radar contact at six miles [10km] and directed me to 3000ft [900m] directly behind and slightly below the Bogey, where I got a visual. I closed to 300ft [90m] and fired one burst, and enemy aircraft exploded and fell to the water burning. Kill was made approximately five miles [8km] west of Mindoro coast. E/A was identified as a Tony. Violent evasive action was used.'

Although the Tu-2 never met the Black Widow in combat after the war – and the big Northrop fighter was replaced by the more capable North American F-82 Twin Mustang by mid-1950 – the Russian-built bomber did encounter American fighters during the Korean War, with disastrous results. On 30 November 1951, 31 F-86 Sabres of the 4th Fighter-Interceptor Group, led by Colonel Benjamin S. Preston, sighted a formation of 12 Tu-2s escorted by 16 piston-engined Lavochkin La-9s and 16 MiG-15 jet fighters, heading south across the Yalu river from Manchuria.

One of the Sabre pilots, Major Winton W. 'Bones' Marshall, described what happened next.

'The Colonel called for a head-on pass by two squadrons of the Sabres. I came over the bombers just as the Sabres struck. As our fighters poured it on, the whole sky became alive with smoke and flame. It was really a sight – our boys scoring hits all over the bombers, and their fighters could do nothing because of the Sabres' superior speed.'

'As our fighters poured it on, the whole sky became alive with smoke and flame... their fighters could do nothing'

The brief, one-sided battle cost the Chinese eight Tu-2s, three La-9s and a MiG-15. Three Tu-2s and the MiG had been claimed by one pilot, Major George A. Davis, who would go on to win the Medal of Honor – and lose his own life in air combat.

Armstrong Whitworth Meteor NF.12

Gloster's first fighter aircraft since the biplane Gladiator, the Meteor first flew in March 1942 and was the first operational jet fighter. It saw limited service in its initial day-fighter form in the last months of World War II. Many improved models followed and, by the mid-1950s, Meteors were the mainstay of Royal Air Force (RAF) Fighter Command and were sold to several foreign air forces including Israel, Argentina and Australia.

The Armstrong Whitworth Company built many Meteors under licence and developed the NF.11, NF.12, NF.13 and NF.14 radar-equipped night-fighters. Armament remained four 20mm (0.79in) cannon, now mounted in the wings to leave room for the AI Mk 21 nose radar. None had ejection seats. These variants differed visually mainly in fuselage length and canopy detail. Different models of engine and radar were the main internal differences.

Egypt, Syria and Israel received a few Armstrong Whitworth NF.13s. One of the few actual combats for the NF Meteors saw an Israeli aircraft shoot down an Egyptian Il-14 transport in 1956. No. 153 Squadron flew Defiant, Blenheim and Beaufighter night fighters from 1941–44. From October that year, it flew Lancaster bombers until it was disbanded in September 1945. Nearly a decade later, in February 1955, it was reformed at West Mailing, Kent, as a night-fighter squadron, although its Meteor night-fighters were not delivered until September.

ARMSTRONG WHITWORTH METEOR NF.MK 12

Specification

Type: twin-engined, two-seat night-fighter

Crew: 2

Powerplant: two 17.48kN (3800lb thrust) Derwent 9 turbojet
  engines

Performance: max speed 940km/h (584mph); service ceiling
  12,200m (40,028ft); range 2590km (1610 miles)

Dimensions: wing span 13.11m (43ft); length 14.80m (48ft 6in);
  height 4.24m (13ft 9in)

Weight: 9456kg (20,830lb) loaded

Armament: four 20mm (0.79in) Hispano cannons with 195 rounds
  each

No. 153 Squadron, No. 11 Group, RAF Fighter Command, Royal Air Force, West Malling, 1957
This particular NF.12 was delivered from the factory in July 1953 and operated by Nos 125 and 25 Squadrons, as well as No. 153, between then and July 1958, when the latter unit disbanded. Stored with No. 60 Maintenance Unit, Rufforth, it was sold for scrap in April 1959.

Ilyushin Il-28 Beagle

The Il-28 was the Soviet Union's first jet bomber, and regarded as the Eastern Bloc's equivalent of the English Electric Canberra, which it preceded into flight by nearly a year. First flown in July 1948, using British Nene engines, the Il-28 entered service with Soviet bomber squadrons in 1950 and remained in production for many years. NATO gave it the reporting name 'Beagle'. Over 6000 were built by the Soviet Union and (without a licence) in China, where it was designated the Harbin H-5. The basic bomber was modified for a variety of roles, including reconnaissance, torpedo bombing, anti-submarine warfare, training, transport, target tug and even as an unpiloted target drone. The 'Beagle' was exported to more than 20 countries.

The IL-28 was introduced into Polish service in 1953 and the *Ludowe Lotnictwo Polskie* (air force) and *Lotnictwo Marynarki Wojennej* (naval aviation) operated the Il-28 bomber, Il-28R reconnaissance aircraft and the Il-28U 'Mascot' trainer with a raised rear cockpit. The Il-28R variant was a three-seat tactical reconnaissance version containing four or five cameras. The tail of the 'Beagle' contains the rear gunner/radio operator and two 23mm (0.91in) NR-23 cannon. The pilot had a fighter-type cockpit and an ejection seat. The Il-28R introduced wingtip fuel tanks, which were also used on electronic intelligence versions, which were based on the R and the Il-28T target tug.

ILYUSHIN IL-28R BEAGLE

Specification

Type: twin-engined jet reconnaissance aircraft

Crew: 3

Powerplant: two 26.48kN (5952lb thrust) Klimov VK-1A turbojet engines

Performance: max speed 902km/h (560mph); service ceiling 12,300m (40,350ft); range 2400km (1491 miles)

Dimensions: wing span 21.45m (70ft 4.5in); length 17.65m (57ft 11in); height 6.7m (21ft 11.75in)

Weight: 18,400kg (40,564lb) loaded

Armament: two 23mm (0.91mm) NR-23 cannon in tail and two in nose; bomber versions can carry up to 3000kg (6614lb) of bombs

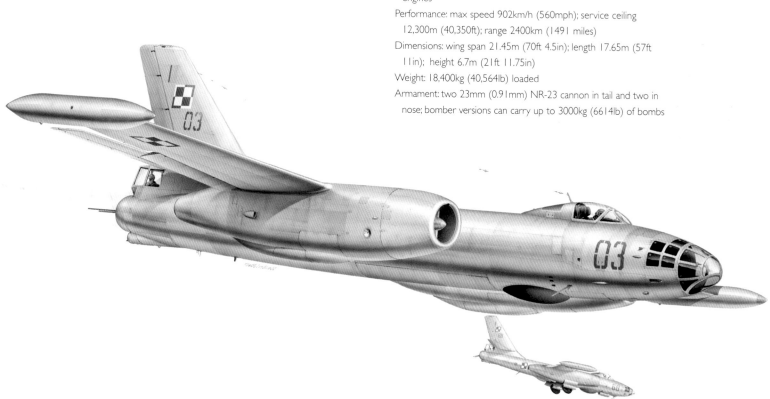

7 Brygada Lotnictwa Bombowego, Bombowo-Rozpoznawczego Ludowe Lotnictwo Polskie, (Polish People's Aviation) Powidz, Poland, 1960s

The Polish Air Force's Il-28Rs served with 7 BLB (*Brygada Lotnictwa Bombowego* – Bomber Brigade) at Powidz Air Base from 1953. The Navy also used the Il-28R with the 15 selr MW (*samodzielna eskadra rozpoznawcza Marynarki Wojennej* – Navy Aviation independent reconnaissance squadron).

METEOR NF.12 VS IL-28

IN THE EARLY 1950s, the presence of large numbers of Il-28 jet bombers in Eastern Europe was seen by the RAF Air Staff as a substantial threat to the United Kingdom.

In fact this threat had been envisaged for some time, and in December 1946 the Air Staff had issued Operational Requirement OR227, calling for a jet-propelled, twin-engined, two-seat night-fighter. In January 1947 OR227 crystallized into Specification F44/66, modified to F4/48 a year or so later. None of the early proposals submitted satisfied the requirement, however, so the Gloster Aircraft Company was asked to investigate the possibility of developing a night/all-weather version of the Meteor to bridge the gap. Gloster had already carried out radar installation trials on Meteor F.3 and F.4 aircraft in conjunction with the Telecommunications Research Establishment (TRE), and the company now looked to the two-seat Meteor T7 airframe as a suitable vehicle for adaptation to night-fighter configuration.

BELOW: *The increased fin area identifies WS697 as being a Meteor NF.12. The unit is No 25 Squadron, based at West Malling, and the fuselage markings are black bars on a silver background.*

Specification F24/48 was issued and written around the Gloster aircraft, and the fourth prototype Meteor T7 was converted as an aerodynamic prototype, flying in October 1949. The first true prototype of the Meteor NF.11, as the night-fighter variant was designated, flew on 31 May 1950.

The viability of Britain's air defences continued to be of serious concern throughout most of the 1950s.

The aircraft featured the T7's tandem cockpit, the F.8's tail unit and long-span wings similar to those of the PR10 high-altitude photo-reconnaissance version, and was fitted with a lengthened di-electric nose containing the scanner for the AI Mk X radar. This equipment, of American origin (it was the SCR720 set carried by the Northrop P-61 Black Widow) was the same as that fitted in the Mosquito NF.36; it had proved very effective in the closing stages of World War

ABOVE: *Ilyushin Il-28 Beagles of AURI, the Indonesian Air Force. The Il-28 was widely exported to countries within the Soviet sphere of influence.*

II, but by 1950 its performance was rapidly degrading. Its use was dictated by the failure of the British Mk IXc, developed by the TRE at Malvern; far better AI equipment was being produced by the American company, Westinghouse, but although it would be ordered later for use in subsequent marks of Meteor, no attempt to purchase it was made at this stage.

Armstrong Whitworth Takes Over

As Gloster was fully occupied in building the F8 day-fighter, and in working on the prototype of the aircraft that would eventually meet F4/48 – the GA5, later to be called the Javelin – it was decided to transfer responsibility for NF.11 production to Armstrong Whitworth. The first production Meteor NF.11 was delivered to No. 29 Squadron at Tangmere in August 1951.

> **In Germany, the Meteor night-fighter squadrons were trained to operate in the intruder role, their targets mainly being the Il-28 bomber bases in eastern Germany.**

The shortcomings of the RAF's night-fighter force were soon demonstrated by its inability, during air exercises, to get to grips with high-flying Canberra jet bombers, of which the Il-28 was roughly the Soviet equivalent. The RAF's other principal night-fighter type, the de Havilland Venom NF.3, could intercept Canberras at up to 13,106m (43,000ft), but the Meteor NF.11 had little chance. Indeed, on many occasions NF.11 crews suffered the ignominy of having a Canberra turning the tables on them at high altitude and claiming them as its victim.

Interception rates improved somewhat with the introduction of the Meteor NF.12, with its improved AI Mk 21 radar, but the viability of Britain's air defences continued to be of serious concern throughout most of the 1950s.

Meteor Night Missions

In Germany, the Meteor night-fighter squadrons were trained to operate in the intruder role, their targets mainly being the Il-28 bomber bases in eastern Germany. 'On a night intruder mission,' one former Meteor NF.12 pilot recalled, 'you would take off in the dark, fly without lights in a fairly loose formation hoping to keep radar separation between aircraft. There were usually six of us and we would orbit the (target) airfield hoping to catch the aircraft operating in the circuit, or failing that, wait until dawn to carry out a strike.' One Meteor night-fighter squadron, No. 39, which was equipped with the NF.13 (basically a tropicalized version of the NF.11) was based on Malta in 1955–58, and in 1956 during the Suez Crisis this unit might well have seen action against the Il-28, which had been supplied to the Egyptians in substantial numbers. Once the Anglo-French invasion of the Suez Canal Zone began, it was anticipated that the Egyptians might use their jet bombers to attack the British airfields on Malta and Cyprus, but instead they chose to evacuate their Il-28s to Luxor, where most of them were destroyed in an attack by French F-84F Thunderstreaks.

Lockheed F-80 Shooting Star

The prototype Lockheed XP-80 Shooting Star first flew on 9 January 1944, with early production P-80As entering US Army Air Forces (USAAF) service late in 1945 with the 412th Fighter Group, which became the 1st Fighter Group in July 1946 and comprised the 27th, 71st and 94th Fighter Squadrons.

The P-80A was followed by the P-80B; the major production version was the F-80C (the P for 'pursuit' prefix having changed to the much more logical F for 'fighter' in the meantime). The F-80C was the fighter-bomber workhorse of the Korean War, flying 15,000 sorties in the first four months alone.

On 28 June 1950, the third day of the Korean War, the 35th Fighter Squadron, nicknamed the 'Panthers' and operating out of Itazuke in Japan, became the first American jet squadron to destroy an enemy aircraft. The engagement took place while the F-80s were protecting a flight of North American Twin Mustangs. Captain Raymond E. Schillereff led four aircraft into the Seoul area and caught a quartet of Ilyushin Il-10s which were attempting to interfere with US transport aircraft embarking civilians at Seoul's Kimpo airfield; all four Il-10s were shot down.

The Shooting Star was assured of its place in history when First Lieutenant Russell Brown of the 51st Fighter Wing shot down a MiG-15 jet fighter on 8 November 1950, during history's first jet-versus-jet battle. The F-80 held the line in Korea until the arrival of the first North American F-86 Sabres.

LOCKHEED F-80 SHOOTING STAR

Specification
Type: fighter-bomber
Crew: 1
Powerplant: one 2449kg (5400lb thrust) Allison J33-A-35 turbojet
Performance: max speed 966km/h (594mph); service ceiling
  14,265m (46,800ft); range 1328km (825 miles)
Dimensions: wing span 11.81m (38ft 9in); length 10.49m (34ft 5in);
  height 3.43m (11ft 3in); wing area 22.07m² (237.6sq ft)
Weight: 7646kg (16,856lb) loaded
Armament: six 12.7mm (0.50in) machine guns, plus two 454kg
  (1000lb) bombs and eight rockets

36TH FIGHTER-BOMBER SQUADRON, 8TH FIGHTER-BOMBER WING, USAF ITAZUKE, JAPAN, JUNE 1950

de Havilland DH.100 Vampire

The de Havilland DH.100 Vampire was Britain's second jet fighter after the Gloster Meteor. The Meteor received priority for engines and did not enter service until after the war, despite having first flown in September 1943. Sharing many components with the Mosquito, the Vampire's fuselage pod was of plywood and balsa construction with armour plate bulkheads. The wings, control surfaces, tailplane and tailbooms were metal. Production examples had a quartet of 20mm (0.79in) Hispano cannon under the forward fuselage, as on the Mosquito.

The most important version was the FB.5, of which 888 were built from 1948. Strengthened for the ground-attack role, the FB.5 and related FB.50-series were exported to New Zealand, South Africa, France, Italy, India, Finland, Iraq and other countries. A number of countries licence-built Vampires. Australian production was undertaken by de Havilland Australia at Bankstown, Sydney, and Swiss aircraft were built by F+W at Emmen. The French Mistral was built by SNCASE, and HAL produced nearly 300 Vampires at Bangalore.

The Royal Auxiliary Air Force (RAuxAF) was integrated into the regular RAF during the war, but was reformed in 1946. In May that year, No. 607 Squadron was re-established at Ouston in Yorkshire as a day-fighter squadron with Mk 14 and Mk 22 Spitfires. In June 1951, Vampire FB.5s were received and these were supplemented by FB.9s from April 1956. In February 1957, along with all the other flying units of the RAuxAF, it was disbanded.

DE HAVILLAND VAMPIRE FB.9

Specification

Type: single-seat day-fighter

Crew: 1

Powerplant: one 19.57kN (4400lb thrust) Rolls-Royce Goblin 2/2 turbojet

Performance: max speed 853km/h (530mph); service ceiling 12,500m (41,000ft); range 1842km (1145 miles)

Dimensions: wing span 11.58m (38ft); length 11.58 m (30ft 9in); height 1.91m (6ft 3in)

Weight: 5606kg (12,360lb) loaded

Armament: four 20mm (0.79in) Hispano cannon, eight 27kg (60lb) rockets and two 227kg (500lb) bombs or two 454kg (1000lb) bombs

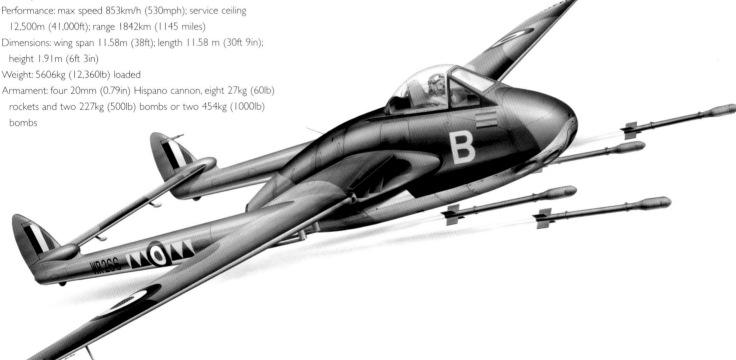

NO. 607 (COUNTY OF DURHAM) SQUADRON, ROYAL AUXILIARY AIR FORCE, RAF OUSTON, YORKSHIRE, 1950S
Vampire FB.9 WR266 was first issued to No. 203 Advanced Flying School, then to No. 607 Squadron, with which it served from 1956 to 1957. It was used by training units until being struck off charge in 1960.

F-80 Shooting Star vs DH.100 Vampire

In the early 1950s, two aircraft – one American, the other British – performed sterling service for their respective air forces.

The American type was the Lockheed F-80 Shooting Star, which was literally the Fifth Air Force's workhorse in the early period of the Korean War.

A good 70 per cent of all combat missions over Korea during the first two weeks of July 1950, as the American and South Korean forces strove to halt the North Korean invaders, were flown by the Fifth Air Force's Shooting Stars. Although they had next to no experience in ground-attack techniques the F-80 pilots quickly built up a high degree of proficiency in their unaccustomed fighter-bomber role, particularly in the use of the 12.7cm (5in) high-velocity aircraft rocket (HVAR) against enemy armour. Each Shooting Star could carry eight of these projectiles in addition to its primary armament of six 12.7mm (0.5in) machine guns.

Because there was no propeller torque to cope with, it was a far better gun platform than any conventional propeller-driven machine.

The Fifth Air Force pilots were unanimous in their praise of the F-80 as a ground-attack aircraft; its high speed gave it the all-important element of surprise, and because there was no propeller torque to cope with it was a far better gun platform than any conventional propeller-driven machine.

Loiter Time

The F-80C could also carry a pair of 454kg (1000lb) bombs in place of its 625-litre (165-gallon) wing-tip tanks, but this reduced the radius of action to approximately 160km (100 miles). Normally, with a full fuel load and eight rockets the radius of action was 362km (225 miles); in this configuration the aircraft had a loiter time over the target of something like 15 minutes. It was not enough, and Fifth Air Force Commander General Earle E. Partridge, conscious of the fact that a few more minutes in the target area would double the F-80's success rate, gave the 49th Fighter-Bomber Wing, the main F-80 ground-attack unit, the task of finding a solution.

BELOW: The Lockheed F-80(P-80) Shooting Star was the USAF's 'workhorse' of the Korean War. In its ground attack role, it played a key part in slowing down the North Korean invasion.

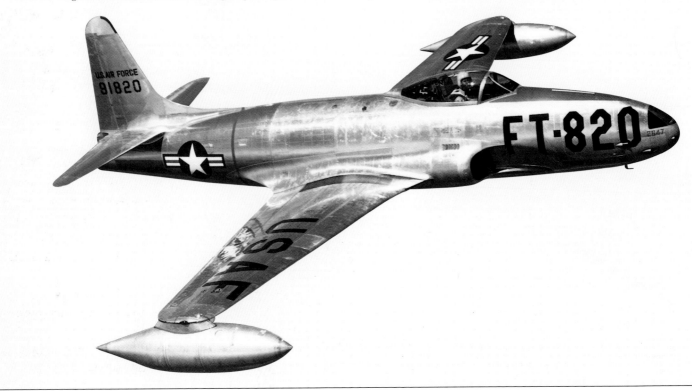

It was not long before the 49th's engineer officers came up with an answer. They found that the two centre sections of a Fletcher fuel tank could be fitted into the middle of the standard Lockheed tank carried by the Shooting Stars, creating a modified tank holding 1003 litres (265 gallons) of fuel. Tests showed that the F-80 was quite capable of carrying these modified tanks. Although there were fears that the heavier load would overstress the F-80's wing tips, Far East Air Force ordered the manufacture of one pair of tanks for every Shooting Star in the Far East Command to go ahead. About 25 per cent of the Japan-based F-80 units had received the modified tanks by the end of July, and pilots now found that they were able to spend up to 45 minutes in the combat area.

Counter-Insurgency Air War
While the F-80 fought on in Korea, its British equivalent, the de Havilland Vampire, was in action against Communist insurgents in Malaya, but with less success. No. 60 Squadron, which equipped with Vampire FB.5s (and later FB.9s) in 1951, experienced problems with the aircraft's ammunition chute doors, and its bomb-carrying mechanism developed faults that required design modifications.

'The tribes did not see sufficient of these little fighters to become overfamiliar with them and... when they did appear, they knew that trouble was afoot...'

Nevertheless, on 14 August 1951 the squadron's Vampires joined other British aircraft in a successful strike against a terrorist camp near Sitiawan in south-west Perak, dislodging a strong force of guerrillas. In 1955 No. 45 Squadron also received Vampires, but in October it re-equipped with the more powerful de

ABOVE: *Nimble and pleasant to fly, with excellent visibility from the cockpit, the Vampire FB.5 equipped the RAF's jet ground attack squadrons in Germany in the dangerous post-war era.*

Havilland Venom FB.1 and was established at Butterworth with 16 of these aircraft. In April 1955 No. 60 Squadron also exchanged its Vampires for Venom FB.1s, and in that month the Venoms of No. 14 Squadron RNZAF were deployed to Tengah, Singapore, from Cyprus, so that by the end of the year the fighter-bomber squadrons of the offensive support force in Malaya were equipped entirely with Venoms.

Some of the RAF's most effective Vampire operations were carried out in the Middle East, where they were sometimes used to quell unrest without a shot being fired. Such was certainly the case in 1951, when a place called the Buraimi Oasis became the subject of dispute between Saudi Arabia and the Trucial Oman. In the words of Air Chief Marshal Sir David Lee:

'The Trucial Coast was by now becoming accustomed to the Vampire, which, with its high speed and the characteristic whine of its Goblin engine created a feeling of confidence among friends and apprehension among potential offenders. The sudden but infrequent appearances of the Vampires at Sharjah probably created a better impression than would have been the case if the Squadron [No. 6] had been permanently located there.

'The tribes did not see sufficient of these little fighters to become over familiar with them and, in consequence, when they did appear, they knew that trouble was afoot...'

As the Shooting Star fulfilled its task admirably in Korea, so did the Vampire in the Middle East – albeit in a very different way.

Avro Shackleton

Often said to have been derived from the Avro Lancaster, the Shackleton patrol aircraft in fact owed more to the Lincoln, with which it shared wings, engines, tail surfaces and landing gear. The fuselage of the Shackleton Mk 1 was shorter and more capacious, with a more oval cross-section compared to that of the Lincoln. The first Mk 1 flew in March 1949 and deliveries began in April 1951. The

MR (maritime reconnaissance) Mk 2 had a redesigned, longer fuselage with the radar moved from the nose to a ventral 'dustbin' position, and a turret with two 20mm (0.79in) cannon in the nose, rather than tail guns. The bomb bay could carry up to three torpedoes or a variety of bombs and depth charges. Two fixed cameras were usually mounted in the tail.

AVRO SHACKLETON MR. MK 2

Specification
Type: long-range maritime patrol aircraft
Crew: 8–10
Powerplant: four 1831kW (2455hp) Rolls-Royce Griffon 57A V-12
  piston engines
Performance: max speed 500km/h (311mph); service ceiling 6400m
  (21,000ft); range 5440km (3380 miles)
Dimensions: wing span 36.58m (120ft); length 26.59m (87ft 3in);
  height 5.1m (16ft 9in)
Weight: 39010kg (86,000lb) loaded
Armament: two Hispano No. 1 Mk 5 20mm (0.79in) cannon in
  nose turret; up to 4536kg (10,000lb)

NO. 205 SQUADRON, FAR EAST AIR FORCE, RAF, RAF CHANGI, SINGAPORE, LATE 1960S
Following conversion of an MR Mk 1 in June 1952, the first new production MR Mk 2 was WG530, seen here. It was delivered to the Aircraft and Armaments Experimental Establishment (A&AEE) in September 1952 and later served with Nos. 120, 224 and 42 Squadrons. No. 205 was its last unit before it was sold for scrap in September 1968. No. 205 Squadron was the first RAF unit to be based in the Far East, being formed in Singapore in 1928. It remained in the region as a maritime patrol squadron for its whole existence, operating Southampton, Singapore, Catalina and Sunderland flying boats. The Sunderlands were used in the Korean War and were the last examples in the RAF when the squadron transitioned to the Shackleton in 1958–9. No. 208 flew the Mk 1A, then the Mk 2, until the squadron disbanded and the RAF withdrew from a permanent presence in the Far East in October 1971.

Lockheed P-3 Orion

A development of the Lockheed Electra airliner, the P-3 (formerly P3V-1) Orion was Lockheed's winning submission in a 1958 US Navy contest for a new off-the-shelf ASW aircraft which could be brought into service very rapidly by modifying an existing type. The first of two YP3V-1 prototypes flew on 19 August 1958, and deliveries of production P-3As began in August 1962.

The WP-3A was a weather reconnaissance version, the next patrol variant being the P-3A. Total P-3A/B production ran to 286 aircraft for the US Navy, plus five for the Royal New Zealand Air Force (RNZAF), 10 for the Royal Australian Air Force (RAAF) and five for Norway. The definitive P-3C variant appeared in 1969; in addition to the 132 P-3Cs delivered to the US Navy, 10 aircraft were ordered by the RAAF.

Further variants of the Orion include the EP-3A electronic intelligence aircraft, the P-3F, six of which were delivered to the Imperial Iranian Air Force in 1975, and the CP-140 Aurora for the Canadian Armed Forces. The Orion was built under licence in Japan, and also serves with the RAAF, the RNZAF, the Republic of Korea, the Netherlands, Pakistan, Portugal and Spain. Foreign-operated Orions have all undergone upgrades over the years.

LOCKHEED P-3C ORION

Specification

Type: maritime patrol aircraft

Crew: 10

Powerplant: four 3661kW (4910hp) Allison T56-A-14 turboprop
engines

Performance: max speed 761km/h (473mph); service ceiling 8625m
(28,300ft); range 3835km (2383 miles)

Dimensions: wing span 30.37m (99ft 8in); length 35.61m (116ft
10in); height 10.29m (33ft 8in)

Weight: 61,235kg (135,000lb) loaded

Armament: up to 8735kg (19,250lb) of ASW stores

US Navy Patrol Squadron 19 (VP-19), United States Navy, Naval Air Station Moffett Field, California, 1963
The Lockheed Orion shown here, 159511, is an early production P-3C. The type replaced the P2V Neptune in service with US Navy Patrol Squadron 19 (VP-19). One of the squadron's Neptunes was shot down by Soviet MiG-17s off the Siberian coast in September 1954.

AVRO SHACKLETON VS LOCKHEED P-3 ORION

ALTHOUGH SOMEWHAT ARCHAIC in appearance compared to the P-3 Orion, the Shackleton remained a viable maritime reconnaissance platfom and submarine hunter until the end of its career, when the task was handed over to the BAe Nimrod.

During most of the Shackleton's working life the Soviet Navy was still reliant on diesel-electric submarines, which had to deploy their schnorkel device for about 20 minutes every few hours to recharge their on-board systems. The maritime reconnaissance task was to search a patrol area with radar so as to detect a submarine during this relatively short schnorkelling period. Under favourable conditions the aircraft's ASV 21 radar might pick up a schnorkel at up to 28km (17 miles), but the range was usually much shorter in the sea states nomally experienced in the North Atlantic.

BELOW: *Avro Shackleton MR.Mk.3 of No 206 Squadron, RAF Kinloss, Scotland.*

Cat and Mouse

Another problem was that submarines had radar intercept equipment that could detect ASV radar at a much greater range than the aircraft's radar could detect the submarine. As one former Shackleton crew member explains:

'It became a game of cat and mouse, on top of hunting for a needle in a haystack. We used various tactics such as switching on the radar intermittently for short periods and/or scanning it in a sector behind the beam of the aircraft, in an attempt to counter the range advantage enjoyed by the submarine.

'Each homing culminated in a visual attack with practice bombs...'

'The hope was that we would detect the submarine before it had time to submerge in reaction to intercepting the aircraft radar. We could then home on to the radar contact for a direct attack, or, if it had submerged, lay sonobuoys on the datum to relocate and attack. We practised this endlessly, homing on to radar buoys located near the main maritime bases or on to a skid target towed behind RAF marine craft that produced a wake effect similar to that of a snorting submarine. Each homing culminated in a visual attack with practice bombs, aimed by the pilot from a height of 100 feet [30m] in daylight or the bomb-aimer from 300 feet [90m] at night.'

In the early years the weapons used in the attack would have been a stick of depth charges, but in the 1960s the weapon would have been a passive Mk 30 homing torpedo or a Mk 44 active homing torpedo.

Cold War Encounters

As well as operating in the Atlantic, US maritime patrol aircraft flew reconnaissance and anti-submarine patrols over the Sea of Japan, and in the Tsugaru and Soya Straits, the former between the Japanese islands of Honshu and Hokkaido and the latter between Hokkaido and the southern tip of Sakhalin. This was a sensitive area to the Russians, whose fighters frequently intercepted Lockheed P-2V Neptunes and P-3 Orions, as these extracts from the patrol logs of various P-3s reveal.

'3 May 1965. Time 0458Z (GMT). Position 43.24N 136.40E. Two Russian Frescoes (MiG-17s) intercepted QA-3 which was heading 045 at 180 knots. The Frescoes initially passed abeam to port, heading 235 degrees T, then orbited aft of the P-3 and passed again abeam to port. The Frescoes then crossed the bow and ascended from 1500 to 2500ft [450 to 750m]. During all the passes, abeam, forward and aft, distance was approximately 1000 yards [900m]. During the intercept,

ABOVE: *Lockheed P-3C Orions firing Harpoon anti-ship missiles. Based on the Lockheed Electra commercial airliner, the P-3 became an excellent ASW platform.*

QA-3 maintained 1500 ft [450m], course 045, speed 180 knots. The total time held was eleven minutes.'

'6 May 1965. Time 0258Z. Position 42.32N 135.40E. Two Russian Frescoes intercepted QA-8 while rigging (identifying and photographing) the Russian freighter *Uman*. The P-3 was at 200ft [60m], course/airspeed 051/160 knots… During the intercept, QA-8 ascended to 12500 ft [3800m] and altered heading to 071 degrees T. The total time held was ten minutes.'

'8 May 1965. Time 0225Z. Position 44.27N 138.10E. Two Russian Frescoes (side numbers 31 and 51) intercepted QA-2. QA-2 was tracking a Russian freighter. The Frescoes were in a loose tail chase formation approx eight miles apart. No 31 passed 100 yards [90m] to starboard at 200 ft [60m] above the P-3, then orbited 2500 yards [2300m] to starboard then to port. No 51 passed abeam to port at approx one mile [1600m]. During the intercept, QA-3 completed the rig and proceeded on track. The total time held was eight minutes.'

Such interceptions occurred on an almost daily basis, and the Americans had every right to be nervous, for several US reconnaissance aircraft had been shot down during the years since the Korean War and others damaged. On 27 April 1965, for example, an RB-47 Stratojet had fought a furious running battle with two North Korean MiG-17s and had returned to its base at Yokota, Japan, with two engines knocked out. Only the skilful use of the RB-47's 20mm (0.78in) tail cannon had saved the aircraft from destruction.

Lockheed C-130 Hercules

Without doubt the most versatile tactical transport aircraft ever built, the Lockheed C-130 Hercules flew for the first time on 23 August 1954, and many different variants were produced over the next half-century. The initial production versions were the C-130A and C130B, of which 461 were built. These were followed by the major production variant, the C-130E, 510 examples of which were produced.

The first C-130E flew on 15 August 1961, deliveries to the 4442nd Combat Crew Training Group, Tactical Air Command, began in April 1962, and the first export C-130E went to the Royal Canadian Air Force (RCAF) in December 1964. The C-130E can carry a maximum of 92 troops, 64 paratroops or 70 stretchers with six attendants. Other versions include the AC-130E gunship, the WC-130E weather reconnaissance aircraft, the KC-130F assault transport for the US Marine Corps (USMC), the HC-130H for aerospace rescue and recovery, the C-130K for the Royal Air Force (RAF), and the LC-130R, which has wheel/ski landing gear.

Total production of the Hercules, all variants, was some 2000 aircraft. As well as the US forces and the RAF, the Hercules was supplied to no fewer than 61 air forces around the world. The RAF is the second-largest Hercules user, operating 80 aircraft.

LOCKHEED C-130E HERCULES

Specification
Type: transport aircraft
Crew: 4
Powerplant: four 3020kW (4050hp) Allison T56-A-7 turboprop
   engines
Performance: max speed 547km/h (340mph); service ceiling
   10,060m (33,000ft); range 6145km (3820 miles)
Dimensions: wing span 40.41m (132ft 7in); length 29.79m (97ft 9in);
   height 11.68m (38ft 4in)
Weight: 70,308kg (155,000lb) loaded
Payload: 19,051kg (42,000lb)

UNITED STATES AIR FORCE, VIETNAM, 1966

Antonov An-12 'Cub'

The Antonov An-12 could be said to be the Soviet Union's equivalent of the C-130 Hercules, although it is slightly smaller and lighter than the basic Lockheed product. First flown in December 1957 in the Ukraine, around 1300 An-12s were built in the Soviet Union and a further 100 or so unlicenced copies in China as the Shaanxi Y-8. Versions of the Y-8 serve as transports, maritime patrol aircraft and drone launchers.

Soviet-built An-12s (Nato code name 'Cub') were exported to Algeria, Bulgaria, China, Cuba, Czechoslovakia, Egypt, Ghana, Guinea, India, Indonesia, Iraq, Poland, Yemen and Yugoslavia. Many specialist variants were delivered for roles including airborne command post, radiation and chemical sampling, ejection-seat testing, weather research and even (in

China) for the seasonal movement of animals. Since the dissolution of the Soviet Union, many An-12s have entered the civil market.

Ostensibly used for the search and rescue (SAR) role, the An-12PS was in fact generally employed on electronic intelligence (Elint) duties. The radio locator equipment could home in not only on rescue beacons, but also on Nato transmitters. It was said that this variant carried a droppable rescue boat in the freight hold. The full Aeroflot markings and civil registrations were often seen on An-12s that on closer inspection had a definite military role. These aircraft were frequently intercepted by Western fighters over the Baltic Sea and other locations, particularly during Nato naval manoeuvres.

ANTONOV AN-12PS CUB-B

Specification
Type: four-engined Elint aircraft
Crew: five in cockpit, unknown number of operators in cabin
Powerplant: four 2983kW (4000hp) Ivchencko AI-20K turboprop
  engines
Performance: max speed 777km/h (482mph); service ceiling
  10,200m (33,465ft); range 5700km (3542 miles)
Dimensions: wing span 38.10m (124 ft 8in); length 33.10m (108ft
  7in); height 10.53m (34ft 6.5in)
Weight: 61,000kg (134,480lb) loaded
Payload: 20,000kg (44,092lb) cargo

SOVIET NAVAL AVIATION, 1980s

LOCKHEED C-130 HERCULES VS ANTONOV AN-12 'CUB'

SOME OF THE MOST INTENSIVE combat operations flown by the USAF's Hercules fleet in Vietnam took place during the siege of Khe Sanh, a US Marine Corps' combat base close to the De-Militarized Zone (DMZ) that marked the border between North and South Vietnam and Laos.

The base came under heavy attack during the Communist Tet Offensive of 1968. The USAF replenished the Marine base using C-130 and smaller C-123 aircraft. Three techniques were used: normal landings, when the aircraft's cargo would be unloaded by huge articulated fork-lift trucks; low-level parachute drop; and by one of the two newly developed low-level extraction systems, LAPES (Low Altitude Parachute Extraction System) and GPSE (Ground Proximity Extraction System). Both allowed palletized loads to be pulled out of an aircraft flying only a few feet above the drop zone.

BELOW: *A Lockheed C-130E with the collapsed crater of Mount St. Helens in the background.*

Breaking the Siege

Every mission into Khe Sanh was fraught with danger for the transport crews, as one C-130 pilot explains.

'At Khe Sanh, the problems were as much to do with air traffic control as anything. The operations were carried out by multiple aircraft, radar controlled and sequenced at time intervals. You'd be given an approach class, and then you stacked up in a holding pattern. Your worst fear was missing an approach, because then you'd have to go back to the top of the stack, and maybe you had enough fuel to wait out ten other aircraft, and maybe you didn't. The secret was to make your approach good the first time.

ABOVE: *An Antonov An-12 Cub in the markings of the Iraqi Air Force. The Cub ideally suited Iraq's air transport requirements.*

'Whether you used the falling leaf or the random steep approach, the object was to get down just as close to the runway as you could, pointed in the right direction. Then you'd slow the aircraft right down to touchdown speed, get the nose just over the end of the runway, watch it disappear and then drop the aircraft.

'On the ground it looks like a waddling duck, but in the air it's as graceful and manoeuvrable as a ballerina.'

'If you were a little long you would compensate by cross-controlling, dropping the right wing, adding left rudder, but by that time you'd be in a very critical situation, and you could stall the aircraft very, very easily. You're starving the flight surfaces of air flow, so you had to be very careful. Dropping the right wing means you mask the rudder, and you could get into a rudder stall, and come down very rapidly.

'You'd be doing this all the way down from maybe five thousand feet, losing around two thousand feet a minute. The Hercules handled it so well. I don't know any other aircraft of anything like its size that could have done it. That's what made the aircraft unique. It was so versatile and powerful. On the ground it looks like a waddling duck, but in the air it's as graceful and manoeuvrable as a ballerina.'

Antonov Operation

The Soviet Air Force was also adept in the use of rapid troop deployment and resupply by air, using its Antonov An-12 transports, as it demonstrated during the invasion of Czechoslovakia in 1968. In the evening of 20 August, the air traffic control staff at Prague-Ruzyne Airport received an urgent signal from the Department of the Interior, prohibiting all aircraft movements until further notice. The following is an eyewitness account of what happened next.

'Things began to happen quickly. A huge dark shape slid down out of the eastern sky, and rolled along the main runway, its landing lights ablaze. The shocked controllers recognized the bulky contours of an Antonov An-12 transport. A giant's roar split the night as its four powerful Ivchenko turboprops were slammed into reverse pitch, bringing it to a stop quickly. The loading ramp that fitted snugly under the big upswept tail unit came down slowly and a host of shadowy figures came running out of the transport's massive belly. There were forty or fifty of them: Russian paratroops, wearing camouflaged smocks and in full battle order. Now, as the An-12 thundered down the runway and climbed away into the night, they fanned out in an extended line and advanced rapidly towards the airport buildings.

'The night now reverberated with the roar of engines as a constant stream of Soviet transport aircraft, mostly An-12s and An-24s, thundered out of the darkness.'

'A second aircraft roared in from the darkness, followed quickly by a third. With near-incredible speed, they discharged their cargoes of men and equipment before taking off again to make room for more. Within minutes, the Russian paratroops had secured the control tower, the airport switchboard and other strategic points on Ruzyne. The night now reverberated with the roar of engines as a constant stream of Soviet transport aircraft, mostly An-12s and An-24s, thundered out of darkness, touching down at the rate of one every fifty seconds.'

A little over 10 years later, the Soviet Air Force's An-12 fleet was active in Afghanistan, the transport crews using tactics that were strangely reminiscent of those used by the American C-130 crews in Vietnam, a war which by then had been ignominiously lost.

Hawker Hunter

Hawker's classic Hunter first flew in July 1951, sharing a common ancestor with the Sea Hawk naval fighter in the P.1040 prototype of 1947. At this time, the British aviation industry led the world in jet engines, but came to swept wings later than the United States and Soviet. The Hunter became the first British-built swept-wing fighter and was the backbone of Royal Air Force (RAF) day-fighter squadrons from 1954.

The definitive RAF Hunter was the F.Mk 6, powered by the Avon 203 engine rated at 44.48kN (10,000lb thrust). The so-called 'big-bore' Hunter equipped eighteen RAF squadrons and was the only pure fighter version in British use after 1963. Derivatives of the F.6 were exported to a number of countries, including Belgium, Denmark, India, Oman, Peru, Saudi Arabia, Sweden and Switzerland.

HAWKER HUNTER F.MK 56

Specification
Type: single-seat day fighter
Crew: 1
Powerplant: one 44.48kN (10,000lb thrust) Rolls Royce Avon 203
    turbojet engine
Performance: max speed 1150km/h (715mph); service ceiling
    15,707m (51,000ft); combat radius 713km (443 miles)
Dimensions: wing span 10.2m (33ft 8in); length 14m (45ft 11in);
    height 4.01m (13ft 2in)
Weight: 5795kg (12,760lb) loaded
Armament: four 30mm (1.18in) Aden cannon

NO. 122 SQUADRON, INDIAN AIR FORCE JAISALMER, 1971
India took more than 200 Hunters, which equipped seven squadrons and saw considerable action in the 1965 and 1971 wars with Pakistan. The bulk of India's Hunters were F.6s delivered as the F.Mk 56. Deliveries after the 1965 war were mostly the F.Mk 56A, which was equivalent to the FGA.9, optimized for ground attack and operations in 'hot and high' conditions. In air combat, the Hunter came off second-best to the F-86F Sabre, but was extremely effective at destroying armoured vehicles and was in fact instrumental on one occasion in preventing the capture of an important fort by driving off the attacking forces. The Indian Hunters had an especially long career, and were used as conversion trainers for the Indian Air Force's Western aircraft types and for target towing and general duties at least until 1999.

North American F-86 Sabre

The most famous of the early generation of jet fighters, the F-86 Sabre flew for the first time on 1 October 1947, powered by a General Electric J35 turbojet. The first operational F-86As were delivered to the 1st Fighter Group early in 1949. During the Korean War, Sabres claimed the destruction of 810 enemy aircraft, 792 of them MiG-15s.

The next Sabre variants were the F-86C penetration fighter (which was redesignated YF-93A and which flew only as a prototype) and the F-86D all-weather fighter, which had a complex fire control system and a ventral rocket pack; 2201 were built, the F-86L being an updated version. The F-86E was basically an F-86A

with power-operated controls and an all-flying tail; it was replaced by the F-86F, the major production version, with 2247 examples being delivered. The F-86H was a specialized fighter-bomber capable of carrying a tactical nuclear weapon; the F-86K was essentially a simplified F-86D; and the designation F-86J was applied to the Canadair-built Sabre Mk 3. Most of the Sabres built by Canadair were destined for Nato air forces; the Royal Air Force, for example, received 427. The Sabre was also built under licence in Australia as the Sabre Mk 30/32, powered by a Rolls-Royce Avon turbojet.

NORTH AMERICAN F-86D SABRE

Specification

Type: night and all-weather interceptor (F-86D)

Crew: 1

Powerplant: one 3402kg (7500lb thrust) General Electric J47-GE-17B turbojet

Performance: max speed 1138km/h (707mph); service ceiling 16,640m (54,600ft); range 1344km (835 miles)

Dimensions: wing span 11.30m (37ft 1in); length 12.29m (40ft 4in); height 4.57m (15ft)

Weight: 7756kg (17,100lb) loaded

Armament: 24 70mm (2.75in) 'Mighty Mouse' air-to-air unguided rocket projectiles

498TH FIGHTER INTERCEPTOR SQUADRON 84TH FIGHTER GROUP, UNITED STATES AIR FORCE, GEIGER FIELD, WASHINGTON, 1955
Known as the 'Geiger Tigers', the 498th Fighter Interceptor Squadron was activated on 18 August 1955, equipped with F-86Ds inherited from the 520th Fighter Interceptor Squadron. Its Sabres were replaced by F-102 Delta Daggers in 1956.

HAWKER HUNTER VS NORTH AMERICAN F-86 SABRE

IN 1965, HAWKER HUNTERS of the Indian Air Force came into violent conflict with F-86F Sabres of the Pakistan Air Force.

On the evening of 6 September, three F-86s of No. 5 Squadron, Pakistan Air Force, flown by Squadron Leader S.A. Rafiqui, Flight Lieutenant C. Choudhry and Flight Lieutenant Y. Hussain, were heading towards Halwara in rapidly fading light. Because of the poor visibility they were unable to locate their target, but as they searched for it, flying at about 61m (200ft), they sighted a pair of Hunters a few hundred feet higher up and Rafiqui decided to attack them. Rafiqui engaged the lead Hunter, which exploded. At this point, it is interesting to look at the official Indian Air Force report of the engagement. It is at variance with the

PakAF version on a number of points, but in places the two agree and it is possible to obtain an accurate picture of what actually happened.

> **'The Pakistani Sabres were in fact pursuing the surviving Hunter of their engagement, which had broken hard right...'**

Opposing Reports

'Patrolling over the Indian air base at Halwara on the evening of 6 September in Hunter F.56s were Flt Lt D.N. Rathore and Flg Off V.K. Neb as No 2. At about 18.40 hours, when the sun had gone down and the horizon was lit only by twilight, Rathore, who was about three miles from the airfield, caught a flash in the air in the vicinity of the airfield. A second look confirmed that the base was under attack by

BELOW: Hawker Hunter F.Mk.56 of the Indian Air Force. The Hunter saw substantial combat against Pakistan during the conflicts between the two nations.

ABOVE: *The North American F-86 Sabre first saw action over Korea. A beautiful aircraft to fly, it went on to form the first line of defence in many air forces, including that of Pakistan.*

Pakistani Sabres and that a dogfight was in progress with another section of two Hunters, led by Flg Off Ghandi, who was also airborne on patrol duty. Rathore, warning Neb, immediately turned towards the airfield. In the first skirmish, however, one Sabre had been downed by ground fire, and the second had fallen to Ghandi's guns.'

This was incorrect. The only aircraft destroyed was Ghandi's, hit by one of the Pakistani pilots, Squadron Leader Rafiqui. Ghandi ejected and made a safe descent. The report goes on:

'The remaining two Sabres were strafing the airfield and bombing it from a very low level. Jockeying for position was not difficult as the two Pakistani pilots were concentrating on their ground attacks.'

This was also incorrect. The Pakistani Sabres were in fact pursuing the surviving Hunter of their engagement, which had broken hard right, when they saw the other two Hunters pulling up from the right. Squadron Leader Rafiqui managed to get on the tail of one of them, only to discover that his guns had jammed. Despite this he elected to remain with the other two Sabres. At this point the PakAF report mentions four more Hunters, closing from the left, but the IAF report makes no mention of these.

Dogfight Confusion

The Pakistani account also describes a low-level dogfight between the Sabres and Hunters in which Flight Lieutenants Choudhry and Hussain claimed one each – no such losses were admitted by the IAF. The sight of gunfire and possible aircraft exploding on the ground might account for Rathore and Neb's impression that the airfield was

under attack, because by now, from a distance, low-flying aircraft would be barely visible in the shadows.

'There was a puff of smoke which rapidly turned into a sheet of flame as the last of the four Pakistani Sabres disintegrated in mid-air...'

The IASF report continues:

'Getting behind the Sabre which was on his right, Rathore closed in to 1000 yards [900m], at the same time instructing Neb to take the Sabre on his left. Overtaking his victim fast, Rathore closed in to 650 yards [600m] before opening fire. He saw the hits registering on the Pakistani Sabre… Closing in still further, Rathore fired again from 500 yards [450m]. This time the Sabre was mortally hit. It started banking to the left and then turned into the ground, exploding in a huge sheet of flame some five or six miles [8–10km] away from the airfield.'

This was almost certainly Rafiqui's aircraft. The next part of the IAF account, apart from the recurring mention of the Sabres attacking the airfield, dovetails nicely into the Pakistani report.

'Meanwhile, Neb had closed in behind the second Pakistani Sabre which, like the first one, was intent on strafing the airfield below… Closing in on the Pakistani Sabre to about 400 yards [365m] he fired a burst. The Pakistani pilot at once abandoned his attack and pulled up sharply. Neb rapidly closed in to less than 100 yards [90m] and fired again on the sharply climbing Sabre, which presented a much better target this time. He saw pieces fly off the Sabre as his cannon shells found their mark on the Sabre's left wing. There was a puff of smoke which rapidly turned into a sheet of flame as the last of the four Pakistani Sabres disintegrated in mid-air and fell to the ground.'

Neb's victim was Flight Lieutenant Hussain.

Mikoyan-Gurevich MiG-17

Thought at first by Western observers to be just an improved MiG-15, the MiG-17 was in fact a new design, incorporating a number of aerodynamic refinements that included a new tail on a longer fuselage and a thinner wing with different section and planform, and with three boundary layer fences to improve handling at high speed. The prototype flew in January 1950, and the basic version of the MiG-17, known to Nato as Fresco-A, entered service in 1952; this was followed by the MiG-17P all-weather interceptor (Fresco-B), and then the major production variant, the MiG-17F (Fresco-C), which had structural refinements

and was fitted with an afterburner. The last variant, the MiG-17PFU, was armed with air-to-air missiles.

Full-scale production of the MiG-17 in the Soviet Union lasted only five years before the type was superseded by the supersonic MiG-19 and MiG-21, but it has been estimated that around 8800 were built in that time, many of these being exported. MiG-17s saw action in the Congo, in the Nigerian civil war, in the Middle East and over North Vietnam, where they they were used in considerable numbers and proved tough and nimble opponents even for more modern types such as the F-4 Phantom. The MiG-17 was built in China as the J-5.

MIKOYAN-GUREVICH MIG-17 FRESCO-A

Specification

Type: fighter

Crew: 1

Powerplant: one 3383kg (7452lb) thrust Klimov VK-1F turbojet

Performance: max speed 1145km/h (711mph); service ceiling 16,600m (54,560ft); range 1470km (913 miles)

Dimensions: wing span 9.45m (31ft); length 11.05m (36ft 3in); height 3.35m (11ft)

Weight: 6000kg (14,770lb) loaded

Armament: one 37mm (1.46in) N-37 and two 23mm (0.91in) NS-23 cannon; up to 500kg (1102lb) of underwing stores

FORCA POPULAR AÉREA DE LIBERATACO DE MOCAMBIQUE (MOZAMBIQUE AIR FORCE) 1980
The example seen here, 'Red 21', was one of 48 examples which were delivered to Mozambique in the late 1970s and early 1980s. Several aircraft were shot down by anti-government Renamo guerrillas, and one was flown to South Africa by a defecting pilot.

Dassault Mystère IV

The Mystère was France's first indigenous swept-wing fighter, and its later versions were the first quantity-built European aircraft capable of level supersonic flight. Following 150 Mystère IIs, production switched to the definitive Mystère IV, with a thinner wing with slightly more sweep and a new, oval section fuselage containing a Rolls-Royce Tay engine, or the Hispano Verdon, a licence-built version.

The prototype Mystère IV first flew in September 1952. The first production aircraft flew in May 1954 and the production Mystère IVA entered Armée de l'Air service in 1955, seeing action over Suez in 1956.

Under the Nato assistance programme, the United States paid for the first 225 Mystères, followed by 100 bought with French funds. Escadron de Chasse 1/8 'Maghreb' was based in Morocco when it replaced its Mistrals (licence-built Vampires) with Mystères in 1960.

It saw some action with them against Algerian rebels before the 1961 cease-fire. The squadron returned to France and was renamed 'Saintonge', flying the Mystère (latterly in the operational training role) until the type was finally retired in 1981.

Israeli Mystère IV fighters also saw combat in 1956, claiming a number of Egyptian MiG-15s, MiG-17s and Vampires, and again in 1967 mainly in a ground support role. India's 110 Mystères were in action against Pakistan in 1965.

As an interceptor, the Mystère IV was replaced by the Mirage III in the early 1960s, but carried on in the ground-attack role until 1975 when replaced by the Jaguar. The Super Mystère B2 with afterburner and guided missiles was the first supersonic version. The career of the 180 French examples spanned 1957–77, and Israeli versions with American engines saw much action.

DASSAULT MYSTÈRE IVA

Specification

Type: single-seat fighter-bomber

Crew: 1

Powerplant: one 34.3kN (7716lb thrust) Hispano-Suiza Verdon 350 turbojet engine

Performance: max speed 1120km/h (696mph); service ceiling 15000m (49,214ft); range 916km (569 miles)

Dimensions: wing span 11.09m (36ft 5in); length 12.8m (42ft 2in); height 4.6m (15ft 1in)

Weight: 9499kg (20,941lb) loaded

Armament: Two 30mm (1.18in) DEFA cannon; optional 35-round SNEB rocket pack, rocket pods or up to 1000kg (2204lb) of bombs

ESCADRON DE CHASSE 1/8 NO. 25 SQUADRON, ARMÉE DE L'AIR ORANGE, FRANCE, 1960S

MiG-17 vs Dassault Mystère IV

ON THE MORNING of 25 May 1960, two Israeli Air Force Mystère IVA jet fighters were scrambled to intercept a pair of Egyptian MiG-17s. An Israeli source gives the following account of what happened, identifying the Israeli pilots only as Captain Aharon and Lieutenant Yadin.

'The Israeli pilots levelled out at 16,000 feet [5000m] and headed towards the south-west, searching for their quarry. Three minutes later, Aharon spotted two glittering dots at two o'clock, slightly lower down. The Mystères at once turned towards them and the distance closed rapidly, revealing the "bogeys" to be a pair of MiG-17s. The Egyptian pilots did not appear to be

aware of the danger, continuing serenely on their course. Like a whirlwind, Aharon shot over the top of the rearmost MiG, leaving his wingman to deal with it, and closed in on the leading Egyptian aircraft. The Egyptian pilot spotted him now and broke frantically to starboard at the last moment, but it was too late. A burst of shells from the Mystère's two 30mm [1.18in] cannon slammed into his port wing root; pieces whirled away in the slipstream and a ribbon of flame streamed back. The MiG turned over and went into a fast spin, leaving a spiral of oily smoke in its wake.

BELOW: *Egyptian Air Force MiG-17s. In the background at the end of the line are examples of its predecessor, the MiG-15.*

'Aharon pulled his aircraft round in a tight turn, looking for the second MiG. It was heading south-westwards at high speed, closely pursued by Yadin. As Aharon watched, Yadin opened fire, the Egyptian took violent evasive action and the Israeli's shells went wide of the mark. They were over Egyptian territory now, and following his instructions Aharon reluctantly ordered Yadin to abandon the chase. The two pilots returned to their base at Hatzerim, elated by Aharon's success.'

'...a dogfight developed over the Sea of Galilee.'

Increasing Tensions

In a second serious clash between Egyptian and Israeli aircraft over the Negev nearly a year later, Mystères from Hatzerim were again the victors. It happened on 28 April 1961, when two MiG-17s penetrated Israeli air space and were engaged by the IAF fighters. One of the MiGs escaped, but the other was trapped by the two Mystères, whose pilots signalled the Egyptian to land. Instead, he tried to turn away towards Egyptian territory and was promptly shot down. The pilot baled out and was seen to land safely.

In 1966, there was a marked deterioration in the already strained relations between Israel and Syria, and on 14 July, partly as a reprisal for a raid by saboteurs across the border in which two Israelis were killed, the Israeli Chief of Staff authorized the IAF to attack a Syrian construction project near the Sea of Galilee.

'At 11.00 hours, four Mystères, escorted by four Super Mystères, attacked the Syrian plant with rockets and cannon fire, causing considerable damage. As they were flying away from the target area, they were attacked by four Syrian MiG-17s, which dived out of the sun and hit one Mystère, damaging it slightly.

'The MiGs were immediately engaged by the Super Mystère escort, and a dogfight developed over the Sea of Galilee. It lasted less than three minutes; one MiG was hit and the pilot ejected, and the others broke off the action and headed for home.'

ABOVE: Dassault Mystère IVA fighters of the French Air Force. The type was delivered to Israel just in time to counter the threat posed by Egypt's Soviet-supplied MiGs.

Cannon Battle

A month later, on 15 August, the Sea of Galilee was the scene of yet another Israeli–Syrian clash. Shortly before dawn, an Israeli patrol boat ran aground on a sandbank near the eastern shore of the lake. At first light, the Syrians opened up on the craft with small-arms fire, wounding two crew members. Shortly afterwards, two MiG-17s appeared over the lake and made several strafing attacks on the craft, causing more damage, but one of the Syrian aircraft ran into a stream of shells from the boat's solitary 20mm (0.79in) cannon and crashed in the lake. The second MiG turned to make another run and its pilot, intent on the boat, never saw the Mystère that came curving down behind him. Battered by 30mm (1.18in) shells, the MiG exploded.

Towards the end of the year Egyptian aircraft became increasingly active over the Negev.

> **...one of the Syrian aircraft ran into a stream of shells from the boat's solitary 20mm [0.79in] cannon and crashed in the lake.**

'On the morning of 29 November,' an Israeli report states, 'two Mystère IVA interceptors led by Captain Michael were on patrol at 25,000 feet [7620m] over the southern tip of the Negev when they sighted two Egyptian MiG-17s heading into Israeli territory. The Mystère pilots manoeuvred themselves into a favourable position to attack and then closed in from behind. Both MiGs were shot down by cannon fire.'

By now, the Israeli Mystères were encountering growing numbers of supersonic MiG-21s, which outclassed them. But the Israelis had a powerful supersonic weapon in their own arsenal – the Dassault Mirage III. In June 1967, in the remarkable offensive known as the Six-Day War, it would play a leading part in removing the threat to Israel's frontiers.

Avro Vulcan

The Avro Vulcan was the most distinctive of the three Royal Air Force (RAF) V-bombers and the one that served the longest in the bombing role. Built to a 1947 specification, the prototype flew in August 1952, but the first training unit was not equipped with the production Vulcan B.Mk 1 until 1957. The B.Mk 2 with a revised wing flew the following year, and after 1956 many were able to carry the Blue Steel stand-off missile. Otherwise the Vulcan could carry freefall nuclear weapons or up to 21 454kg (1000lb) bombs in its

bomb bay. The delta wing gave a smooth ride at low level and was less prone to stress than the more conventional Vickers Valiant, which had to be withdrawn due to fatigue.

The Vulcan was approaching retirement in 1982 when the Falklands War saw it participate in its only combat missions. Flying from Ascension Island in the South Atlantic, the Vulcans flew five 'Black Buck' missions against Argentine forces in the Falklands, at the time the longest bombing raids in history.

AVRO VULCAN B.MK 2A

Specification

Type: strategic bomber

Crew: 5

Powerplant: four 78.8kN (17,000lb thrust) Bristol Olympus 201
   turbo jets

Performance: max speed 1038km/h (645mph); service ceiling
   19,812m (65,000ft); range 7400 km (4600 miles)

Dimensions: wing span 38.83m (111ft); length 32.15m (105ft 6in);
   height 7.94m (26ft 1in)

Weight: 92,534kg (204,000lb) max take-off

Armament: Blue Danube or Yellow Sun nuclear weapons, up to
   21 454kg (1,000lb) bombs

No. 101 Squadron, Royal Air Force Wideawake Airfield, Ascension Island, 1982

Vulcan B.2 XM597 entered service in 1963 with No. 12 Squadron and went on to serve with Nos. 35, 50, 9, and 101 Squadrons. During the Falklands War, it was used on two missions to attack Argentine radars around Stanley Airfield, modified to carry four AGM-45A Shrike anti-radiation missiles on underwing pylons. On the night of 2/3 June 1982, the Vulcan destroyed a Skyguard radar with two Shrikes, but damaged its refuelling probe while connecting to the Victor tanker. Without enough fuel for a return to Ascension Island, XM597 diverted to Rio de Janeiro and landed with very little fuel and one missile which would not fire, causing something of a diplomatic incident. The pilot, Squadron Leader Neil McDougall, was awarded the Distinguished Flying Cross.

Tupolev Tu-16 'Badger'

The Tupolev Tu-16 jet bomber flew for the first time in 1952, and production of the type, which was allocated the Nato reporting name 'Badger', began in 1953. The principal subvariant of the Badger-A was the Tu-16A, configured to carry the Soviet Union's air-deliverable nuclear weapons.

The next major variant, the Tu-16KS-1 Badger-B, was similar to Badger-A, but was equipped initially to carry the KS 1 Komet III (AS 1 Kennel) anti-shipping missile, with retractable dustbin radome aft of bomb bay. The Tu-16K-10 Badger-C was an anti-shipping version armed with the K-10 (AS-2 Kipper) air-to-surface missile beneath the fuselage. The Tu-16K-26 Badger-C Mod was a conversion of the Tu-16K-10 with provision for the smaller K-26 (AS-6 Kingfish) air-to-surface missile under

the wings instead of, or in addition to, the centreline-mounted K-10.

The Tu-16R Badger-D was a conversion of the Badger-C for maritime reconnaissance, while the Badger-E was basically a Badger-A with a battery of cameras in the bomb bay. The Badger-G was armed with two AS-5 Kelt or AS-6 Kingfish air-to-surface missiles and was a dedicated anti-shipping version, while the Badger-J was equipped for barrage jamming in the A- to I-bands. The Badger-L was one of the last variants in a long line of electronic intelligence gatherers.

Some Badgers were converted to flight refuelling tankers, and still served in that role in the 1990s. The Tu-16, more than 2000 examples of which are thought to have been produced, was also licence-built in China as the Xian H-6.

TUPOLEV TU-16 'BADGER'

Specification

Type: strategic bomber/maritime warfare aircraft

Crew: 7

Powerplant: two 9500kg (20,944lb) thrust Mikulin RD-3M turbojets

Performance: max speed 960km/h (597mph); service ceiling 15,000m (49,200ft); range 4800km (2983 miles)

Dimensions: wing span 32.99m (108ft 3in); length 34.80m (114ft 2in); height 10.36m (34ft 2in)

Weight: 75,800kg (167,110lb) loaded

Armament: two 23mm (0.91in) cannon in radar-controlled barbettes in lower ventral fuselage and tail positions

967TH LONG-RANGE AIR RECONNAISSANCE REGIMENT, NORTHERN FLEET, MURMANSK, LATE 1960S
Illustrated here is a Tupolev Tu-16 Badger-C Mod of the Soviet Union's 967th Long-Range Air Reconnaissance Regiment.

AVRO VULCAN VS TUPOLEV TU-16 'BADGER'

JUST AS THE BOEING B-52 and the Tupolev Tu-95 'Bear' symbolized the awesome power of strategic heavy bombers during the Cold War, the Avro Vulcan and Tu-16 'Badger' represented the medium bomber forces which would probably have formed the first wave of any nuclear exchange.

The prototypes of the Tu-16 and the Vulcan flew within a few months of each other: the Tu-16 in April 1952, and Avro's delta-wing bomber in August of the same year. By mid-1955 the Tu-16 was the spearhead of the Soviet Union's nuclear strike force, and in that year Tu-16s took part in a series of exercises involving the delivery of nuclear weapons by aircraft. These culminated in two significant shots, both occurring in November. The first, on 6 November, was a thermonuclear bomb reduced in size to fit the bomb bays of the Tu-16 and other Soviet jet bombers; it produced a yield of 215 kilotons. The second, which took place on 22 November, was the first Soviet high-yield (1.6 megaton) weapon test, which occurred at an elevation of several thousand metres.

By the end of 1955, therefore, the Russians had an effective nuclear strike force in place, and were about to deploy nuclear weapons. In Britain, the first of the RAF's so-called V-bombers, the Vickers Valiant, was just becoming operational, armed with the first British atomic bomb, the 'Blue Danube'. It was to be another two years before the first Vulcan squadrons became operational, and in the meantime the Tu-16 Badger remained a significant threat.

By the end of 1955, the Russians had an effective nuclear strike force in place, and were about to deploy nuclear weapons. It was to be another two years before the first Vulcan squadrons became operational.

By the time the Mk.2 version of the Vulcan – designed to deliver stand-off missiles – assumed full operational capability, the V-Force had years of experience behind it, its operational techniques having been pioneered by the Vickers Valiant. By 1963 the V-Force had

BELOW: *Resplendent in its white anti-nuclear-flash paintwork, this Vulcan B.1A is pictured over Canada for an air exercise.*

ABOVE: A Tupolev Tu-16 'Badger' photographed over the Pacific in 1963 by US Navy aircraft from the carrier USS Kitty Hawk. *Badgers frequently 'shadowed' US warships.*

become an extremely efficient organisation, with a strong nucleus of 'Select Star' crews – this being the highest V-Force crew classification, the others being 'Combat' and 'Select'.

This expertise was embodied in and reflected by the QRA (Quick Reaction Alert) concept and in the ability of the V-bombers to 'scramble' in ninety seconds. Crews were assigned to QRA on a one-a-week basis, plus one weekend in every three. For the most part, there was little to do except read and play cards, the crews living in their QRA caravans beside the 'Bomber Box', the teletalk system connecting the crew to the Bomber Controller in the Bomber Command Operations Room.

Fifteen-Minute Readiness
When a crew was called to readiness or summoned for an alert exercise, crew members reported to the Operations Wing (with sufficient kit for an indefinite stay away from base) and were briefed on the nature of the alert. Each crew would undergo the usual pre-flight briefing routine, and then all the crews would be subjected to further specialist briefings; the Air Electronics Officers (AEOs) would be briefed by the Wing AEO, for example. The crews would then go into a waiting posture while the aircraft was made combat ready, each having to meet a stringent preparation level. When this was achieved, crews would go out to their aircraft to carry out the appropriate checks; the cockpit door would then be locked and no one allowed inside except crew members.

'The crews would then await the alert call,' explains a former Vulcan AEO, 'which was sounded either by klaxon or station broadcast over the tannoy. The initial call brought them to

'Readiness One-Five' (15 minutes) and they would remain inside the cockpit with the door locked and ground crew standing by, the bomber crew connected to the Bomber Command Operations Room via the 'Bomber Box'. Over the teletalk, the crew would be able to hear dispersal instructions being issued to other units; these usually followed a set pattern, with units being brought to five-minute readiness, followed by two-minute readiness, then scrambled. Engines were started at Readiness Zero Two; later, a simultaneous start technique (Mass Rapid Start) was evolved, enabling all four engines to be started at the same time.

In the early 1960s, Vulcans and Tu-16s faced up to each other in the Far East, when Vulcans were deployed to Singapore...

'Once a scramble had been ordered, all the pilot had to do was to press the Mass Rapid Start Button and everything else happened automatically, the engines lighting up and the aircraft starting to move off the Operational Readiness Platform, set at an angle to the runway, as thrust developed. The cockpit of the Vulcan was fitted with shields for protection against nuclear flash; only the forward vision panels were exposed during take-off and initial climb. During the remainder of the sortie the whole of the cockpit was blacked out, the route being flown by radar. The crew's task in this respect became more exacting when the V-Force went over to the low-level role, for the continual use of terrain-following radar required a high level of concentration on the part of the two pilots.'

In the early 1960s, Vulcans and Tu-16s faced up to each other in the Far East, when RAF Vulcans were deployed to Singapore – together with the third V-bomber type, the Handley Page Victor – to counter the threat posed by Tu-16s serving with the air force of Indonesia, then in a state of confrontation with Malaysia.

English Electric Canberra

The first photoreconnaissance (PR) Canberras were the PR.3 and PR.7, the latter having extra wing fuel and more powerful engines. The PR.57 was an export version of the Mk 7 for India of which a dozen were supplied. The PR.9 introduced a revised wing with a broader-chord inner wing and extended outer wings. A new nose section was fitted, which hinged to the right to allow entry by the navigator. The pilot's canopy opened unlike that on the B(I)8. The new nose housed an F95 forward-facing camera at the tip and another oblique F95 at the rear of the compartment. Two F96 cameras with lenses up to 1220mm (48in) focal length were mounted in front of the wing roots. Up to three more F96s could be carried in the rear fuselage. An infrared linescan system allowed the terrain under the

flight path to be mapped by day or night. An optional Electro-Optical Long-Range Oblique Photographic sensor (EO-LOROP) records imagery in digital format on magnetic tape.

Twenty-three production PR.9s were built under licence by Shorts in Belfast between 1958 and 1962. No. 39 Squadron (also known as 1 Photo Reconnaissance Unit) has operated this version since 1962 and have taken part in many operations, from monitoring Soviet ports during the Cuban Missile Crisis in 1962 to tracking refugee movements in the Congo in the late 1990s. Chile received two ex-RAF PR. 9s after the Falklands War, but it seems likely that RAF aircraft were also operated in Chilean markings during the conflict to keep an eye on bases in neighbouring Argentina.

ENGLISH ELECTRIC (BAC) CANBERRA PR.9

Specification

Type: jet reconnaissance aircraft

Crew: 2

Powerplant: two 50kN (11,250lb thrust) Rolls-Royce RA24 Avon Mk 26 turbojets

Performance: max speed 901km/h (560mph); service ceiling over 18,288m (60,000ft); range 8159km (5,070 miles)

Dimensions: wing span 22.30m (69ft 5in); length 20.31m (66ft 8in); height 4.77m (15ft 8in)

Weight: 26,082kg (57,500lb) loaded

Armament: none

No. 39 Squadron (1 PRU) Royal Air Force, Wyton, Cambridgeshire, 1980s
During the 1980s the RAF greatly reduced its Canberra force and XH174 was one of many aircraft scrapped.

Boeing RB-47 Stratojet

The XB-47 prototype first flew in December 1947 and was unlike any previous bomber. The three crew sat one behind the other under a fighter-style bubble canopy, while the swept wings were so thin that they flexed greatly in flight. This was to cause some control problems at high speeds. Small outrigger wheels were fitted under the outer engines to prevent the wingtips touching the ground.

More than 1300 of the main production B-47E were built out of 2032 of all versions. They never saw combat as bombers, but specialized reconnaissance and Elint (electronic intelligence) versions were active around the periphery of the Soviet Union and several were shot down by Soviet fighters. The RB-47H was an electronic reconnaissance and countermeasures version of the B-47E. A specialist crew of three 'crows', or electronics operators, was carried in a pressurized compartment in the bomb bay, and its job was to locate and analyse radar signals. Equipment was also carried to jam and spoof radar transmitters during wartime. The RB-47 had no bombing capability, but retained a pair of 20mm (0.79in) cannon in a remotely operated tail turret for self-defence.

BOEING B-47H STRATOJET

Specification

Type: strategic reconnaissance aircraft
Crew: 6
Powerplant: six 33.4 kN (7200lb thrust) General Electric J47-GE-25 turbojets
Performance: max speed 975km/h (605mph); service ceiling 12,345m (40,500ft); range 6437km (4000 miles)
Dimensions: wing span 35.36m (116ft); length 33.48m (109ft 10in); height 8.50m (17ft 11in)
Weight: 36,630kg (80,756lb) empty
Armament: two 20mm (0.79in) cannon with 350 rounds

338TH STRATEGIC RECONNAISSANCE SQUADRON, 55TH STRATEGIC RECONNAISSANCE WING, STRATEGIC AIR COMMAND, UNITED STATES AIR FORCE, FORBES AIR FORCE BASE, KANSAS, 1962
The first RB-47H of 35 built entered service with the 55th Strategic Reconnaissance Wing in August 1955. The 338th Strategic Reconnaissance Squadron, one of whose RB-47Hs is illustrated here, was particularly active during the Cuban Missile Crisis in 1962. The 338th survives today as the crew training squadron for the 55th Wing, based at Offutt AFB, Nebraska.

ENGLISH ELECTRIC CANBERRA VS BOEING RB-47

AT THE HEIGHT OF THE COLD WAR, while the notorious Lockheed U-2 and its exploits claimed the headlines, other reconnaissance aircraft were quietly going about their business.

The principal reconnaissance types used in the West were the English Electric Canberra and the Boeing RB-47 Stratojet. The last photo-recce Canberra variant, the PR.9, far outlived the RB-47, the last examples being withdrawn from use only in 2006.

Although the Canberra PR.9 could not reach the same altitudes as the U-2, it was nevertheless an impressive aircraft, with a good performance, although the latter fell short of expectations. Its Rolls-Royce Avon Mk 206 engines gave a good rate of climb to 15,000m (50,000ft), but it fell off rapidly above that altitude, and further tests revealed that the induced drag from the new wing centre section at high altitude was virtually cancelling out the increased thrust margin. On 18 September 1956 English Electric

Chief Test Pilot Roland Beamont reached 18,000m (59,000ft) in a PR.9, but the aircraft would go no higher and it had used a great deal of fuel in getting there.

In carrying out their missions, the British and American photo-recce aircraft were always in danger of being intercepted by hostile fighters, sometimes with fatal consequences.

BELOW: *The English Electric (BAC) Canberra PR.9 provided the RAF with a very viable photo-reconnaissance system. Note the increased wing area between the fuselage and engine nacelles.*

ABOVE: RB-47 crews sometimes ran enormous risks in carrying out their reconnaissance task.

By July 1960 No 58 Squadron at RAF Wyton had six PR.9s on strength, and now embarked on a period of intensive flying. The aircrews were impressed by the PR.9, and in particular by its rate of climb. It could reach 9100m (30,000ft) in two and a half minutes. High level operations meant the use of partial pressure helmets and jerkins, and crews had to attend a course on the theory of high-altitude flight and its effects on the human body at the RAF Aeromedical Centre at Upwood, where they were subjected to simulated high-altitude decompression. Most of the training flights undertaken by No 58 Squadron were by single aircraft, flying 'Lone Ranger' sorties to El Adem, Cyprus, Nairobi and the Gulf, or 'Polar Bear' sorties to Norway. Frequent sorties were also flown to the 2nd Allied Tactical Air Force operational area in Germany.

Typically, a Canberra would fly at high level to a point off the north coast of Germany, followed by a let-down into the recognized 2 ATAF low-level routes and a landing on a German airfield. On the way back to the UK from Germany a similar profile was used, the Canberra flying at high level and then descending to make use of the UK low level routes. Sometimes the PR Canberras, operating from Bodø or Andoya in Norway, ventured deep inside the Arctic Circle; one long mission, in December 1960, involved an overflight of Jan Mayen Island, 800km (500 miles) north-north-east of Iceland.

In carrying out their missions, the British and American photo-recce aircraft were always in danger of being intercepted by hostile fighters, sometimes with fatal consequences.

Barents Sea Mission

On 1 July 1960, an RB-47H of the 343rd Reconnaissance Squadron, 55th Strategic Reconnaissance Wing, took off from Brize Norton in Oxfordshire to carry out a mission over the Barents Sea, with special reference to Soviet naval facilities on the Kola peninsula and the nuclear test facility on Novaya Zemlya. The RB-47 carried a crew of six, comprising Captain Willard Palm (aircraft commander); Lt Bruce Olmstead (pilot); Lt John McKone (navigator); and three signals specialists, Captain Eugene Posa, Lt Dean Phillips and Lt Oscar Goforth.

As the RB-47 approached the target area, it was intercepted by a Soviet MiG-19 fighter.

'I heard the aircraft commander, Bill Palm, say, "Where in the hell did that guy come from?" Like it was a surprise. Suddenly, we had a fighter off our right wing.'

'We were two minutes early at the turning point,' McKone remembered. 'I told the aircraft commander, "OK Bill, start your left turn now." I'd already given him the heading to take. As we started the left turn, over the intercom I heard the copilot say, "Check, check, check, right wing." I heard the aircraft commander, Bill Palm, say, "Where in the hell did that guy come from?" Like it was a surprise. Suddenly, we had a fighter off our right wing.'

It was at this moment that Olmstead spotted the lone MiG-19 for the second time. 'We'd already seen him once before. We watched him for a while; then he disappeared. Then all of a sudden, he appeared on our right wing. Then he came right up the cone behind us and started firing!'

The MiG-19's cannon shells put two of the RB-47's engines out of action and threw the aircraft into a flat spin.

'I remember a second burst of fire,' McKone recalled, 'and I saw some holes opening around my position – in the nose of the airplane – that were about the size of cannon shells. Then I heard the aircraft commander say, "Bail out, bail out, bail out," and I heard alarm bells ring and saw red alarm lights come on for bailing out. I heard a couple of explosions behind me; they sounded like ejection seats and the canopy going off. I figured it was time to get out of there. So I bailed out.'

Olmstead and McKone were fished out of the sea by the Russians and taken to Moscow for interrogation. They were eventually repatriated in January 1961. They were the only two survivors.

AIRCRAFT OF THE VIETNAM ERA 1964–74

For a decade, from 1964 to 1974, the eyes of the world were focused on the war in Vietnam, where the United States hurled the full weight of its weapons technology against a guerrilla army that refused to be beaten. It was a war that demonstrated the awesome striking power of the Boeing B-52 Stratofortress when used in the conventional bombing role – and also revealed its vulnerability to surface-to-air missiles when it operated against the heaviest concentration of anti-aircraft weaponry in the world.

Vietnam was a war in which the United States Air Force, Navy and Marine Corps suffered appalling losses in attacks on heavily-

lessons that were quickly picked up and assimilated by both East and West. One of the principal lessons was that ground forces needed the support of heavily-armoured, heavily armed and dedicated attack aircraft. The United States and USSR moved quickly to develop such aircraft, resulting in the Fairchild A-10 Thunderbolt II on the one hand and the Sukhoi Su-25 'Frogfoot' on the other. Both were to see much action in the limited wars of the late 20th century, and both were to emerge from these conflicts with credit.

Vietnam was the proving ground

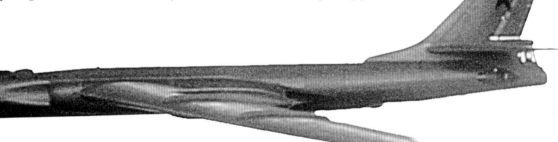

defended North Vietnam, where F-4 Phantoms battled with MiG-21s and American pilots found themselves locked in combat with highly competent and skilled adversaries.

The United States lost 2400 jet aircraft during the war, 1800 of them to enemy action. To that total must be added some 4500 helicopters, about half of which were lost in accidents.

The Vietnam War threw many lessons into the combat arena,

LEFT: *The F4 Phantom II was the workhorse multi-role aircraft of the Vietnam era. Typical armament was a 20mm (0.79in) Vulcan cannon, four AAMs and nearly 6000kg (13,200lb) of ordnance.*

ABOVE RIGHT: *The Tupolev Tu-16 'Badger' was a Soviet medium bomber and reconnaissance aircraft that had a maximum range of 4800km (2983 miles).*

for sophisticated weapons systems like the Grumman A-6 Intruder and its derivatives, aircraft capable of weaving their way through the most advanced air defence systems undetected to deliver their war load with extreme accuracy.

The period of the Vietnam War was one of change in the world of military aviation. Not only did the performance, manoevrability and armament of jet combat aircraft undergo dramatic changes in the space of a decade, the lessons learned in the skies of Southeast Asia showed an urgent need for much more emphasis to be placed on air combat tactics and training, resulting in the creation of air combat schools like Red Flag at Nellis Air Force Base in Nevada and the US Navy's 'Top Gun' equivalent at Miramar in Florida. Never again would fighter pilots go into combat using the tactics of yesteryear, and never again would the air defences of a potential enemy be underestimated. The air combat revolution came just in time to face the challenges of the 1990s, over Iraq and elsewhere.

Tupolev Tu-95/Tu-142 'Bear'

Given the Nato reporting name 'Bear', the Tupolev Tu-95 flew for the first time on 12 November 1952. It entered service with the Soviet Strategic Air Forces (Dal'naya Aviatsiya) in 1957, early examples having played a prominent part in Soviet nuclear weapons trials.

The initial Tupolev Tu-95M Bear-A freefall nuclear bomber was followed by the Tu-95K-20 Bear-B of 1961, this being a maritime attack and reconnaissance version with a large radome under the nose and a Kh-20 (AS-3 Kangaroo) cruise missile. The Tu-95KD was similar, but was fitted with a flight refuelling probe. The Tu-95KM Bear-C, thought to be a new-build variant, was a specialized maritime reconnaissance version, as was the similar Bear-D, while the Bear-E and Bear-F were upgraded variants with a new electronics suite. These and later aircraft were designated Tu-142. Later models include the Bear-H, equipped to carry up to four cruise missiles, and the Tu-142MR Bear-J, a very long frequency (VLF) communications platform based on the Bear-F. This variant is tasked with providing a secure communications link with Russian submarines using an 8-km (5-mile) long antenna which is stowed in a container beneath the fuselage. Eight Tu-142s were supplied to the Indian Navy.

TUPOLEV TU-95/TU-142 'BEAR'

Specification

Type: strategic bomber/maritime warfare aircraft

Crew: 10

Powerplant: four 11,186kW (15,000hp) Kuznetsov NK-12MV
  turboprop engines

Performance: max speed 805km/h (500mph); service ceiling
  13,400m (44,000ft); range 12,550km (7800 miles)

Dimensions: wing span 48.50m (159ft); length 47.50m (155ft 10in);
  height 11.78m (38ft 8in)

Weight: 154,000kg (340,000lb) loaded

Armament: six 23mm (0.91in) cannon; weapons load of up to
  11,340kg (25,000lb)

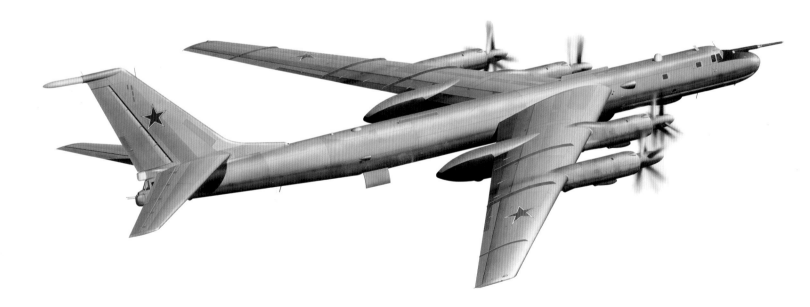

135TH LONG-RANGE ASW REGIMENT 206TH SOVIET NAVAL AIR DIVISION VOLGODSKAYA, 1985
The 206th Naval Air Division, based on the Murmansk Peninsula, was responsible for long-range maritime reconnaissance and anti-submarine warfare operations. Pictured here is a Tu-142M Bear-F Mod 3 of the division's 135th Long-Range ASW Regiment

Boeing B-52 Stratofortress

The B-52G version of the long-lived Stratofortress bomber was intended as a stopgap measure while troubles with the B-58 Hustler were worked out. Work began in 1956, and the first of 193 B-52Gs was completed in October 1958. It had the same engines as the preceding B-52F, but a lighter structure and a shorter tailfin. The tail-gunner's position was moved from the rear fuselage to a seat in the main forward cabin, and he operated the guns using a video monitor or radar. Larger fuel tanks were installed and spoilers replaced ailerons for roll control. The capability to carry the AGM-28 Hound Dog missile was added during production, and later the AGM-69A short-range attack missile (SRAM).

Although intended as a nuclear bomber and missile launcher, the B-52 entered combat as a conventional 'dumb' bomber. In April 1972, 28 (of an eventual 98) B-52Gs were sent to Guam to support the B-52D and F in operations against North Vietnam. Most were equipped with a more sophisticated ECM suite, but the G could not carry bombs externally and was generally less effective as a conventional bomber.

In an effort to move stalled peace talks, the United States launched Operation Linebacker II in December 1972; the B-52s were used to attack targets around the heavily defended capital, Hanoi, in what was called the 'Eleven-Day War'. The B-52s dropped over 15,000 tons of bombs and flew nearly 730 sorties during these raids. Six B-52Gs were shot down by surface-to-air missiles and one was damaged out of a total of 15 'Buff' losses.

BOEING B-52G STRATOFORTRESS

Specification
Type: strategic bomber
Crew: 5
Powerplant eight 61.2kN (13,750lb thrust) Pratt & Whitney J57-P-43WB turbojet engines
Performance: max speed 1024km/h (636mph); service ceiling 14,326m (47,000ft); ferry range 12836km (7976 miles)
Dimensions: wing span 56.4m (185ft); length 48.0m (157ft 7in); height 12.4m (40ft 8in)
Weight: 137,275kg (302,634lb) loaded
Armament: four 12.7mm (0.50in) Browning M3 machine guns with 600 rounds each in tail turret; maximum ordnance 22,680kg (50,000 lb)

72ND STRATEGIC WING (PROVISIONAL), STRATEGIC AIR COMMAND UNITED STATES AIR FORCE ANDERSEN AIR FORCE BASE, GUAM, 1972

TU-95/TU-142 'BEAR' VS B-52 STRATOFORTRESS

THE KEY to the Bear's long-term success is its powerplant. The Nk-12 turboprop engine was developed from 1947 by the newly established Nikolai D. Kuznetsov Engine Design Bureau at Kuibyshev.

Many members of the original NK-12 design team were Germans, forcibly removed from their homeland to work in the USSR at the end of World War II. A massive engine, the NK-12 was designed with a single shaft, the five-stage turbine driving a 14-stage compressor, with variable guide vanes and blow-off valves, and a complex power-dividing gearbox that coupled the power into tandem co-axial propellers. The huge AV-60 series propellers have two units each with four blades, with a diameter of 5.6m (18ft 4in). Each propeller is independent of its partner, though once the engine is running an electronic control maintains propeller pitch at values giving constant rotational speed.

In terms of longevity the Bear has matched Boeing's venerable B-52.

A crucial factor in the design of all aircraft powered by this engine/propeller combination is that the propeller pitch is very coarse. When the Bear is in flight, its propeller blades look as though they are almost

BELOW: A Russian Tu-142 Bear-F seen at the International Air Tattoo, Fairford, in 1994. The Bear provided the Russians with an unparalleled maritime surveillance capability.

feathered (turned edge-on to the airflow). This indicates a slow rotational speed, which in turn means that without greatly exceeding the speed of sound at the tips of the blades, the aircraft can be made to fly at jet speeds.

US Interest

When the potential of the Bear was first assessed by the US Department of Defense, American analysts refused to believe that a slow-turning propeller operating in a very high pitch range could be efficient, and assumed that the aircraft's maximum speed would be in the region of 644km/h (400mph). Information on the quality of the NK-12 and its propellers, supplied by German engineers who had been released from captivity, was ignored, and the analysts concluded that the USSR had spent a great deal of time and effort in developing an aircraft that was both vulnerable and unable to compete with the strategic jet bombers that were appearing in the mid-1950s.

History has proved how wrong they were. In terms of longevity the Bear has matched Boeing's venerable B-52, and time and again has shown its effectiveness in the maritime surveillance role, for which its extremely long range makes it eminently suitable. During the Cold War, Bears making the long transit from Murmansk to Cuba

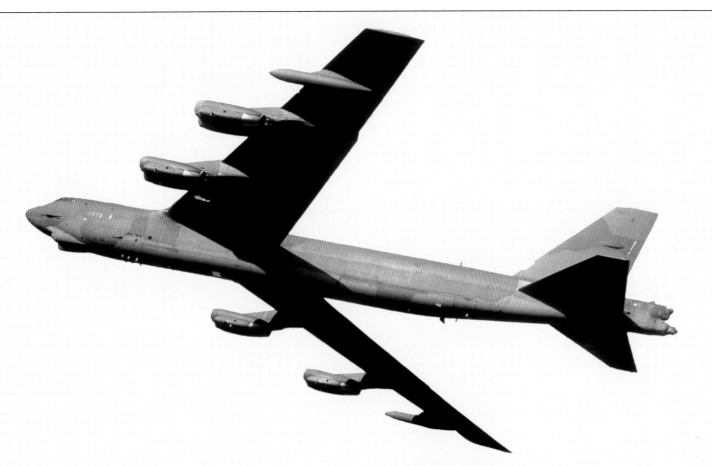

non-stop and without refuelling were a frequent sight; few other aircraft could have matched that.

B-52 Maritime Operations

Although – unlike the Tu-142 – no variant was developed specifically for the task, the B-52 also had a secondary maritime role. On 15 January 1964, the USAF directed Strategic Air Command to adopt an anti-submarine warfare role in defence of the Continental United States, and in September that year, during trials, a B-52 dropped eight types of mine at the Air Proving Ground Center, Eglin Air Force Base, Florida. In March and April 1965, SAC B-52s, supported by KC-135 tankers, took part in an extensive visual and photographic sea-search exercise code-named Water Gap. It was the first time that B-52s had been used in this way.

> **It is for its nuclear deterrent role that Boeing's big bomber will always be remembered – and for its blistering, high-altitude bombing attacks on terrorist strongholds in Afghanistan and elsewhere in more recent times.**

Maritime exercises soon became a regular feature of SAC's activities and continued throughout the most dangerous period of the Cold War into the 1980s. On 12–14 March 1980, for example, two B-52H aircraft of the 410th Bomb Wing set off from K.I. Sawyer AFB, Michigan, on a 42-hour, 35,816km (22,260-mile) round-the world flight that took them across Canada, the North Atlantic, several

ABOVE: The Boeing B-52G was the penultimate version of the Stratofortress. It carried two Hound Dog air-to-surface missiles on wing pylons. The last B-52G was completed late in 1960.

European countries, the Mediterranean, the Indian Ocean, the Strait of Malacca, the South China Sea and the North Pacific before ending at the starting point, Sawyer AFB.

'In contrast to earlier round-the-world missions,' the SAC summary of the flight reads, 'this flight included reconnaissance/surveillance activities which had become increasingly important to SAC, in conjunction with US naval forces in the Indian Ocean.'

In March 1983, in the largest B-52 mining exercise of its kind so far, ten SAC B-52Ds and Gs from the 43rd Strategic Wing and the 2nd and 19th Bomb Wings dropped mines off the coast of South Korea. Also in March, in addition to sea search and surveillance, SAC's collateral maritime mission was also expanded to include an anti-shipping role when some B-52Gs were modified to carry the AGM-84 Harpoon anti-ship missile. The first launch trials from a B-52 took place between 15 and 28 March 1983 on the Pacific Missile Test Range, and a limited operational capability with the Harpoon was achieved by the 42nd Bomb Wing's B-52Gs on 6 October.

The B-52, then, fulfilled a maritime mission that remained relatively unknown during the long years of the Cold War. But it is for its nuclear deterrent role that Boeing's big bomber will always be remembered – and for its blistering, high-altitude bombing attacks on terrorist strongholds in Afghanistan and elsewhere in more recent times.

Grumman A-6 Intruder

The Grumman A-6 Intruder was originally flown as the YA2F-1 in April 1960, having been selected for the US Navy's all-weather attack aircraft requirement in 1957. Unlike previous navy jet bombers, it was relatively small, with only a two-man crew, seated side by side. All weapons were carried externally on wing and fuselage pylons, rather than in an internal bomb bay. The bulbous nose contained a powerful Norden multi-mode radar with terrain-following capability. As part of a sophisticated navigation and attack package, this allowed the Intruder to strike targets at night and in bad weather, following a long run at low level to avoid radar detection.

Despite some initial problems, and a high initial loss rate, the A-6 went on to be the most effective night-attack platform in Vietnam. In all, 69 US Navy and 25 US Marine Corps (USMC) Intruders were lost on combat missions, a low figure in relation to their total numbers.

GRUMMAN A-6E INTRUDER

Specification

Type: all-weather carrier-based attack bomber

Crew: 2

Powerplant: two Pratt & Whitney J52-P-8B turbojets rated
  at 41.4kN (9300lb thrust)

Performance: max speed 1297km/h (806mph); service ceiling
  12,925m (42,200ft); range (fully loaded) 1627km (1011 miles)

Dimensions: wing span 16.15m (53ft); length 16.69m (54ft 9in);
  height 4.93m (16ft 2in)

Weight: 27,397kg (60,400lb) loaded

Armament up to 8165kg (18,000lb) of conventional or precision
  bombs, guided missiles including AGM-62 Walleye, AGM-84
  Harpoon, AGM-88 HARM and AGM-123 Skipper

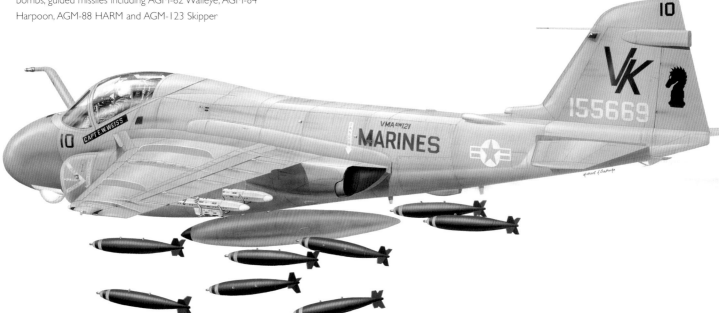

MARINE ATTACK SQUADRON (ALL WEATHER) 121, 'GREEN KNIGHTS', UNITED STATES MARINE CORPS, MARINE CORPS AIR STATION CHERRY POINT, SOUTH CAROLINA, LATE 1980S

In 1969, USMC Skyhawk squadron VMA-121 made the transition to the A-6A, and it was reconstituted as Marine Attack Squadron (All Weather) 121, or VMA(AW)-121, the additional letters signifying its new all-weather role. For the next 20 years, the 'Green Knights' flew the A-6 until they became the first USMC squadron to fly the two-seat night-attack version of the F/A-18 Hornet in 1993. Built as an A-6A, this particular aircraft was one of those upgraded to A-6E configuration. VMA(AW)-121 was the first Intruder squadron to receive the TRAM system.

Blackburn (BAe) Buccaneer ⊞

The Blackburn Buccaneer originated in the early 1950s as a design for a carrier-borne attack aircraft able to carry a nuclear bomb below radar coverage. As the NA.39, the prototype flew in April 1958 and was followed by an order for 50 Buccaneer S.Mk 1s for the Royal Navy. From 1962 until 1978, the S.1 and the improved S.Mk 2 flew from the Royal Navy's large-deck aircraft carriers. The Royal Air Force (RAF) took over some of the Royal Navy's 'Buccs' in 1969 and ordered more, most of them the S.Mk 2B version with a bulged bomb bay and Martel guided missile capability. The Buccaneer was famed for its smooth low-level ride and was one of the best strike aircraft of the 1960s and 1970s. The Navy gave its remaining aircraft to the RAF in 1978. South Africa was the only export user, purchasing 15 S.Mk 50s, which saw action over Angola.

BLACKBURN (BAE) BUCCANEER
S.MK 2B

Specification

Type: maritime strike aircraft

Crew: 2

Powerplant: two 51.5kN (11,000lb thrust) Rolls-Royce RB.168-1A
  Spey turbofans

Performance: max speed 1112km/h (691mph); service ceiling
  12,192m (40,000ft); range 3701km (2300 miles)

Dimensions: wing span 13.41m (44ft); length 19.33m (64ft 5in);
  height 4.95m (16ft 3in)

Weight: 25,402kg (56,000lb) loaded

Armament: up to 7264kg (16,000lb) of bombs, or rocket pods or
  Martel or Sea Eagle air-to-surface missiles, or two WE.177 nuclear
  weapons

No. 12 Squadron, Strike Command, Royal Air Force, RAF Lossiemouth, late 1980s

This Buccaneer, XW530 was built for the RAF and was one of 12 that served in the 1991 Gulf War, where she was known as Guinness Girl and Pauline. The Buccaneers initially designated targets for the laser guided bombs (LGBs) of Tornadoes, but later in the war dropped LGBs themselves. Depicted here firing a TV-guided Martel anti-ship missile, this aircraft is in the markings of No. 12 Squadron, which was re-formed with Buccaneers in 1969 as a dedicated maritime attack unit. The fox badge originated when the squadron operated the Fairey Fox bomber in the 1930s.

 With the imminent arrival of the maritime attack version of the Tornado, the GR.1B, No. 12 Squadron was disbanded in October 1993, marking the end of the Buccaneer in regular RAF service. XW530 is preserved at the Buccaneer Petrol Station in the town of Elgin, near Lossiemouth.

A-6 INTRUDER VS BUCCANEER

Although there was a gap of only two years between the first flights of the A-6 Intruder and the Buccaneer, there was a huge disparity in terms of equipment between the American and British aircraft, the A-6 having the benefit of far more sophisticated avionics.

Yet each fulfilled a crucial low-level strike role during some of the most dangerous years of the Cold War, and each went on to participate in one of the 20th century's later conflicts, the 1991 Gulf War.

The A-6A Intruder saw extensive action over Vietnam, providing the US Seventh Fleet with a formidable striking force. For the first time in the Vietnam War, the Americans had an aircraft with an advanced avionics weapon system. It was the only operational aircraft that possessed a self-contained all-weather bombing capability, permitting its use in the monsoon season, not only in South Vietnam, but also in Laos and in the heavily-defended environment of North Vietnam.

The A-6 Intruder revolutionized night and all-weather close support techniques when operating with US Marine ground forces, whose forward air controllers (FACs) deployed small radar beacons known as RABFACs. With these, the precise position of a FAC could be displayed on the A-6's radar scope. The FAC could thus

BELOW: A Grumman A-6E Intruder pictured during the Gulf War of 1991. The Intruder's amazing weapon system gave the US Navy the capability to strike targets at low level, at night and in all weathers.

provide the bearing and distance of a target from the beacon, plus the elevation difference between the two; the bombardier/navigator in the A-6A could enter this data into the weapon system computer and bomb the target in bad weather or at night with an accuracy that could only be achieved by other strike aircraft – such as the Buccaneer – in broad daylight.

At one point five SAMs were heading for him, but each one exploded directly overhead...

In the hostile environment of North Vietnam, Intruders operated singly against high-value targets or used their advanced avionics to guide other attack aircraft. On one particularly difficult mission, flown on the night of 30 October 1967 by an Intruder of VA-196 against a vital railway target in Hanoi, the crew (Lt Cdr Charles B. Hunter and Lt Lyle F. Bull) had to evade no fewer than 16 surface-to-air missiles, as well as a fearsome concentration of AAA. Hunter avoided the first salvo of SAM by barrel-rolling the Intruder with 4,000kg (9,000lb) of bombs under its wings, an extremely dangerous manoeuvre and one that testified to the ruggedness of the aircraft.

ABOVE: *A Blackburn (BAe) Buccaneer S.2B of No 12 Squadron RAF. The Buccaneer was an excellent low-level strike aircraft, and extremely stable at low level and high speed.*

It also kept the aircraft on course for the target, so that Lt Bull could continue to compute his attack pattern. By this time, the AAA fire was so heavy that it lit up the countryside, so much so that Lt Cdr Hunter stayed right down 'on the deck'. At one point five SAMs were heading for him but each one exploded directly overhead, filling the cockpit with an orange glow and making the aircraft shudder. Despite all the opposition, Hunter and Bull bombed the target accurately and returned safely to their carrier, the USS *Constellation*.

Anti-Shipping Buccaneer

Although it lacked the Intruder's sophisticated avionics, the Blackburn (later British Aerospace) Buccaneer was intended to perform much the same tasks, and it was in the anti-shipping role that the aircraft really came into its own. A former Buccaneer navigator explains how an attack profile was set up.

'With large areas of ocean devoid of enemy activity, the standard profile adopted by a Buccaneer maritime attack formation was a Hi-Lo-Hi. At a range of 240 miles [390km] from the target the Buccaneer formation, which would be six or eight aircraft, started a descent to sea level to stay outside the enemy's detection range. At 30 miles [50km] the leader 'popped up' and the navigator switched on his 'Blue Parrot' air-to-surface radar for two or three sweeps during which time he identified and 'marked' the target before descending back to 100 feet [30m]. The lead navigator then had to inform the rest of the formation.

'Once we had penetrated the target ship's weapons engagement zones, we used the exceptional low-flying performance of the Buccaneer to fly at high speed and ultra-low-level while sustaining high-g manoeuvres to increase the tracking problems of the enemy radars. The first attacks were delivered from a toss delivery at three miles on converging headings. Each 1000lb [454kg] bomb was fused to explode at a height of 60 feet [18m] above the target, the aim being to destroy the fire-control radars and incapacitate the missile and gun crews.

> **'we used the exceptional low-flying performance of the Buccaneer to fly at high speed and ultra-low-level while sustaining high-g manoeuvres to increase the tracking problems of the enemy radars.'**

'In the meantime, the attack force had turned starboard through 90 degrees before rolling in to release four to six 1000lb [454kg] bombs independently from a low-level dive or laydown attack that provided the killing blow. Timing was critical if the aircraft were to avoid the debris from the preceding attack.'

Aermacchi MB-326

Still in service in many countries, the design of the MB-326 jet trainer dates back nearly half a century, with the prototype flying in December 1957. The first production examples were delivered to the Italian Air Force in early 1962, but it was in the export market where the 'Macchi' had its greatest success, being supplied to Argentina, Australia, Brazil, Dubai, Ghana, Paraguay, South Africa, Tunisia, Zaire and Zambia. In all, about 800 MB-326s have been built, and the basic design formed the basis of the successful MB-339, which has also been widely exported. A single-seat attack

version of the MB-326 was built as the MB-326K and known as the Impala in South Africa, where many were built under licence by Atlas.

Embraer of Brazil acquired a licence to build the MB-326 as the T-26 Xavante (the name of a Brazilian Indian tribe) and constructed 166 for its own air force, 10 for Paraguay and six for Togo. The Brazilian aircraft are usually known as the AT-26 to signify their secondary attack role. Some have reconnaissance cameras and refuelling probes and are known as the RT-26.

AERMACCHI (EMBRAER) EMB-326GB/AT-26 XAVANTE

Specification

Type: two-seat jet trainer/light attack aircraft

Crew: 2

Powerplant: one 15.17kN (3410lb thrust) Rolls-Royce Viper 20 Mk 540 turbojet engine

Performance: max speed 867km/h (539mph); service ceiling 11,890m (39,000ft); range with external fuel 2446km (1520 miles)

Dimensions: wing span 10.85m (35ft 7.25in); length 10.67m (35ft 0.25in); height 3.72m (12ft 2in)

Weight: 4211kg (9285lb) loaded

Armament: up to 1962kg (4352lb) of bombs or rockets; 12.7mm (0.50in) gun pods

2° ESQUADRÃO, 5° GRUPO DE AVIAÇIO GAV COMANDO, AÉREO DE TREINAMENTO FORÇA AÉREA BRASILEIRA, BASE AÉREA DE NATAL, BRAZIL, LATE 1980S

This Xavante belongs to the 2nd Squadron of the 5th Air Group (2° Esquadrão, 5°Grupo de Aviaçio, or 2°/5° GAv) at Natal, on the furthest eastern point of Brazil. The squadron uses the call sign 'Joker' and is one of two units at Natal which train pilots for the operational AT-26 units and other combat aircraft. For the weapons training role, the Xavante often carries Avbras SBAT-70 rocket launchers, as seen here. Other options include up to six 118kg (260lb) bombs or 12.7mm (0.50in) gun pods. It is planned that 2°/5°GAv will receive the AT-29 Super Tucano to replace the AT-26 in the coming years.

BAC Strikemaster

The basic design of the British Aircraft Corporation (BAC) Strikemaster can be traced to the piston-engined Percival Provost trainer of 1950. Hunting Aviation took the wings and tail, and created a jet version with the Bristol-Siddeley (later Rolls-Royce) Viper engine in 1954. The Jet Provost became the Royal Air Force's most numerous advanced trainer and served in this role into the 1990s, the later versions being pressurized with wingtip fuel tanks.

In 1967, BAC flew a strengthened version of the 'JP' Mk 5 as the Strikemaster, intended for the export market as a light attack aircraft and weapons trainer. With a more powerful Viper and extra wing hardpoints, the Strikemaster could carry a useful weapons load and over 100 were sold, to Ecuador, Kenya, Kuwait, New Zealand, Oman, Saudi Arabia, Singapore, Sudan and South Yemen. Botswana later acquired some ex-Kuwaiti aircraft.

BAC STRIKEMASTER MK 88

Specification

Type: advanced jet trainer/light attack aircraft

Crew: 2

Powerplant: one 15.17kN (3410lb thrust) Rolls-Royce Viper 20 Mk 525 turbojet engine

Performance: max speed 724km/h (450mph); service ceiling 12,190m (40,000ft); ferry range 2224km (1382 miles)

Dimensions: wing span 11.23m (36ft 10in); length 10.36m (34ft); height 3.10m (10ft 2in)

Weight: 5216kg (11,500lb) loaded

Armament: up to 1361kg (3000lb) of ordnance, including bombs, rockets or gun pods

NO. 14 SQUADRON ROYAL NEW ZEALAND AIR FORCE, OHAKEA NEW ZEALAND, 1970

This is one of 16 Strikemaster Mk 88s acquired by the Royal New Zealand Air Force (RNZAF) in the 1970s to replace the two-seat Vampire in the advanced training, jet conversion and weapons training roles. During this time, all RNZAF trainee pilots flew the 'Blunty', as it was known, whether they were destined for the A-4, C-130, P-3, Andover, 727 or the UH-1. NZ6376 was delivered in June 1975 and served with No. 14 Squadron at Ohakea in the central North Island.

In the late 1980s, the Strikemasters suffered from fatigue problems and were phased out in favour of the Aermacchi MB-339 by 1993. NZ6376 was in the final flypast of four Strikemasters on 17 December 1992 and later converted to an instructional airframe for use at No. 4 Technical Training School at Woodbourne.

AERMACCHI MB-326 VS BAC STRIKEMASTER

THE MB-326 and the Strikemaster both saw considerable operational service with foreign air forces.

The South African Air Force's single-seat MB-326s, known as the Impala Mk II, were operated by Nos 4 and 8 Squadrons and were first deployed in support of the army's cross-border operations in neighbouring Angola in August 1978. The flat and featureless nature of the border area made the Impalas easy targets for small-arms fire and shoulder-launched missiles, and the SAAF pilots became adept at delivering their weapons from ultra-low level; 15m (50ft) above ground level at full throttle was the normal operating procedure.

Low-Level Attacks

Fast low-level attack techniques assumed a new importance from 1980, when the rebel forces in Angola (aided by Cuban 'advisers')

BELOW: *The Aermacchi MB.326 was a simple and straightforward design. Easy to handle and very manoeuvrable, it was readily adapted to the light attack role.*

fielded more advanced Soviet weaponry against the SAAF. Shoulder-launched SAMs claimed three Impala Mk IIs during 1980, all three pilots being lost. Two succeeded in ejecting, but one was was killed by his captors and the other died of injuries sustained during the ejection sequence. In December 1983 two Impalas were hit by SAMs, but in both cases the missiles failed to explode and the pilots managed to recover to their airfields.

Attrition caused by combat losses and accidents gradually reduced the size of the SAAF's Impala fleet.

In May 1983, in retaliation for an ANC car bomb attack on the SAAF headquarters in Pretoria, Impala Mk IIs attacked ANC bases in Mozambique, and in September Impalas shot down six Soviet-built helicopters (four Mil Mi-25s and two Mi-17s) with cannon fire, the first time in history that the attack variant of a trainer

aircraft was credited with an air-to-air victory. These successful actions were the fruit of a SAAF training policy that laid emphasis on aircraft vs helicopter combat techniques.

Attrition caused by combat losses and accidents gradually reduced the size of the SAAF's Impala fleet, and cost considerations brought about a large force reduction at the end of the border war. Another primary reason for the reduction was that there had been substantial cuts in the size of the South African Army, so there was no longer a need for substantial numbers of close support aircraft.

Strikemaster in Oman

The British Aircraft Corporation's Strikemaster was used operationally for a long time by the Sultan of Oman's Air Force (SOAF), the aircraft being flown by RAF personnel under contract. The presence of the Strikemasters in Oman was a direct result of a rebellion, supported by Yemen, which broke out in Dhofar province in 1965. The situation worsened in 1967 when the British vacated Aden, and the Dhofar Liberation Front (DLF) established a number of bases inside what became South Yemen.

> The involvement of SOAF Hawker Hunters and Strikemasters, but also IIAF F-4 Phantoms, as well as numerous Omani and Iranian attack and transport helicopters, proved decisive in ending the rebellion in Dhofar.

British personnel working with the SOAF were sufficiently concerned by such developments that they convinced the Sultan to place an initial order for four BAC 167 Strikemaster Mk 82 trainers and light tactical support aircraft. In April 1968, before the first of these aircraft was delivered, the planning began for establishing a whole Strike Squadron within the SOAF, and the order was increased to 12 as a consequence. The Strikemasters flew their first offensive operations in February 1971, in support of ground forces (mainly Special Air Service) who launched an offensive aimed at securing the areas east of Salalah, the main SOAF air base, and cutting off the flow of arms and supplies from Yemen. The Strikemasters also bombed and made rocket attacks on artillery positions inside Yemen.

SOAF suffered its first loss on 9 July 1973, when a Strikemaster was shot down by ground fire and its British pilot killed. By this time the Imperial Iranian Air Force had become involved in operations against the Yemenis, its F-4 Phantoms flying combat air patrols along the border. The Phantoms also carried out some bombing attacks, reducing the Strikemasters' workload.

In 1975 there came a new and dangerous development. On 9 August a SOAF Strikemaster was shot down by a Soviet SA-7 shoulder-launched surface-to-air missile. The pilot ejected safely and a number of helicopters and additional Strikemasters were deployed to rescue the pilot while he was floating down to the ground. Although being targeted by a number of SA-7s, no other aircraft was damaged and the British pilot was safely recovered.

The involvement of SOAF Hawker Hunters and Strikemasters, but also IIAF F-4 Phantoms, as well as numerous Omani and Iranian attack and transport helicopters, proved decisive in ending the rebellion in Dhofar. Without them the isolated outposts along the main rebel supply routes would have been unable to survive. These outposts were essential in weakening the rebels: they effectively cut off their supply routes, while forcing them to commit their forces in frontal attacks against well-defended positions, and exposing them to superior firepower.

In 1977, the Strikemasters were replaced by the first of a batch of SEPECAT Jaguar International aircraft, marking an important step forward in the modernization of the Sultan of Oman's Air Force.

Antonov An-26 'Curl'

Originally designed as a civil transport to replace the piston-engined Ilyushin Il-12 and Il-14s in Aeroflot service, the Antonov An-24 of 1959 was soon adapted to become a military transport with a side freight door. The similar-looking An-26 (Nato code name 'Curl') was in fact an all-new design with a rear loading ramp, a pressurized cargo hold and more powerful engines. A small turbojet auxiliary power unit (APU) in the tail provides electrical power on the ground, but also can be used to supplement the main turboprop engines on take-off.

The aircraft was used by the Soviet Union and most of the Warsaw Pact nations and was exported to more than 20 foreign air forces. Many of these continue to fly the An-26 and/or its successor the An-32 'Cline', which remains in production in the Ukraine. A derivative is the An-30 'Clank', which is a purpose-built survey aircraft with a raised cockpit and glazed nose. The An-26 is still produced in China as the Xian Y-7H-500.

ANTONOV AN-26 'CURL'

Specification

Type: twin-engined transport aircraft

Crew: 5–6

Powerplant: two 2103kW (2820hp) Ivchencko AI-24VT turboprop engines

Performance: max speed 540km/h (336mph); service ceiling 7400m (24,605ft); range 2550km (1585 miles)

Dimensions: wing span 29.20m (95ft 9.5in); length 23.80m (78ft 1in); height 8.58m (28ft 1.5in)

Weight: 24,400kg (53,790lb) loaded

Payload: 40 passengers or 5500kg (12,100lb) cargo

TRANSPORTFLIEGERSTAFFEL 24 DDR LUFTSTREITKRÄFTE, DRESDEN-KLOTSCHE, GERMAN DEMOCRATIC REPUBLIC, 1980S

The aircraft illustrated is an early model An-26, delivered in 1980 to the Luftstreitkräfte (air force) of the German Democratic Republic, which had at least 12 'Curls'. As well as standard transports, the East Germans had special variants for electronic intelligence gathering and calibrating aeronautical navigation aids. Some of the An-26s were retained by the Luftwaffe after the reunification of Germany, but they were soon put in museums or sold on to Russian airline Komi Avia. In 1991, No. 371 here became 52+01 with the Luftwaffe, then in 1993 RA-49264 with Komi Avia. It spent two years working with the United Nations as UN-488 before being returned to Russia.

Transall C-160

The Transall C-160 tactical transport was designed and produced as a joint venture between France and Federal Germany, Transall being an abbreviation of the specially formed consortium Transporter Allianz, comprising the companies of MBB, Aerospatiale and VFW-Fokker. The prototype flew for the first time on 25 February 1963, and series production began four years later.

The principal variants were the C-160A, consisting of six pre-series aircraft; the C-160D for the Luftwaffe (90 built); the C-160F for France (60 built); the C-160T (20 built for export to Turkey); and the C-160Z (nine built for South Africa). Production of a second series was authorized in 1977 following an additional French order and requests by other countries including Turkey and South Africa. The new version was designated the C.160NG (Nouvelle Generation) and

was fitted with improved avionics and a reinforced wing with additional fuel tanks for extended range, as well as flight refuelling equipment.

Six second-generation French Transalls were specially modified for two types of special duty; two were equipped for electronic intelligence (Elint) and jamming operations, and four were fitted with VLF transmission equipment, including a long, trailing aerial which enabled the aircraft to communicate with nuclear submarines of France's Force Océanique Stratégique without the need for them to surface. The aerial platform was known as ASTARTE (Avion STAtion Relais de Transmissions Exceptionelles – aircraft relay station for special transmissions). This system was due to be replaced by a ground-based communication system.

TRANSALL C-160NG

Specification
Type: transport aircraft
Crew: 4
Powerplant: two 4548kW (6100hp) Rolls-Royce Tyne RTy.20 Mk 22
  turboprop engines
Performance: max speed 536km/h (333mph); service ceiling 8500m
  (27,900ft); range 4558km (2832 miles)
Dimensions: wing span 40m (131ft 3in); length 32.40m (106ft 3in);
  height 11.65m (38ft 5in)
Weight: 16,000kg (35,270lb) loaded
Payload: 93 troops, 68 paratroops, 62 stretchers

64E ESCADRE DE TRANSPORT, ARMÉE DE L'AIR, EVREUX/FAUVILLE, FRANCE, 1990S

ANTONOV AN-26 'CURL' VS TRANSALL C-160

FOR NATO, ONE OF THE MOST alarming aspects of the Cold War was the Warsaw Pact's huge air transport capability, mainly due to the fact that literally hundreds of civil transport aircraft could be called on for military use at very short notice.

The An-26 provides a good example of this dual role. The Transall C-160, in contrast, provides an example of a type that has seen much military service, but has never been a civil success, despite much marketing.

Antonovs in the Balkans

The Antonov An-26 saw a great deal of operational service in the former Yugoslavia, where it served as the principal transport type in the Yugoslav Air Force from 1976, replacing the Douglas C-47s which had been in use since the end of World War II. At one time some 30 aircraft were in service, divided between No 677 Transport Squadron based at Nis and No 679 Transport Squadron at Zagreb. During the bitter civil war, these aircraft transported thousands of refugees and hundreds of tons of material from the republics that had declared their independence; no losses were sustained. However, the An-26 force suffered badly during the NATO bombing campaign of 1999. In August

BELOW: *An Antonov An-26 of the Afghan Air Force.*

1994, an An-26 owned by a Ukrainian air charter company was shot down by the Bosnian Serb Army while en route from Croatia to Bihac.

Although the An-26 is a fine aircraft in its own right, the German Luftwaffe considered the C-160 Transall to be better, which is why the An-26 fleet inherited from the former East Germany was quickly scrapped or sold off to civil operators.

French Transalls to Africa

The Transall has seen much operational service with the French Air Force, in Africa and elsewhere. One of its more recent operations took place in 1995, when the French government authorized military action to restore order in the Comoros Islands in the Indian Ocean, which had been seized by a mercenary-backed coup. On 3 October 1995, a French special forces' unit known as the Commando Hubert made a reconnaissance of two key airfields; shortly afterwards, at around 02.30 on 4 October, three Puma helicopters airlifted troops of the French Foreign Legion and a force of French Marines to Hahaya airport. They initially came under fire from few heavy machine-guns,

but using the cover of darkness and night-vision gear the French troops were able to secure the whole airport and the local area, capturing some twenty enemy troops in the process.

By 03.00 the Commando Hubert had secured Iconi airport as well, and subsequently further French Foreign Legion paratroop units were deployed aboard Transall C-160 transports to guard both airfields, while the Commando Hubert was sent to capture Kandani barracks. This operation was executed very swiftly, and thirty more rebel troops were captured in the process.

A steady stream of Transalls flew in supplies while the French troops moved on the capital, Moroni. The French Air Force Transall C-160 transports proved indispensable during this operation.

The main air assault began around 05.00hrs, when two Transalls delivered elements of the Foreign Legion to Hahaya. 30 minutes later the Legionnaires were joined by Marines, supported by artillery. By 05.50hrs the French had established a secure zone around the airport, and a steady stream of Transalls flew in supplies while the French troops moved on the capital, Moroni. The French Air Force C-160 transports proved indispensable during this operation. Having a capability of carrying loads of up to 16,000kg (35,275lb) or 68 fully-equipped troops, they were the main means of reaching the Comoros for the French troops of the first attack wave.

Nearly a decade later, the French Air Force's Transalls were active

ABOVE: *The Transall C-160, seen here in German markings, saw much combat duty with the French Air Force, supporting ground operations in Africa and elsewhere.*

in Kosovo, as this new report explains. The date was 6 October 2004.

'STANOVC, Serbia and Montenegro, Oct 6 (Reuters) – Hundreds of French troops parachuted into Kosovo on Wednesday in the first major operational drop by the French military since intervention in Zaire in 1978. The mid-morning calm in open meadows north of the U.N.-governed province's capital, Pristina, was shattered by the thunder of seven Transall C-160 planes arriving at the end of a five-hour flight from bases in France. Arching low over cornfields, they emptied their human cargo, filling the skies with the dirty-white canopies of 361 French paratroopers, each with combat rifle and 50 kg [110lb] of equipment strapped to his back.

'The units included marines, signals, a medical team and an Air Force squadron. Their 200m [600ft[jump into a drop zone guarded by Moroccan troops marked the start of a 2,000-strong reinforcement of the NATO-led KFOR peacekeeping force ahead of a general election in Kosovo on 23 October.'

It was France's first large airborne operation since 1978, when paratroops were deployed to rescue French and other foreign nationals from war-torn Zaire. During that operation the French used Lockheed C-130 Hercules transports rather than Transalls, which did not have sufficient range to reach Zaire from French bases, but one Transall belonging to the Zaire Air Force was used as an airborne command post.

Sukhoi Su-15 'Flagon'

The Sukhoi Su-15 'Flagon' traces its ancestry back to the Sukhoi Su-9, known to Nato as 'Fishpot'. Fishpot-A was a single-seat interceptor; to some extent, an Su-7 with a delta wing. It was armed with the first Soviet air-to-air missile, the semi-active radar homing Alkali, four of which were carried under the wings. In 1961, a new model, the Su-11 Fishpot-B, was developed from the Su-9, and was followed into service by the Fishpot-C, which had an uprated engine. A tandem two-seat trainer variant of the Su-9 was given the Nato reporting name 'Maiden'.

The Su-9 flew for the first time in 1955 and entered service in the following year. The follow-on to the Su-11 aircraft was the Su-15, a twin-engined delta-wing interceptor that first flew in 1965 and was in Soviet Air Force service by 1969. Capable of carrying two air-to-air missiles, the Flagon was numerically the Soviet Union's most important all-weather interceptor by the mid-1970s, some 1500 being produced in total.

The T-5 prototype from which the Su-15 was developed was basically an enlarged version of the Su-11 with the same nose intake, but the T-58 which followed had a 'solid' nose housing AI radar equipment and intakes on the fuselage sides. A number of Flagon variants were produced, culminating in the definitive Su-15TM Flagon-F of 1971.

SUKHOI SU-15TM FLAGON-F

Specification

Type: all-weather interceptor
Crew: 1
Powerplant: two 6205kg (13,668lb) thrust Tumanskii R-11F2S
   turbojets
Performance: max speed 2230km/h (1386mph); service ceiling
   20,000m (65,615ft); combat radius 725km (450 miles)
Dimensions: wing span 8.61m (28ft 3in); length 21.33m (70ft);
   height 5.10m (16ft 8in)
Weight: 18,000kg (39,680lb) loaded
Armament: four external pylons for medium-range air-to-air missiles

SOVIET AIR DEFENCE FORCES, DOLINSK-SOKOL, SAKHALIN, EARLY 1980s
On 1 September 1983, an Su-15TM like the aircraft illustrated here, and based at Dolinsk-Sokol on Sakhalin, achieved notoriety by shooting down a Korean Air Lines Boeing 747 over the Sea of Japan.

Convair F-106 Delta Dart

Begun as the '1954 Ultimate Interceptor', and for a time known as the F-102B, the F-106 emerged as a much more capable and long-lived interceptor than its predecessor, and also proved to be a useful dogfighter in its later years. The prototype YF-106 flew in December 1956 and was similar in configuration and dimensions to the F-102A, but with refined aerodynamics, a square-topped fin, completely revised intakes and a more powerful Pratt & Whitney J75 engine.

The airframe was regarded as just one component of the MA-1 integrated weapons system. The MA-1 included an automated interception system that would fly the aircraft 'hands off' to the firing point. Weapons included the same Falcon missiles as the F-102A, but also the MB-1 Genie rocket with a nuclear warhead. Late in their careers, some aircraft such as this one had a Vulcan cannon fitted between the bomb bay doors and a clear-topped canopy installed.

Mainly based in the United States, F-106 units were sent to South Korea to bolster local air defence during the 1968–70 period of tension with North Korea over the capture of the intelligence ship USS *Pueblo*.

CONVAIR F-102A DELTA DART

Specification

Type: supersonic interceptor fighter

Crew: 1

Powerplant: one Pratt & Whitney J75-P-17 turbojet rated at 76.50kN (17,200lb thrust) static and 108.98kN (24,500 lb thrust) with afterburner

Performance: max speed 2137km/h (1328mph); combat radius 925km (575 miles); service ceiling 17,374m (57,000ft)

Dimensions: wing span 11.67m (38ft 3.5in); length 21.56m (70ft 8.75in); height 6.18m (20ft 3.5in)

Weight: loaded 17,779 kg (39,195 lb)

Armament: one MB-1 Genie nuclear-tipped air-to-air missile and four AIM-4 Falcon radar or IR-guided air-to-air missiles; later models also had one M61A1 Vulcan 20-mm (0.79in) cannon

49TH FIGHTER INTERCEPTOR SQUADRON TACTICAL AIR COMMAND GRIFFISS AIR FORCE BASE, NEW YORK, 1983

Delta Dart 58-0780 was the 140th of 330 F-106s to be built and was delivered in November 1959 to the 27th Fighter Interceptor Squadron (FIS) at Loring Air Force Base (AFB), Maine. It moved between units quite regularly, serving with the 94th, 71st, 319th, 460th, 159th, 194th and the Air Development Weapons Center (AWDC). In 1983, it joined the 49th FIS at Griffiss AFB, New York, and served there until 1987 when the unit disbanded. After four years in storage it was converted to a QF-106 drone for weapons tests. Many of these aircraft were used for years and survived many missile engagements, but 0780 was shot down by an AIM-7 Sparrow in its first unmanned mission on 9 March 1993.

SU-15 'FLAGON' VS F-106 DELTA DART

IN THE MID-1950S, the threat of the long-range strategic bomber armed with stand-off nuclear missiles produced alarm in both the USA and USSR, and led to an urgent requirement for supersonic long-range interceptors, resulting in the Convair F-106 and Sukhoi Su-15 'Flagon'.

The destruction of the Korean Air Lines Boeing 747 in September 1983 has tended to eclipse an earlier incident, also involving an Su-15 and a Korean Air Lines airliner – on this occasion a Boeing 707. It happened on 20 April 1978, when Korean Air Lines Flight 902 departed Paris for a flight to Seoul with an intermediate stop at Anchorage, Alaska. The aircraft passed the Canadian Station 'Alert' early warning station, located 640km (400 miles) from the North Pole where the crew corrected their course. However, this brought them on a course directly across the Barents Sea towards Soviet airspace.

The aircraft was initially identified by Soviet anti-aircraft defence radars as a Boeing 747, and two Sukhoi Su-15TM interceptor jets were sent to intercept the intruder. When both Su-15s were flying next to the Korean airliner, the captain said he slowed down the aircraft and switched on his landing lights. Despite this, the Su-15

BELOW: The Sukhoi Su-15 'Flagon' achieved notoriety in two missile attacks on Korean airlines. Its real function was to destroy Strategic Air Command's B-52 Stratofortresses.

crews were ordered to shoot down the airliner. For several minutes, according to US sources, the leading Russian Su-15 pilot tried to convince his superiors that the order to shoot down the 707 should be countermanded, the Korean aircraft having now been positively identified as a civilian Boeing 707 rather than a Boeing RC-135 electronic intelligence aircraft, a military variant of the 707.

The order to destroy the Boeing was confirmed and one of the Su-15s fired two P-60 air-to-air missiles.

The order to destroy the Boeing was confirmed and one of the Su-15s fired two P-60 air-to-air missiles. One of them missed the 707 but the other rocket exploded, severely damaging part of the left wing. Shrapnel punctured the fuselage, causing rapid decompression and killing two passengers. The Korean pilot initiated an emergency descent from 10,600m (35,000ft) to 1500m (5000ft) and entered clouds, where both Su-15s lost contact with the airliner. The aircraft continued at low altitude, crossing the Kola Peninsula while the crew looked for a suitable place to make an emergency landing. After several unsuccessful attempts

ABOVE: *The Convair F-106 Delta Dart was developed from the less-than-successful F-102 Delta Dagger. This F-106 is seen landing at Edwards AFB, California, after a test flight.*

in the evening dusk the pilot, in a remarkable feat of airmanship, made a successful landing on the ice of Korpijärvi lake, on the Finnish border. All 107 passengers and crew were rescued by Russian helicopters.

Delta Dart Flight Test

The Convair F-106 Delta Dart, was very similar in performance to the Russian fighter, although its weapons system was much more reliable. British test pilot Wing Commander Roland Beamont had the opportunity to fly an F-106 during a visit to the United States, and recorded his impressions. He was also able to compare it with the English Electric P.1B Lightning, which he tested.

'The basic characteristics of the F-106 are similar to those of the F-102, as are the systems and cockpit layout, and it was possible to make some attempt at measuring performance from the start on this one flight. From this limited experience it was clear that the F-106 contained many control features which were developments from and improvements on the F-102 production standard; in particular transition trim changes had been reduced (stabilisers IN) to insignificant proportions, and the turn co-ordinator clearly takes care of the adverse yaw characteristics which are still quite apparent on the F-102.

> **'The handling qualities of this second generation delta-wing fighter were already excellent and likely to result in a practical and formidable Mach 2 all-weather fighter.'**

'The result is a balanced aircraft, which is easy to control and pleasant to fly throughout the limited conditions experienced. Performance,

which during the climb phase promises well, is disappointing at altitude and as measured does not approach the standard at present achieved with the P.1B series.

'In the cockpit, seat comfort and control layout were good, but forward vision through the Convair 'V' windscreen was found to be very restricting. It can be said, therefore, that at the present time on the F-106, a high standard of artificial stability and control has been achieved, and that in its present form the aircraft is already likely to be suitable for all-weather operation up to and including supersonic speeds.

'Although limited by the current engine and intake development problems, it was clear that the handling qualities of this second generation delta-wing fighter were already excellent and likely to result in a practical and formidable Mach 2 all-weather fighter when the specified power became available.

'It seemed likely also that the Hughes MA1 weapons system would provide some advantages over the Ferranti AirPass system of the Lightning, but that otherwise in direct comparison the Lightning was likely to remain superior on many counts. These included acceleration and time to altitude, hard-turning capability and sustained g at all altitudes due to the Lightning's low-tailplane configuration, which produced significantly less lift loss and induced drag in the turn than did the all-elevon delta wing of the F-106. Also the Lightning's inherent stability was a marked safety and reliability factor, in contrast to the auto-stabiliser-dependent F-106 (on all axes).

'This interesting visit to the centre of American military test flying ended on a high note, with the sheer enjoyment of landing this fine new fighter easily and without complication on the wide expanse of Edwards AFB under the brilliant afternoon sky. But, on the way back to the UK, it was also pleasant to reflect that in the Lightning the RAF would clearly now have a fighter which could handle anything in the USAF inventory up to and including the F-106.'

Mikoyan-Gurevich MiG-21

Known by the Nato reporting name 'Fishbed,' the MiG-21 was a child of the Korean War, where Soviet air combat experience had identified a need for a light, single-seat target defence interceptor with high supersonic manoeuvrability. Two prototypes were ordered, both appearing early in 1956; one, code-named 'Faceplate,' featured sharply swept wings and was not developed further.

The initial production versions (Fishbed-A and Fishbed-B) were built in only limited numbers, being short-range day fighters with a comparatively light armament of two 30mm (1.18in) NR-30 cannon. The next variant, however, the MiG-21F Fishbed-C, carried two K-13 Atoll infrared homing air-to-air missiles, and had an uprated Tumansky R-11 turbojet as well as improved avionics.

The MiG-21F was the first major production version; it entered service in 1960 and was progressively modified and updated over the years that followed. In the early 1970s, the MiG-21 was virtually redesigned, re-emerging as the MiG-21B (Fishbed-L) multi-role air superiority fighter and ground-attack version. In its several versions, the MiG-21 became the most widely used jet fighter in the world, being licence-built in India, Czechoslovakia and China. In Vietnam, the MiG-21 was the Americans' deadliest opponent.

MIKOYAN-GUREVICH MIG-21MF FISHBED-J

Specification

Type: fighter

Crew: 1

Powerplant: one 6600kg (14,553lb) thrust Tumanski R-13-300 turbojet

Performance: max speed 2230km/h (1384mph); service ceiling 15,250m (50,000ft); range 1800km (1118 miles)

Dimensions: wing span 7.15m (23ft 5in); length 15.76m (51ft 9in); height 4.02m (14ft 9in)

Weight: 9400kg (20,727lb) loaded

Armament: one 23mm (0.9in) GSh-23 cannon; two K-13A air-to-air missiles on underwing pylons

NO. 7 'BATTLE AXES' SQUADRON INDIAN AIR FORCE, GWALIOR, 1980S
One of the major customers was India, the MiG-21MFs of which were equipped to carry a wide range of weaponry, reflecting their multi-role capability. For air-to-air combat, the Indian Air Force used the Soviet K-13A Atoll and R-60 Aphid, as well as the French Matra R550 Magic. The MiG-21MF Fishbed-J here is seen in the markings of the Indian Air Force's No. 7 'Battle Axes' Squadron.

McDonnell Douglas F-4 Phantom II

As a result of the lessons learned in Vietnam, the provision of airborne equipment to fulfil the defence suppression role, and the modification of aircraft to carry it, assumed top priority in US Air Force (USAF) Tactical Air Command planning in 1975. What Tactical Air Command needed was a self-contained weapon system – an aircraft capable of carrying both the necessary electronics and the weaponry to hit enemy surface-to-air missile radars, and the F-4 Phantom was the best choice available.

'Wild Weasel' trials had already been carried out with two F-4Ds in 1968, but later studies showed that the F-4E variant was easier to modify. USAF funding was consequently obtained to convert 116 F-4Es to F-4G standard under the Advanced Wild Weasel Programme. Modfications included the addition of a torpedo-shaped fairing on top of the fin to house APR-38 radar antennae, and the F-4E's M61A1 cannon installation was deleted to permit the installation of the computer systems associated with the F-4G's sensory radar. With this equipment, the Wild Weasel crew could detect, identify and locate hostile radar emitters and select the appropriate weapons package for use against them.

MCDONNELL DOUGLAS F-4G 'WILD WEASEL' PHANTOM

Specification

Type: defence suppression aircraft

Crew: 2

Powerplant: two 8119kg (17,900lb) thrust General Electric J79-GE-17 turbojets

Performance: max speed 2390km/h (1485mph); service ceiling 17,678m (58,000ft); range 2817km (1750 miles)

Dimensions: wing span 11.70m (38ft 5in); length 17.76m (58ft 3in); height 4.96m (16ft 3in)

Weight: 26,308kg (58,000lb) loaded

Armament: up to 5888kg (12,980lb) of ordnance and stores on underwing pylons, including AGM-88 HARM anti-radiation missiles

35TH TACTICAL FIGHTER WING (PROVISIONAL) UNITED STATES AIR FORCE, SHEIKH ISA AIR BASE, BAHRAIN, JANUARY 1991
The F-4G pictured here, normally based at Spangdahlem in Germany with the 23rd Tactical Fighter Squadron (TFS), 52nd Tactical Fighter Wing (TFW), was assigned to the 35th TFW for operations during Desert Storm in 1991. It carries 27 mission marks in the form of a 'spook' figure. The 'Night Stalker' artwork is an allusion to the 'Rhino' nickname adopted by the Phantoms.

MiG-21 vs F-4 Phantom II

THE HEAVY, MULTI-ROLE F-4 Phantom provided the answer to almost all the air combat requirements of the USAF, USN, USMC, and many other air forces in the 1960s and for twenty years thereafter.

In Vietnam, it proved capable of outfighting the small and nimble MiG-21 – but often, it was only because the American pilots had the benefit of superior tactics and training.

Phantoms flew their first combat mission over South Vietnam on 13 April 1965, when twelve F-4Bs of Marine Fighter/Attack Squadron VMFA-531, normally based at Atsugi in Japan, operated out of Da Nang in support of US Marine ground troops. In November 1965, the Phantom strength in Vietnam was boosted with the arrival of the 12th Tactical Fighter Wing, with F-4Cs.

In September 1966, with the USAF's 'Rolling Thunder' air strike operations against North Vietnam in full swing, the North Vietnamese Air Force suddenly began to fight back in strength, and the F-4Cs were temporarily diverted from their primary strike mission to air combat against the MiGs. The latter were mainly MiG-21s, armed with Atoll infrared homing missiles and operating from five bases in the Hanoi area.

Early in 1967, the Americans devised a ruse code-named Operation Bolo, which was designed to bring the MiGs to battle. F-105 Thunderchief strike aircraft were used as bait, and were supported by

BELOW: A MiG-21 'Fishbed-J'. The MiG-21 was a simple, robust and highly effective combat aircraft.

56 Phantoms of the 8th and 366th Tactical Fighter Wings as well as by defence suppression aircraft. The 8th TFW's Phantoms were led by Colonel Robin Olds, a highly experienced fighter leader with eight victories to his credit during World War II. In the air battle that took place on that day, 2 January 1967, he and his Phantom pilots destroyed seven MiGs in twelve minutes for no loss.

'the F-4 had a good solid head-on or tail shot against any MiG he could find and get close enough to shoot at.'

Olds himself went after a MiG-21 which disappeared into the clouds, but another emerged off to his left, in a hard turn towards him. Olds pulled the nose of his Phantom up to about 45 degrees and rolled to the right. Half inverted, he waited until the MiG passed beneath, then rolled down astern. At just under a mile [1600m] range he launched two Sidewinders, one of which hit and blew the MiG's right wing off.

Neither the MiG-17 nor the MiG-21 were specialised night fighters, but they often operated in that capacity, particularly when the American night bombing campaign against the North intensified during 1972. One US Navy pilot, Captain R.E. Tucker, recalled that: 'During 1972, when Navy A-6s were making a number of single

ABOVE: *An F-4E Phantom releases its substantial bomb load over a weapons range. Tail markings reveal that this is an aircraft of the 52nd TFW, Spangdahlem, Germany.*

aircraft low-level night strikes all over the area between Haiphong and Hanoi, MiGs were known to launch, making the A-6 drivers nervous (although I personally felt that the MiGs had no night/IFR capability against an A-6 at 300 feet). As a result, we started positioning a single F-4 on MIGCAP along the coastline at night. We figured a single F-4 didn't have to worry about a mid-air with his wingman and had plenty of potential at night against a single MiG. If a MiG launched and headed towards an A-6, the F-4 would vector for the MiG. Invariably MiGs would run for home when the F-4 got to within 25–30 miles [40–50km] of them. Some pilots weren't too overjoyed about the night MIGCAP missions, but I personally felt it was a golden opportunity and my MiG kill proved it. I figured that the MiG had a negligible opportunity to do anyone bodily harm at night with his limited weapons system and Atoll/guns load, whereas the F-4 had a good solid head-on or tail shot against any MiG he could find and get close enough to shoot at.'

Tucker, then a Lieutenant-Commander, was flying an F-4 Phantom of VF-103, operating from the USS *Saratoga*, when he destroyed a MiG-21 on the night of 10/11 August 1972. The Phantom was armed with two AIM-7E Sparrows and two AIM-9D Sidewinders. Tucker was refuelling from a KA-6D tanker when he heard the fighter controller vector another Phantom on to a MiG. He immediately broke contact and joined the other F-4 in the search, the controller advising him that the enemy aircraft was at 2,500m (8,000ft), 140 degrees at 19km (12 miles) range.

> **'The MiG-21 pilot did not survive. If he ejected after the first missile, the second missile must have done him in. We couldn't see any debris in the dark...'**

Tucker descended to 2,500m (8,000ft) and his RIO, Lt (JG) Bruce Edens, got a radar contact at once. Lighting his afterburners, Tucker accelerated to 650 knots and closed to within five miles of the MiG, at which point Edens advised the pilot that he had lost radar contact. Realizing that the MiG pilot had probably descended, Tucker went down to 1000m (3500ft); Edens announced that he had regained contact and that the MiG was 11–13km (7–8 miles) ahead. Tucker jettisoned his centreline fuel tanks and accelerated to 750 knots, overtaking the MiG from directly astern. At a range of about two miles the pilot launched two Sparrows, the second one leaving the under-fuselage rack just as the first warhead detonated. 'There was a large fireball,' Tucker reported, and the second missile impacted in the same spot. I came right slightly to avoid any debris. The target on our radar appeared to stop in mid-air and within a second or two the radar broke lock. The MiG-21 pilot did not survive. If he ejected after the first missile, the second missile must have done him in. We couldn't see any debris in the dark...The kill was confirmed three days later.'

Sukhoi Su-25 'Frogfoot'

A Russian requirement for an attack aircraft in the A-10 Thunderbolt II class materialized in the Sukhoi Su-25 'Frogfoot,' which was selected in preference to a rival design, the Ilyushin Il-102. As a result of lessons learned during the Afghan conflict, an upgraded version known as the Su-25T was produced, with improved defensive systems to counter weapons such as the Stinger.

The improvements included the insertion of steel plates, several millimetres thick, between the engine bays and below the fuel cell. After this modification, no further Su-25s were lost to shoulder-launched missiles. In total, 22 Su-25s were lost in the nine years of the Afghan conflict.

The Su-25UBK is a two-seat export variant, while the Su-25UBT is a navalized version with a strengthened undercarriage and arrester gear. The Su-25UT (Su-28) was a trainer version, lacking the weapons pylons and combat capability of the standard Su-25UBK, but retaining the original aircraft's rough field capability and endurance. Only one aircraft was flown in August 1985, appearing in the colours of DOSAAF, the Soviet Union's paramilitary 'private flying' organization.

In service with the Soviet Air Force, the Su-25 was nicknamed 'Grach' ('Rook'), and most aircraft deployed to Afghanistan featured a cartoon rook design. Russian infantrymen called the aircraft *Rascheska* ('The Comb') because of its 10 weapon pylons.

SUKHOI SU-25 'FROGFOOT'

Specification
Type: close support aircraft
Crew: 1
Powerplant: two 4500kg (9921lb) Tumanskii R-195 turbojets
Performance: max speed 975km/h (606mph); service ceiling 7000m (22,965ft); combat radius 750km (466 miles)
Dimensions: wing span 14.36m (47ft 1in); length 15.53m (50ft 11in); height 4.80m (15ft 9in)
Weight: 17,600kg (38,800lb) loaded
Armament: one 30mm (1.18in) GSh-30-2 cannon; eight external pylons with provision for up to 4400kg (9700lb) of stores

STATE FLIGHT TEST CENTRE, AKHTUBINSK, RUSSIA, 1980s
Operated by the Sukhoi OKB Flight Test Department, this Su-25TM was detached to the State Flight Test Centre at Akhtubinsk, situated between Volgograd and Astrakhan. Known as 'Blue 10', the aircraft was used for weapons trials and also undertook overseas demonstration flights on behalf of potential customers.

Fairchild A-10 Thunderbolt II 🇺🇸

The Fairchild A-10A is one of the most specialized modern combat aircraft to enter service, having been designed to destroy Soviet armour on the European central front using its massive 30mm (1.18in) cannon as its primary weapon. The first A-10 flew in May 1972 and beat the Northrop A-9 to win a US Air Force (USAF) competition in early 1973.

The A-10's unusual appearance, which resulted in the nickname 'Warthog', resulted largely from the need to duplicate and separate critical systems such as engines and control surfaces. The pilot is protected by a 'bathtub' of titanium armour to protect against ground fire, and the wing and fuselage have 11 weapons pylons that can carry a combination of bombs, rockets and missiles. The A-10 saw a great deal of action in both US–Iraq wars and proved its ability to absorb large amounts of battle damage and keep flying. One was credited with an air-to-air kill in 1991, when it destroyed an Iraqi Mi-8 helicopter with its cannon.

FAIRCHILD A-10A THUNDERBOLT II

Specification

Type: close support aircraft

Crew: 1

Powerplant two 40.32kN (9065lb thrust) General Electric TF34-GE-100 turbofans

Performance: max speed 706km/h (439mph); service ceiling 13,636m (45,000ft); range 3947km (2454 miles) ferry range with two drop tanks

Dimensions: wing span 17.53m (57ft 6in); length 16.26m (53ft 6in); height 4.47m (14ft 8in)

Weight: 22,680kg (50,000lb) max take-off

Armament: one GAU-8 Avenger 30mm (1.18in) cannon with 1350 rounds; max ordnance load of 7758kg (16,000lb) including bombs, rockets and AGM-65 Maverick missiles

81ST FIGHTER SQUADRON, 52ND FIGHTER WING USAFE, SPANGDAHLEM, GERMANY, LATE 1980S

This late-production Fairchild A-10A is in the colours of the 81st Fighter Squadron 'Black Panthers' of the 52nd Fighter Wing. The 81st flew the original Republic P-47 Thunderbolt from English bases during World War II and received the A-10 Thunderbolt II in 1993. The 81st's two sister squadrons fly the F-16C in the defence suppression role. The 81st flew many missions over the former Yugoslavia during Operation Allied Force in 1999. One notable mission was in supporting the rescue of an F-117 pilot downed over Serbia, for which the A-10 pilot received the Silver Star.

By July 1994, A-10 82-0646 had joined the 118th Fighter Squadron 'Flying Yankees' of the Connecticut Air National Guard, with which it still serves. The 81st continues to fly the A-10 at Spangdahlem.

Su-25 vs
A-10 Thunderbolt II

IF WAR HAD COME between NATO and the Warsaw Pact, the ability to kill the latest tanks from the air would have assumed the highest priority. The A-10 and the Su-25 were designed to do just that.

Twenty-three Su-25s were lost during the nine years of conflict in Afghanistan, representing a loss rate of one aircraft per 2800 hours of operational flying. Others sustained quite incredible battle damage, yet survived. One aircraft, flown by Colonel Alexander V. Rutskoi, was damaged twice, once by AAA and then by two Sidewinder AAMs launched by Pakistani Air Force F-16s. On both occasions the pilot recovered safely to base. The aircraft was refurbished in Tbilisi, and after receiving a new paint application was displayed at the Paris Air Show in 1989 as Blue 301. It is currently on display at the Khodynka Air Museum.

Rutskoi, however, was not so lucky a third time. During a subsequent sortie, his Frogfoot was hit head-on by a Blowpipe

BELOW: Operations in Afghanistan showed that the Su-25 'Frogfoot' could absorb tremendous punishment and carry on flying. Other air forces operating the type include Peru.

shoulder-launched missile which caused one engine to flame out. The aircraft was then hit by AAA and Rutskoi was forced to eject. He spent a short time as a prisoner in Pakistan before being exchanged.

Unable to stop after landing, the aircraft rolled off the runway and into a minefield...

Other instances that demonstrate the Su-25's ruggedness include one where an aircraft flown by Major Rubalov was hit in one engine, which surged and flooded an engine bay with fuel. The cockpit canopy was shattered, various instruments rendered inoperative and the major's face covered with blood. With his principal flight instruments out of action, Rubalov had to be guided in for a belly landing by his wingman.

Another Su-25 flown by Lieutenant Golubtsov lost half its rudder and its brakes were put out of action. Unable to stop after landing, the aircraft rolled off the runway and into a minefield, where the

ABOVE: *Fairchild A-10A Thunderbolt II of the 23rd Tactical Air Support Squadron, Niagara Falls. This unit took part in operations in Iraq in 1991.*

unfortunate pilot remained marooned for some time until a mine clearance squad arrived to extricate him.

Ground-Attack Specialist

The Frogfoot's American equivalent, the Fairchild A-10, was born out of the Vietnam war, which revealed a serious lack of an aircraft designed specifically for ground attack and close support. The A-10 was designed for a very high sortie rate, so servicing was made as simple as possible to cut down turnround time. Most of the aircraft's panels can be reached by a man standing on the ground, and an automatic system assures rapid reload of the GAU-8/A ammunition drum. The 81st Tactical Fighter Wing, which operated A-10s from Bentwaters and Woodbridge in Suffolk, UK, during the last decade of the Cold War, regularly flew over 80 sorties with eleven aircraft in a single day.

An A-10 pilot of that period described the operational procedure.

'The A-10s operate in two-ship flights and each pair can cover a swathe of ground up to six miles [10km] wide. In practice, however, the best swathe width has been found to be two or three miles, so that an attack can quickly be mounted by the second aircraft once the first pilot has made his firing pass on the target. The A-10 has a combat radius of 250nm [460km], enough to reach a target area on the East German border from a FOL (Forward Operating Location) in central Germany and then move on to another target area in northern Germany. The aircraft has a three-and-a-half hour loiter endurance, although wartime sorties in Europe would probably last from one to two hours. The 30mm [1.18in] ammunition drum carries enough rounds to permit ten to fifteen firing passes.'

1991 Gulf Action

The A-10 was destined never to fulfil its primary mission of engaging Soviet armour on the plains of Europe; instead, it found action in the 1991 Gulf War against Iraq. In that conflict, A-10s, with a mission capable rate of 95.7 percent, flew 8,100 sorties and launched 90 percent of the AGM-65 Maverick missiles – with tragic results on one occasion, when Mavericks launched by A-10s mistakenly engaged two British armoured personnel carriers, killing several soldiers. The A-10 was responsible for more than half of the Iraqi military inventory losses including tanks, Scud missiles and helicopters.

The principal enemy of the A-10 (and for that matter the Su-25) is anti-aircraft artillery, and to stand any chance of survival in a hostile environment dominated by this weapon the pilot must fly at 30m (100ft) or less and never remain straight and level for more than four seconds. Survivability also depends on close co-operation between the two A-10s; while one engages the target, the other stands off and attacks anti-aircraft installations with its Maverick TV-guided missiles, six of which are normally carried on triple launchers slung on pylons under its wings.

'The 30mm ammunition drum carries enough rounds to permit ten to fifteen firing passes.'

If an A-10 is attacked by a hostile fighter, the standard tactic is to turn head-on towards the threat and use 'coarse rudder' – yawing the aircraft from side to side – to spray the attacker with 30mm [1.18in] ammunition, a manoeuvre calculated to unnerve the enemy pilot.

In recent years, A-10s have operated with great success in support of NATO peacekeeping forces in trouble spots such as Kosovo, where – like the Su-25s in Afghanistan – they had to contend with shoulder-launched missiles.

Mil Mi-8 'Hip'

The Mil Mi-8, first seen in public in 1961, is a product of the brilliant Soviet helicopter pioneer Mikhail Leontyevich Mil, who died in 1970. During the early post-war years the Soviet Union lagged far behind the United States in helicopter development. In 1951, therefore, the Soviet Government issued a specification for a medium transport helicopter. Two projects were selected for development, one submitted by Mil and the other by Alexander S. Yakovlev. Mil's design was the Mi-4, which was given the NATO reporting name 'Hound'. It entered service with the Soviet Air Force in the summer of 1953 and production ran into thousands. The success of the Mi-4 persuaded Mil to initiate development of a turbine-powered version. The result was the Mi-8 (NATO reporting name 'Hip'). Although the Mi-8 is intended primarily as a transport helicopter (the Hip-C version), it can perform a wide variety of tasks. The Hip-D, for example, is a gunship, carrying rockets, bombs or anti-tank guided missiles. The Mi-14 is a variant optimized for anti-submarine warfare, while the Mi-17 is an uprated version used for support and attack.

MIL MI-8 'HIP'

Specification

Type: general purpose helicopter

Crew: 2/3

Powerplant: two Klimov (Isotov) TV2-117A turboshafts each rated at 1104kW (1481shp)

Performance: max speed 250km/h (155mph); service ceiling 4500m (14,760ft); range 930km (577 miles)

Dimensions: main rotor diameter 21.291m (69ft 10in); length 25.24m (82ft 9in); height 5.65m (18ft 6in)

Weight: 12,000kg (26,455lb) max take-off

Armament: outriggers carry four pylons each capable of carrying rocket pods or a bomb of up to 250kg (551lb)

FORÇA AÉREA POPULAR DE ANGOLA (ANGOLAN PEOPLE'S AIR FORCE) 1980s
The Mi-8 has been widely exported. The helicopter illustrated here is an Mi-8 'Hip-C' of the Angolan People's Air Force, which acquired abut 25 Mi-8s and Mi-17s. Some are believed to have been destroyed during the government's long struggle against the guerrilla forces of the National Union for Total Independence of Angola (UNITA). Angolan Hips were used mainly in the troop transport and supply roles, but some were fitted with UV-16-57 rocket pods and used in the light attack role against UNITA rebels.

Westland/Aérospatiale Puma

In 1967, Britain and France signed an agreement for the joint production of three helicopter types, the Westland Lynx, the Aérospatiale Gazelle and the Aérospatiale SA330 Puma, the latter being the largest of the three. Its development had begun in 1962, with a French requirement for a new utility transport helicopter capable of carrying up to 20 troops and fulfilling a range of other tasks. The prototype Puma flew on 14 April 1965, powered by two Turboméca Bastan VII turbines.

Sud-Aviation went on to build a series of eight prototypes and soon re-engined the Puma with the Turboméca Turmo IIIC.4 turboshaft, as used in the Super Frelon. As the development programme progressed, UK interest in the new helicopter grew and the last prototype was transferred to Britain for evaluation. It was this that ultimately led to the selection of the Puma by the Royal Air Force as a Whirlwind and

Belvedere replacement, and to the Anglo-French helicopter agreement. French Army Aviation adopted the SA330B Puma as its basic aircraft, and a similar version, designated Puma HC.Mk 1, was acquired by the RAF, being built under licence by Westland.

Aérospatiale went on to build 686 SA330s in successively improved versions for numerous export customers. These included civil operators, notably those in the oilfield support industry, for whom the company produced the all-weather Puma SA330J and L. Between 1970 and 1984 Aerospatiale produced 126 civil Pumas. Further production was undertaken by the Romanian company IAR, which built over 200 Pumas under license between 1977 and 1994. In the late 1970s production switched to the AS332 Super Puma, which has increased power and a larger fuselage.

WESTLAND/AÉROSPATIALE PUMA

Specification

Type: general purpose helicopter

Crew: 3/4

Powerplant: two Turbomeca Turmo IVC turboshafts, each rated at 1175kW (1575 shp)

Performance: maximum speed 293km/h (182mph); service ceiling 6000m (19,685ft); range 572km (355 miles)

Dimensions: main rotor diameter 15m (49ft 2.5in); length 18.15m (59ft 6.5in); height 5.14m (16ft 10.5in)

Weight: maximum take-off 7500kg (16,534lb)

NO.33 SQUADRON, RAF ODIHAM, HAMPSHIRE, 1980s

Mil Mi-8 vs Westland/Aérospatiale Puma

VERY SIMILAR IN SIZE and configuration, the Mil Mi-8 and the Puma were developed to meet the need for a tactical assault helicopter. Both have seen substantial development during their operational careers, and have proved adaptable to roles other than those for which they were intended.

Over 1,600 Mi-8s served with the USSR's Frontal Aviation, 900 with Transport Aviation and a further 100 with Naval Aviation. Many still remain in service with the Russian Federation and former Soviet Bloc states. Mi-8s were also exported to 39 other countries and have seen combat in various parts of the world. During the Yom Kippur War in 1973 a force of about 100 Hips, carrying crack 18-man Egyptian commando teams, crossed the Suez Canal to attack Israeli oilfields and to hinder the movement of reinforcements. The commandos were supported by Mi-8s carrying rockets and bombs, while others were modified to carry two fixed heavy machine guns and up to six light machine guns to provide suppressive fire around the landing zones. Napalm bombs were also

reported to have been rolled out through the clamshell doors onto Israeli positions along the Canal. Egyptian Mi-8s were additionally used for resupply and medevac duties. The Syrians employed about a dozen Hips to deliver commandos 2440m (8,000ft) up Mount Hermon to capture an Israeli observation post.

Multi-role Hip

In the bitter Ogaden war, the Soviet commander of the Ethiopian forces used Mi-8s to airlift troops and light armoured vehicles over a mountain and place them behind forward Somali positions. Earlier, in 1974, two Soviet Hips operated from the deck of the Soviet ASW cruiser *Leningrad* as part of a mission to sweep mines from the southern end of the Suez Canal. The Soviet Union also widely operated the Mi-8 both as a troop transport and gunship in the protracted Afghanistan conflict. More recently, Russia has

BELOW: This dramatic photograph shows Mil Mi-8 helicopters engaged in an amphibious assault exercise with Russian naval forces.

used the Hip in two hard-fought campaigns in the breakaway region of Chechnya.

During the Yom Kippur War in 1973 a force of about 100 Hips, carrying crack 18-man Egyptian commando teams, crossed the Suez Canal to attack Israeli oilfields and to hinder the movement of reinforcements.

Mi-8s have also been used in many humanitarian operations. During 1985, for example, Soviet and Polish Hips took part in famine relief operations in drought-stricken Ethiopia; the Polish Relief Helicopter Squadron arrived at Assab aboard the MV *Wislica* with 100 tons of food and equipment. Within three days, the Mi-9Ts were assembled and able to begin airlifting supplies for distribution to the starving people in the desert.

Puma Development
Just as the Mil Mi-8 was developed into the more powerful Mi-17, in 1974 Aérospatiale drew up proposals for a Super Puma in response to customer demands for more power and lifting capacity.

The Super Puma was completely re-engined with a pair of more powerful Turbomeca Makila 1A turboshafts.

The design that emerged was the SA.332, which shared the uncluttered lines of its predecessor but which incorporated subtle

ABOVE: In the RAF, the Puma is operated by Nos 33 and 230 Squadrons in the tactical support role. This example is carrying out a search and rescue exercise.

differences. From the beginning the Super Puma used the glass-fibre composite rotor blade technology that had been introduced in the late-model SA.330s. The most obvious change was the addition of a nose radome to house a weather radar. The Super Puma was completely re-engined with a pair of more powerful Turbomeca Makila 1A turboshafts. Unlike the Puma, the Super Puma was aimed primarily at the civil market, although it also had considerable military potential.

The first Super Puma took to the air on 13 September 1978, and deliveries began in 1981. The initial production aircraft, the military AS.332B and the civil AS.332C, were no larger than the original Puma and could carry up to 21 passengers or 18 troops. A stretched version appeared in 1979; this was the AS.332M (military) and AS.332L (civil), both of which had an increase in length of 76cm (30in) and could carry four extra passengers. The stretched Super Puma was certified in 1983, and cleared for operations in known icing conditions – a vital capability for offshore work and air-sea rescue operations.

The Puma line underwent further changes in 1990 with the appearance of the AS.532 Cougar. A range of versions appeared, to which Aérospatiale (soon to become Eurocopter France) assigned designation suffixes as follows: U (unarmed military utility); A (armed); S (anti-ship/anti-submarine); C (short fuselage, military transport); and L (long fuselage, military and civil).

COMBAT TYPES FROM 1975 TO THE PRESENT DAY

During the years of the Cold War, prophets of doom were quick to propagate an image of the Warsaw Pact as an inexorable war machine against whose might the North Atlantic Treaty Organization (NATO) countries could put up only a token resistance in a conventional war, leaving NATO with no choice but to resort to nuclear weapons. It was never the case. Not only did the NATO countries spend more on defence than those of the Warsaw Pact, but their combined populations and overall wealth were also greater. The really worrying factor, for the NATO planners, was that the quality of Soviet equipment was beginning to match, and perhaps in some cases outstrip, that of the NATO powers.

Then came the abrupt collapse of the Soviet Union, the end of the Cold War, and a series of limited conflicts, the biggest of which was the 1991 war with Iraq. These conflicts proved conclusively that the latest Russian equipment, both in the air and on the ground, was no match for the devastating firepower that could be brought into action by NATO.

This chapter looks at the relative merits of aircraft that might have come into conflict during the later years of the Cold War, and in some cases did in fact see action in conflicts far removed from the European theatre. The types range from attack helicopters through trainers with a secondary strike role, to front-line air superiority and strike fighters, long-range interdictors and supersonic bombers.

Some of these aircraft saw combat in unlikely places – none more unlikely than the Falklands in 1982, when Royal Navy Sea Harriers fought with Argentine A-4 Skyhawks in a conflict no one had anticipated. A little earlier, another naval fighter, the US Navy's F-14 Tomcat, had showed its awesome capability in action against Libyan Air Force Sukhoi Su-22s over the Gulf of Sirte in a clear demonstration of American superiority in both weapons and tactics.

In other, later conflicts, the bomber that had been designed to replace the B-52 as the main sword of Strategic Air Command (SAC), the supersonic Rockwell B-1B, now found itself operating side by side with the veteran Boeing bomber in punitive combat operations over Afghanistan, assuming what amounted to an anti-terrorist role against forces seeking to destroy the fabric of Western society.

In this chapter we see the last of what may be described as the 'traditional' combat aircraft, machines where the pilot is ultimately responsible for the direction and outcome of air combat. Many of these aircraft, such as the MiG-29, once served a particular and clearly defined master; now they serve alongside former enemies. The combat aircraft of former adversaries may today be called upon to operate in any part of the world, sometimes in concert with one another, sometimes not, in support of a United Nations resolution; and pilots may find themselves locked in combat with aircraft and weapon systems built in their own countries and sold to Third World powers, flown by opposing pilots trained by the same system as themselves.

LEFT: *The General Dynamics F-16 Fighting Falcon can carry up to 9276kg (20,450lb) of ordnance on seven external handpoints. For dogfighting its cannon has a lead-computing sight and snapshot modes.*

ABOVE: *The MiG-29 Fulcrum was designed to counter the US F-15 Eagle and F-14 Tomcat fighters. Its weapon systems have the capability to destroy targets out to 60km (37 miles).*

SAAB Viggen

SAAB's Viggen (named for the Norse god Thor's thunderbolt) was developed as a relatively low-cost Mach 2 fighter for the *Svenska Flygvapnet* (Royal Swedish Air Force), capable of operating from dispersed airfields and even sections of highway. The design pioneered the use of flap-equipped canards with a stable delta-wing configuration. The engine was based on the commercial Pratt & Whitney JT8D-22 turbofan, but equipped with a thrust reverser and Swedish-designed afterburner.

The initial AJ 37 Viggen all-weather attack variant featured sophisticated navigation/attack multi-role radar. The first of seven Viggen prototypes initially flew in February 1967, and deliveries began in 1971. The primary armament comprised SAAB Rb 04E anti-ship missiles (replaced by the far more capable long-range Rbs 15) and

licence-built AGM-65 Maverick air-to-surface missiles. A total of 108 attack Viggens was built, out of 319 of all variants. For most of their careers, the AJ 37s wore the spectacular 'fields and meadows' splinter camouflage pattern seen here.

Flygflottilj (Wing) 6 was based at Karlsborg and consisted of two squadrons, numbered 1 and 2 *Attackflygdivisionen*. Only comparatively recently have squadron badges appeared on Viggens; otherwise the only unit identifier was usually the wing number on the nose. *Flygflottilj* 6 (F6) disbanded at the end of 1993, the first *Flygvapnet* wing to go in a wave of post–Cold War cuts. The unit's Viggens, which were the oldest in service by that time, were either transferred to F10 or F15, or relegated to instruction duties, scrapped or preserved.

SAAB AJ 37 VIGGEN

Specification

Type: ground-attack fighter

Crew: 1

Powerplant: one 125.04kN (28,110lb thrust) Volvo Flygmotor RM8B afterburning turbofan engine

Performance: max speed 2126km/h (1321mph); service ceiling 18,000m (59,055ft); range 2000km (1243 miles)

Dimensions: wing span 10.60m (34ft 9.25in); length 16.40m (53ft 9.75in); height 5.6m (18ft 3in)

Weight: 17,000kg (37,478lb) loaded

Armament: up to 5897kg (13,000lb) of bombs, rockets or air-to-surface missiles

FLYGFLOTTILJ 6, VÄSTGÖTA FLYGFLOTTILJ, SVENSKA FLYGVAPNET, KARLSBORG, SWEDEN, 1992
AJ 37 37034 is on display at Uppsala in northern Sweden, home of the last Viggen unit not disbanded or re-equipped with the JAS 39 Gripen.

SEPECAT Jaguar

Developed jointly by the British Aircraft Corporation and Breguet (later Dassault-Breguet) under the banner of SEPECAT (*Société Europeanne de Production de l'Avion Ecole de Combat et Appui Tactique*), the Jaguar emerged from protracted development as a much more powerful and effective aircraft than originally envisaged.

Service deliveries of the Jaguar E began in May 1972, the first of 160 Jaguar As following in 1973. The British versions, known as the Jaguar S (strike) and Jaguar B (trainer), flew on October 12 1969 and 30 August 1971, respectively, being delivered to the Royal Air Force (RAF) as the Jaguar GR.Mk 1(165 examples) and T.Mk 2 (38 examples). Armée de l'Air Jaguars were fitted with a stand-off bomb release system, while British Jaguars were fitted with two weapon guidance systems: a Laser Ranging and Marked Target Seeker (LRMTS) and a Navigation and Weapon Aiming Subsystem (NAVWASS).

The Jaguar International, first flown in August 1976, was a version developed for the export market. It was purchased by Ecuador (12), Nigeria (18) and Oman (24), and was licence-built in India by HAL (98, including 40 delivered by BAe).

When Britain and France decided to contribute personnel and material to Operation Desert Storm in 1991, it was inevitable that the Jaguar, which was capable of rapid deployment with minimal support and which could function in relatively primitive conditions, should be included in the Coalition Forces' Order of Battle. In the event, the aircraft performed extremely well.

SEPECAT JAGUAR GR.MK IA

Specification
Type: tactical strike aircraft
Crew: I
Powerplant: two 3313kg (7305lb) thrust Rolls-Royce/Turbomeca Adour Mk 102 turbofans
Performance: max speed 1593km/h (990mph); service ceiling 14,000m (50,000ft); combat radius 557km (357 miles)
Dimensions: wing span 8.69m (28ft 6in); length 16.83m (55ft 2in); height 4.89m (16ft)
Weight: 15,500kg (34,172lb) loaded
Armament: two 30mm (1.18in) DEFA cannon five external hardpoints with provision for 4536kg (10,000lb) of underwing stores; two overwing-mounted AIM-9L Sidewinders for self-defence

RAF JAGUAR DETACHMENT, ROYAL AIR FORCE MUHARRAQ, BAHRAIN, 1991

SAAB VIGGEN VS SEPECAT JAGUAR

ALTHOUGH AT FIRST GLANCE they might appear to be completely different in concept, Sweden's SAAB Viggen and the Anglo-French SEPECAT Jaguar actually have a great deal in common, particularly from the operational point of view.

In the event of an east–west confrontation, RAF Jaguars would have found themselves operating under much the same conditions as the Royal Swedish Air Force's Viggens, even though the latter would only have been fighting to guard Sweden's neutrality. The Jaguars, as part of the RAF's Tactical Support Force, would have been rapidly deployed to the Royal Norwegian Air Force base at Andoya, from where they would have flown strike and reconnaissance sorties against enemy invasion forces.

In carrying out its low-level task, the Jaguar would have had one major advantage over the Viggen in that its smaller size would have made it very hard to detect, both visually and on radar. On the other hand, as one Jaguar pilot explains, an adversary at higher level can be readily spotted.

'Operating at low level makes it easier to spot a bogey (unidentified aircraft), especially when he is close to the horizon. Sometimes, the bogey will be leaving a distinctive smoke trail; the trail from a Phantom, for example, can be seen up to thirty miles away under certain lighting conditions, such as the afterglow of the sunset. If the smoke trail is suddenly cut off it means that the aircraft producing it has suddenly gone into reheat, which might mean that he has sighted you and is racing in to the attack.'

AAA Threat

One disadvantage shared by both the Viggen and the Jaguar was that both aircraft originally belonged to an era where ground attack meant releasing the weapons load as the aircraft flew directly over its target; the days of smart weapons that could obliterate an objective after being released from several miles away were still in the future.

> **One disadvantage shared by both the Viggen and the Jaguar was that both aircraft originally belonged to an era where ground attack meant releasing the weapons load as the aircraft flew directly over its target**

BELOW: A unique shape in European skies, Sweden's SAAB Viggen was the result of its country's desire to remain neutral in a world dominated by the East–West conflicts of the Cold War.

ABOVE: *Jaguar GR.1 of No 41 Squadron, RAF Coltishall, camouflaged for Arctic operations in support of a Royal Marines task force on exercise in Norway.*

For tactical pilots, whether they belonged to the air forces of NATO or the Warsaw Pact, the biggest threat when attacking enemy concentrations at low level in the 1970s came from anti-aircraft artillery (AAA), of which there was a formidable variety. As most AAA sites were heavily camouflaged, the first indication a pilot usually had of their presence is when he saw the muzzle flashes; large guns make big, slow-rate flashes, while small-bore rapid fire flashes produce a sparkling effect. Radar-directed guns do not generally use tracer ammunition, but small- and medium-calibre weapons that are visually laid use up to 25 per cent tracer rounds.

'In the heat of the action,' a Jaguar pilot explained during the Cold War era, 'a pilot may tend to forget, to his cost, that the tracer he sees represents only a fraction of the total ammunition that is being thrown in his direction. At dawn, dusk or night, if he is flying directly towards the gun, he may get the visual sensation that he is flying down a tunnel whose walls are made up of tracers; this can produce a mesmerising effect that makes the pilot reluctant to break off for fear of hitting the "wall" and consequently presents the gunners with some excellent no-deflection shooting.

'There have been occasions when pilots, apparently hypnotized, have flown down the tracer stream and into the ground.'

'If a pilot finds himself on the receiving end of airbursts, then he is the target of medium or heavy calibre AAA; small automatic weapons do not produce airbursts. If medium-calibre bursts occur between the aircraft and the gun, then the pilot has little to fear from that particular weapon; the bursts mark the limit of the gun's range. Heavy-calibre shells, on the other hand, generally employ proximity or radar fuses; the latter are probably in use if the altitude of the bursts changes as the target aircraft changes height during evasive manoeuvring.'

SAM Avoidance

The Viggen and the Jaguar both entered service with their respective air forces at a time when the short- and medium-range surface-to-air missile was coming into its own, but even this new threat could be dealt with if a pilot acted in time. In the first few seconds after launch, a SAM's booster rocket leaves a thick grey or white smoke trail which can be easy to see even though the missile itself may be invisible; the smoke is usually accompanied by flame.

'When the smoke trail takes on a wiggly appearance, it means the missile has entered its guidance phase. If the smoke and the bright light of the rocket exhaust remain at about the same spot on your canopy, the odds are that you are the target. This is because a guided SAM attempts to fly a lead pursuit course, holding its target at a constant angle. As SAMs are generally small, it is often difficult to estimate their range, so the sooner you take hard evasive action the better your chances of survival will be.'

Both the Viggen and the Jaguar are now at the end of their operational careers. Of the two, only the Jaguar saw combat; Sweden, thankfully, was never required to defend her neutrality.

Dassault/Dornier Alpha Jet

The Alpha Jet was a collaborative project between Dassault of France and Dornier of Germany to produce a new advanced trainer. During development, which began in 1969, the German requirement diverged so that its aircraft were specified as light attack aircraft to replace the Fiat G-91. The French prototype of the Alpha Jet flew in 1973, with another flying in Germany a year later.

France ordered 175 of the Alpha Jet E (Ecole), while West Germany took the same number of the Alpha Jet A (Appui Tactique). Both aircraft were weapons capable, but the German aircraft had a head up display (HUD) and a navigation/ attack system. The French aircraft had a more rounded nose, which gave better spinning characteristics, and Martin-Baker Mk 4 ejection seats rather than the American Stencel S-111 model.

The Alpha Jet has been nearly as successful as the BAe Hawk in the export market, new examples being sold to Qatar, Ivory Coast, Belgium, Morocco, Togo, Cameroon, Nigeria and Egypt. German service began in 1979, and the last aircraft was delivered in 1985. They were used as light attackers, forward air control trainers, conversion trainers and to give fast jet experience to prospective Tornado navigators. Some crews were trained to destroy enemy helicopters. During the 1991 Gulf War, some Luftwaffe Alpha Jets were despatched to Erhac, Turkey, to maintain Nato's commitment to defend that country. Alpha Jet A 40+15 was assigned to *Jagdbombergeschwader* (JBG) 41, one of three fighter-bomber wings to operate the type. The Luftwaffe withdrew the Alpha Jet from the combat role in 1993 and 50 were given to Portugal, including 40+15, which was issued to one of two squadrons of *Grupo Operativo* 111 at Beja.

DASSAULT/DORNIER ALPHA JET A

Specification

Type: two-seat jet trainer/light attack aircraft

Crew: 2

Powerplant: two 13.24kN (2976lb thrust) SNECMA/Turboméca Larzac 04-C6 turbofan engines

Performance: max speed 1000km/h (621mph); service ceiling 14630m (48,000ft); range 2460km (1780 miles)

Dimensions: wing span 9.11m (29ft 10.75in); length 11.75m (38ft 6.5in); height 4.19m (31ft 9in)

Weight: 8000kg (17,637lb) loaded

Armament: one 27mm (1.06in) IWKA-Mauser cannon in removable pod; up to 2500kg (5511lb) of bombs and rockets

JAGDBOMBERGESCHWADER 41, TAKTISCHE DIVISION LUFTFLOTTEN KOMMANDO, LUFTWAFFE HUSUM, FEDERAL REPUBLIC OF GERMANY, LATE 1980S

British Aerospace Hawk

The first British Aerospace (originally Hawker Siddeley) Hawk flew in August 1974, the culmination of a lengthy process to create a subsonic aircraft to replace the Gnat, Hunter T.7 and some two-seat Jaguars for advanced and weapons training. In various versions, the Hawk has been a great export success, selling to Abu Dhabi, Australia, Canada, Dubai, Finland, Indonesia, Kenya, Kuwait, Saudi Arabia, South Africa, South Korea, Switzerland and Zimbabwe.

BRITISH AEROSPACE HAWK T.1A

Specification

Type: advanced jet trainer

Crew: 2

Powerplant: one 23.13kN (5200lb thrust) Rolls-Royce/Turboméca Adour Mk 1151-01turbofan engine

Performance: max speed 1040km/h (646mph); service ceiling 15,240m (50,000ft); range 2400km (1491 miles)

Dimensions: wing span 9.39m (30ft 10in); length 11.85m (38ft 11in); height 4.00m (13ft 1in)

Weight: 8340kg (18,390lb) loaded

Armament: one 30mm (1.18in) ADEN Mk 4 cannon with 120 rounds in underfuselage pod; two AIM-9 Sidewinders or bombs or rockets up to 680kg (1580lb)

NO. 92 (RESERVE) SQUADRON, NO. 7 FLYING TRAINING SCHOOL, ROYAL AIR FORCE RAF CHIVENOR, DEVON, 1994

XX157 was the third Hawk built and, after evaluation, was delivered to the Royal Air Force (RAF) in December 1979. It was one of 88 updated to T.1A standard between 1983 and 1986. The modifications saw the wing pylons wired for Sidewinder air-to-air missiles, allowing the Hawk to undertake an emergency point defence role to supplement the Phantom and Tornado F.3.

In 1994, No. 7FTS was disbanded, Chivenor was closed and No. 92 Squadron once again went into limbo. With its distinguished history, it is a strong candidate for re-forming as a Eurofighter Typhoon unit in the next few years.

ALPHA JET VS HAWK

DURING THE LATER years of the Cold War, the Luftwaffe's Alpha Jets would have found themselves at the very forefront of ground-attack operations, alongside the RAF's Harrier force.

The two Luftwaffe Alpha Jet attack wings in the north were JaboG (*Jagdbombergeschwader*) 41 at Husum, south-east of Flensburg on the 'neck' of Schleswig-Holstein close to the Danish border, and JaboG 43 at Oldenburg, west of Bremen. The Alpha Jet bases were more or less aligned with Gutersloh, the home of the Harriers, and the three were spaced to give maximum air support to the Allied forces facing the three possible Warsaw Pact thrust lines in the area of 2nd Allied Tactical Air Force.

Each of the two Alpha Jet JaboGs in 2 ATAF had 51 aircraft, so their combined force represented a formidable contribution to NATO close support power. One of their principal roles in wartime was to destroy Warsaw Pact battlefield support helicopters.

In time of war, JaboG 49 would have had the responsibility of confronting any Warsaw Pact thrust from Czechoslovakia towards Munich along the southern flank of the Central Front.

BELOW: *The prototype Alpha Jet trainer for the French Air Force pictured on an early test flight. The type also served as an extremely viable ground attack aircraft with the Luftwaffe.*

Alpha Jet Capabilities

The Alpha Jet had a maximum level speed at sea level, but it manoeuvred well at low speed. Its combat radius on a hi-lo-hi mission, including combat at maximum continuous thrust and a high-speed dash of 100km (62 miles) with belly gun pod and underwing weapons, was 582km (362 miles), increasing to 1073km (667 miles) with underwing tanks as well as weapons. A lo-lo-lo mission with the same configuration produces combat radii of 389 and 629km (242 and 391 miles) respectively.

In the south, the 4th Allied Tactical Air Force was supported by 50 Alpha Jets of JaboG 49, based at Fürstenfeldbruck near Munich. In time of war, JaboG 49 would have had the responsibility of confronting any Warsaw Pact thrust from Czechoslovakia towards Munich along the southern flank of the Central Front, and had the task of destroying key bridges on the river Danube as well as attacking enemy columns at various bottlenecks along the road that ran into German territory from the Bohemian Forest, parallel to the River Iser.

Trainer and Combat Aircraft

As for the BAe Hawk, nothing was more indicative of this excellent aircraft's versatility than an announcement in the British parliament,

ABOVE: *A dramatic picture of a BAe Hawk T.Mk.1 over the Eddystone Lighthouse, off the Cornish coast, southwest England. The Hawk replaced the Hawker Hunter as the RAF's tactical weapons trainer.*

If the incoming hostiles consisted of bombers with a fighter escort, the Hawks were to take on the fighters while the more heavily-armed aircraft went for the bombers.

in 1979, that it was to be armed with AIM-9L Sidewinder AAMs and used to plug a gap in the United Kingdom's air defences. The Hawk War Role Programme, as it was known, went ahead under the joint auspices of the Ministry of Defence Procurement Executive, the RAF and British Aerospace. The aim was to give 89 Hawks, whose sole armament then was a 30mm (1.18in) Aden gun, an air defence capability by fitting two Sidewinder stations to each aircraft. Development was started early in 1980, and as work progressed two important modifications were added to the air defence installation programme: the fitting of strobe lights and a twin gyro platform to provide a high accuracy attitude reference system.

The first test firing of a Sidewinder from a modified Hawk was made in 1980 and, after some problems caused by the effect of the missile smoke trail had been satisfactorily resolved, a useful AIM-9L Sidewinder firing envelope was released for use by the Service in May 1983. By this time British Aerospace had been awarded a contract for the modification of 89 Hawks to War Role standard for the second-line defence of UK installations. Aircraft so modified – those in service with Nos 1 and 2 Tactical Weapons Units at AF Brawdy and RAF Chivenor, together with those of the Central Flying School at RAF Scampton (including the aircraft used by the Red Arrows aerobatic team) – were allocated the designation Hawk T.Mk 1A.

The modification programme was completed in August 1986, by which time the original concept of using the missile-armed Hawks for point defence had undergone changes as a result of lessons learned during air defence exercises. The original idea had been to deploy the first line of defence – the F.3 Tornado and the F.4 Phantom – as far forward as possible, using flight refuelling tankers as necessary.

The second line would be provided by Bloodhound surface-to-air missiles (SAMs), with short-range Rapier SAMs and the Hawks forming the last line. This plan assumed, of course, that the RAF's air defence and strike airfields were the enemy's principal targets; as the Hawk was not equipped with radar, it would fly combat air patrol (CAP) on the threat axis, as far as possible for the airfield it was defending but remaining within the airfield's radar coverage. Alternatively, the Hawk could operate at the limit of its combat radius, two Hawks accompanying a Phantom or a Tornado, which would use their radar to set up an engagement. If the incoming hostiles consisted of bombers with a fighter escort, the Hawks were to take on the fighters while the more heavily-armed aircraft went for the bombers. Once this happened the Hawks would be on their own; after the fight, assuming that they had weapons and fuel remaining, they would return to the CAP.

Aero L-39 Albatros

The Aero L-39 Albatros was developed in Czechoslovakia to meet the needs of the Soviet Union and Warsaw Pact to replace the L-29 Delphin as the main jet training aircraft. The Soviet Union had considerable input into the design and took the great bulk of production. More than 2800 examples were built, making it the most numerous jet trainer ever produced.

The prototype flew in November 1968 and was followed by the L-39C unarmed trainer, the L-39ZO weapons trainer and the L-39ZA ground-attack and reconnaissance aircraft. Czechoslovakia itself introduced the Albatros to service in 1974, but was only one of more than 20 nations around the world to fly the type. The L-39 is simple to maintain and can carry a wide range of weapons for training and light attack missions.

The Czechoslovakian Air Force (*Ceskoslovenske Letectvo*) became the Air Force of the Army of the Czech Republic (Vzdusné Síly ACR) after the dissolution of the union of the Czech Republic and Slovakia in 1993. Many bases were closed and aircraft types retired, and the Czech Republic chose to concentrate in the future on two combat aircraft types. These will be the SAAB Gripen and the L-159 ALCA (Advanced Light Combat Aircraft), a much more capable derivative of the L-39.

AERO L-39ZA ALBATROS

Specification

Type: advanced trainer and light attack/reconnaissance aircraft

Crew: 2

Powerplant: one 16.87kN (3792lb thrust) Ivchencko AI-25TL turbofan engine

Performance: max speed 755km/h (486mph); service ceiling 11,000m (36,090ft); range 1100km (683 miles)

Dimensions: wing span 9.46m (31ft 0.5in); length 12.13m (39ft 9.5in); height 4.77m (15ft 8in)

Weight: 4700kg (10,362lb) loaded

Armament: one GSh-23 twin-barrel 23mm (0.91in) cannon; weapons load of up to 907lb (2000kg) of bombs or rockets

VZDUSNÉ SÍLY ACR, KOSICE, CZECHOSLOVAKIA, 1990S

Depicted in service in the mid-1990s, L-39ZA 2418 was still active in 2003 with 322 *Taktika Letka* (tactical squadron) at Namest nad Oslavou in the southeast of the country. This unit keeps some aircraft on quick-reaction alert to protect the local nuclear power plant. Around 30 L-39s remain in Czech service.

CASA C.101 Aviojet

To replace the elderly Hispano Saeta trainer, Spanish aircraft maker CASA (Construcciones Aeronauticas SA) began work on the C.101 Aviojet in 1975. Germany's MBB and Northrop in the United States helped with the development, and the first of four prototypes flew in June 1977. The design followed that of other jet trainers such as the Hawk and Alpha Jet, but was less aerodynamically sophisticated, with an unswept wing, and it had limited weapons capability. The Ejército del Aire (Spanish Air Force) designated the C.101 as the E-25 Mirlo (Blackbird) and

purchased 88 in two batches. In 1990–92, all had their navigation/attack capability modernized.

Export sales have been limited. Four Aviojets were sold to Honduras, and Jordan bought 16 C.101CC-04 dedicated attack versions. Chile bought four similar aircraft and built a further 19 as the ENAER A-36CC Halcón. A more sophisticated C.101DD variant was developed which had provision for Maverick missiles, a new HUD, a radar warning system and chaff/flare dispensers. It has so far failed to receive any orders.

CASA C.101EB AVIOJET

Specification
Type: advanced jet trainer
Crew: 2
Powerplant: one 20.91kN (4700lb thrust) Garrett TFE-731-5-1J turbofan engine
Performance: max speed 769km/h (478mph); service ceiling 12,800m (42,000ft); range over 1038km (644 miles)
Dimensions: wing span 10.60m (34ft 9.5in); length 12.50m (41ft 5in); height 4.25m (13ft 11.25in)
Weight: 6300kg (13,889lb) loaded
Armament: one 30mm (1.18in) DEFA cannon pod or two 12.7mm (0.50in) machine guns; up to 1840kg (4056lb) of bombs or rockets

ESCUADRÓN 793, ESCUELO DE VUELO BÁSICO ACADEMIA GENERAL DEL AIRE EJÉRCITO DEL AIRE, SAN JAVIER, SPAIN, 1980s
This E-25 is depicted when in service with the Escuelo de Vuelo Básico (Basic Flying School) of the Academia General del Aire (General Air Academy) at San Javier in southeast Spain. The Patrulla Aguila aerobatic team is also based here, and its C.101s are flown by the academy's instructors. This Aviojet was last noted in service with the team.

AERO L-39 ALBATROS VS CASA C.101 AVIOJET

THE LATEST MEMBERS of the Albatros family are the Aero L-59 Super Albatros and the L-159 Albatros II. Developed directly from the L-39, the L-59 features a strengthened fuselage, longer nose, a vastly updated cockpit and a more powerful engine.

In 1992, a dedicated single-seat attack variant of the Albatros was proposed under the project name ALCA (Advanced Light Combat Aircraft), and was successfully marketed to the Czech Air Force. The first flight of this variant (designated L-159A) took place on 2 August, 1997.

The aircraft features mostly Western avionics, with systems integration undertaken by Boeing. The Czech Republic is currently the only operator of the type.

It has been qualified with a variety of weapons, including Sidewinder, Maverick and Brimstone missiles, as well as unguided rockets, bombs and electronic countermeasures or reconnaissance pods.

BELOW: *Although Spain's CASA Aviojet was a very viable combat trainer design, it never achieved the export potential for which its designers had hoped.*

Since then a new two-seat trainer has been flown as the L-159B Albatros II. This aircraft is based on a refinement of the L-59 Super Albatros design, the L-139. This never reached production status. The TFE731 engine installed in the L-139 was in some ways a retrograde step from the Progress DV-2 of the Super Albatros. Although the Western turbofan was more fuel-economical, lighter and in principle more reliable, it also produced significantly less thrust, making the L-139 relatively underpowered.

The ALCA

Although the L-139 did not go into production, it provided the basis for an improved derivative, the ALCA, which is primarily a light attack aircraft that can also be used as a lead-in trainer. It is substantially more optimized for combat than other members of the Albatros family, with cockpit armour protection, plus a centreline stores pylon and three stores pylons under each wing, for a total of seven pylons. It has been qualified with a variety of weapons, including Sidewinder, Maverick and Brimstone missiles, as well as

ABOVE: The L-39 Albatros was yet another successful design to emerge from the Czech aviation industry. It was adopted as the standard jet trainer by many air forces.

unguided rockets, bombs and electronic countermeasures or reconnaissance pods. The standard cannon pod is the ZPL-20 Plamen 20mm (0.79in) gun pod, but others are also compatible. Other stores, such as beyond-visual-range AIM-120 AMRAAM missiles, have been considered.

The L-159 is powered by an Allied Signal / ITEC F124-GA-100 turbofan engine with dual redundant full-authority digital controls (FADEC) and 2860kg (6300lb) thrust. Larger intakes were designed to accommodate the new engine, which is about twice as powerful as the L-39's original AI-25TL engine. The aircraft is fitted with modernized cockpit instrumentation and controls conforming to Western standards, making a suitable combat aircraft for Eastern European nations trying to integrate with NATO.

Spanish Service

The CASA C.101 has enjoyed far less of a success story than the Czech Albatros series; nevertheless, it has served the Spanish Air Force well and has enjoyed some export success. The two Spanish contracts for the C.101EB-01 (the aircraft is designated E.25 Mirlo by the Spanish Air Force) comprised 60 and 28 aircraft. The first four were delivered to the General Air Academy at San Javier on 17 March 1980 and the last in 1984. In the early 1990s the aircraft were assigned to four units: Escuadron 411 and 412 at Matacan for refresher training, Escuadron 793 at San Javier for advanced

training, along with the co-located Patrulla Aguila aerobatic team, and the trials unit Grupo 54 at Torrejon. By mid-2000, the training units had been realigned and the operators consisted of Escuadron 744 at Matacan, the test unit Grupo 44 at Torrejon, and the Escuela de Vuelo Basico (Basic Training Squadron) and the Patrulla Aguila, which became part of the Academia General del Aire at San Javier.

...all versions have a large fuselage bay beneath the rear cockpit in which can be housed armament or a reconnaissance camera, ECM jammer, laser designator and other devices.

The C.101 is of modular construction to reduce cost and complexity, and ample space was deliberately left for avionics and equipment to meet any conceivable requirement. Features include a single turbofan of high bypass ratio for good fuel economy, stepped tandem Martin-Baker Mki 10L zero/zero ejection seats, a pressurized cockpit with separate canopies that hinge to the right, levered-suspension landing gear with a non-steerable nosewheel, fuel contained in integral tanks in the wings and a flexible cell in the fuselage with pressure fuelling, fixed wing leading edge, slotted flaps, powered ailerons but manual elevators and rudder, and a tailplane with electric variable incidence for trimming.

The most unusual feature is that not only is there provision for underwing stores, but all versions have a large fuselage bay beneath the rear cockpit in which can be housed armament or a reconnaissance camera, ECM jammer, laser designator and other devices.

British Aerospace Sea Harrier

Developed from the RAF's Harrier GR.Mk 3, the Sea Harrier FRS.Mk 1 introduced a redesigned forward fuselage and nose fitted with a Ferranti Blue Fox radar, a new canopy and raised cockpit for improved view, and a more powerful Pegasus Mk 104 engine.

An initial order was placed in 1975 for 24 FRS.Mk 1s. Later orders brought the total to 57 for the Royal Navy, and another 24 for India. A two-seat trainer without radar was developed as the Sea Harrier T.4. The first operational squadron (No. 899 Squadron) was commissioned in April 1980 and two units (Nos 800 and 801 Squadrons) were subsequently deployed during the Falklands War aboard HMS *Hermes* and *Invincible* where they served with great distinction, scoring twenty-three confirmed victories against Argentine Air Force and Navy aircraft.

BRITISH AEROSPACE SEA HARRIER FRS.MK I

Specification

Type: carrierborne fighter, reconnaissance and strike aircraft

Crew: 1

Powerplant: one 95.64kN (21,500-lb thrust) Rolls-Royce Pegasus 2 MK 104 non-afterburning turbofan

Performance: Max speed 1183km/h (735mph); service ceiling over 15240m (50,000ft); range 1480km (980 miles)

Dimensions: Wing span 7.7m (25ft 3in); length 14.5m (47ft 7in); height 3.17m (12ft 2in)

Weight: 11,880kg (26,190lb) loaded

Armament: two 30-mm ADEN cannon and up to 3628kg (8,000lb) of ordnance including bombs, rockets, Sea Eagle ASMs or AIM-9 Sidewinder AAMs

NO. 801 SQUADRON, FLEET AIR ARM HMS INVINCIBLE, 1983

Sea Harrier XZ451 was embarked aboard HMS *Invincible* as part of the British Task Force in April 1982. On two missions on 1 May it damaged a T-34 with cannon fire and shot down a Canberra with AIM-9s. On 21 May, Nigel 'Sharkey' Ward destroyed a Pucara attack aircraft with cannon and on 1 June he brought down a C-130 Hercules with Sidewinder and cannon. In both cases he was flying XZ451. In 1983 *Invincible* visited Australia and New Zealand and XZ451 is depicted in the markings it wore at that time, complete with kangaroo 'zap' marking. On 1 December 1999 it crashed into the Mediterranean near Sardinia when a reaction control valve jammed. The pilot ejected. Surviving Sea Harriers have been upgraded to FA.2 standard with new Blue Vixen radar and the ability to carry the AIM-120 AMRAAM missile.

Douglas A-4 Skyhawk

The A-4 Skyhawk is one of the classic designs of post-war military aviation, being both lighter and stronger than the US Navy thought possible when it asked Ed Heinemann for proposals for a new carrier-based attack aircraft in 1952. The X44D-1 Skyhawk prototype was flown in June 1954, and production models entered service in 1956.

The A-4B was the first fully operational model, fitted with an inflight-refueling probe and able to carry a wide range of conventional or nuclear weapons. In all, 2960 Skyhawks were built, 542 of them A-4Bs, but production of new models continued until 1979. Four nations ordered new A-4s from Douglas, but a further five took surplus US Navy and US Marine Corps models. Both Argentina and Singapore bought large numbers of refurbished A-4Bs for their air arms.

In Singapore service, the A-4 has been used in both the fighter and bomber roles and still serves with three squadrons. Until the Royal Singapore Air Force (RSAF) acquired tanker aircraft, it was not uncommon to see some of its A-4Bs without refuelling probes as a weight- and drag-saving measure.

DOUGLAS A-4S SKYHAWK

Specification

Type: jet fighter-bomber

Crew: 1

Powerplant: one 37.37kN (8400lb thrust) Curtiss-Wright J65-W-20 turbojet engine

Performance: max speed 1064km/h (661mph); service ceiling 13,716m (45,000ft); range 2680km (1665 miles)

Dimensions: wing span 8.38m (27ft 6in); length without probe 11.70m (38ft 5in); height 4.27m (14ft 1in)

Weight: 10,206kg (22,500lb) loaded

Armament: two 30mm (1.18in) ADEN cannon; ordnance of up to 2268kg (5000lb) including conventional bombs and rockets and AIM-9P Sidewinder missiles

NO. 143 'PHOENIX' SQUADRON, REPUBLIC OF SINGAPORE AIR FORCE CHANGI AIR BASE, SINGAPORE, LATE 1980S

A-4S number 681 was built for the US Navy as A-4B Bureau Number 145046 and is known to have flown with Reserve squadron VA-209 'Air Barons' before delivery to Singapore in 1972. Although later deliveries of A-4s were converted to 'Super Skyhawk' configuration with F404 turbofans and modern avionics, this was not one of them, being sold to Celtrad Metal Industries for scrap.

No. 143 Squadron moved from Changi to Tengah when the former airfield was rebuilt as the country's international airport. In 1997, it became the first RSAF squadron to make the transition to the F-16C/D Fighting Falcon.

BAe Sea Harrier vs Douglas A-4 Skyhawk

ALTHOUGH BOTH VERSIONS of the Harrier – the GR.Mk.3 and the Sea Harrier – were used in the Falklands War, it was the latter that captured the headlines because of its successful air battles with Argentine fighter-bombers, mostly A-4 Skyhawks.

The Sea Harrier's achievements in the Falklands War were summed up by Lieutenant Commander Nigel 'Sharkey' Ward, commanding No. 801 Squadron of the Fleet Air Arm. 'One frequent comment has been that the enemy aircraft had too little fuel to remain in the target area for more than a few minutes. This was obviously not the case, as any student of Mirage and A-4 Skyhawk performance figures can easily establish. They had almost as much loiter time available over the target as did the Harrier and, most importantly, they had the considerable advantage of being on the offensive and with vastly superior numbers... The Argentines christened Sea Harrier La Muerte Negra – the Black Death – and publicized this fact in their national radio broadcasts. They lived in fear of the Fleet Air Arm, though to their credit they continued with

BELOW: A Sea Harrier is marshalled for launch from the carrier HMS Hermes during the Falklands conflict of 1982.

their almost suicidal offensive against our land and naval forces until Port Stanley fell.'

'We could see the awful sight of the ships burning at Bluff Cove. The smoke was pouring out, black and oily, and the entire after section of the ship was glowing red with the heat.'

Falklands Dogfights

One Argentine Navy Skyhawk pilot, Lieutenant Ruben Zini of Grupo 5, had this to say:

'We were briefed to avoid dogfights and escape at low level and alone. We had a lot of experience of air combat manoeuvring, but in the A-4 there was not much choice. Not only were we too slow, but we knew very well that we could not outmanoeuvre the Sea Harrier. All we could do was try to escape at low level at full throttle. We never

ABOVE: *AQ Douglas A-4B Skyhawk C-207 of the Argentine Navy, seen with its substantial weapons load. This aircraft sank the guided missile destroyer HMS Coventry on 25 May 1982.*

mounted Sidewinders on our Skyhawks because our mission was always one of attack, never air-to-air combat. The Sidewinder L is a very effective missile and our older models could not hope to equal them.'

Just how effective was the combination of Sea Harrier and AIM-9L Sidewinder missile is illustrated by this report of an action fought by Lieutenant Dave Smith, RN, and Flight Lieutenant Dave Morgan, RAF, both of whom were serving with No. 800 Squadron of the Fleet Air Arm, operating from the carrier HMS *Hermes*. It was the squadron's last combat of the Falklands War.

'We could see the awful sight of the ships burning at Bluff Cove. The smoke was pouring out, black and oily, and the entire after section of the ship [the Fleet Logistics Ship *Sir Galahad*] was glowing red with the heat. It was about 1800 hours and getting dark when we noticed some Skyhawks having a go at some landing craft coming down from the direction of Goose Green. Dave Morgan rolled upside down and pulled hard for the surface.

> **'The range was two or two-and-a-half miles, and as I watched the Sidewinder's trail, it seemed to me that it flamed out about 300 yards [275m] short of its target... Evidently it did not, as there was a blinding flash'**

'I followed him down very fast, but he was nearly disappearing in the gloom. It was very hard to keep an eye on him. I slammed the throttle to full power and aimed in the general direction in which Dave had by now disappeared. He must have been about half a mile

[800m] ahead of me. My air speed was just over 600 knots when I saw two bright flashes from the direction of Dave's aircraft – he had fired both Sidewinders. I watched the white smoke trails and they ended in two fireballs as the Skyhawks disintegrated and hit the sea.'

Sidewinder Kill

'Now where had he got to? Fortunately he opened up on the other two Skyhawks with his cannon and I just flew towards the shell splashes in the water – there he was. As I approached for an attack Dave was in the way, but fortunately pulled out and cleared from my sights.

'I pointed the missile at the nearest bogey and heard the growl in my ears as the missile acquired him. I fired, thinking he was too far and going too fast for the missile to get him. The range was two or two-and-a-half miles [3.2 or 4km], and as I watched the Sidewinder's trail, it seemed to me that it flamed out about 300 yards [275m] short of its target. Evidently it did not, as there was a blinding flash, followed fractions of a second later by the Skyhawk impacting on the ground.'

Defending Sea Harriers were steered towards incoming Argentine raiders by radar air defence ships. Pilots then mostly had to rely on their naked eyesight to locate the attackers, who were almost always at low level. The Sea Harrier pilots had to overcome problems of distance, too; at times, their two aircraft carriers were stationed up to 402km (250 miles) east of the Falklands, which meant that for every two Sea Harriers on combat air patrol (CAP), another pair would be returning to the ships, and a third pair would be on the way out. Three CAP stations were normally maintained, so with 18 aircraft needed to patrol those areas, full CAP was only achieved because of the Sea Harrier's excellent serviceability record, which was a remarkable 95 per cent.

Mikoyan-Gurevich MiG-27 'Flogger'

The MiG-23, which flew in prototype form in 1967 and which entered service with the Frontal Aviation's attack units of the 16th Air Army in East Germany in 1973, was a variable-geometry fighter-bomber with wings sweeping from 23 to 71 degrees, and was the Soviet Air Force's first true multi-role combat aircraft. The MiG-23M Flogger-B was the first series production version and equipped all the major Warsaw Pact air forces; a simplified version for export to Libya and other Middle East air forces was designated MiG-23MS Flogger-E.

The MiG-23UB Flogger-C was a two-seat trainer, retaining the combat capability of the single-seat variants, while the MiG-23BN/BM Flogger-F and Flogger-H were fighter-bomber versions for export. The MiG-27, which began to enter service in the late 1970s, was a dedicated battlefield support variant known to Nato as Flogger-D; the MiG-27D and MiG-27K Flogger-J were improved versions, while the MiG-23P was a dedicated air defence variant.

About 5000 MiG-23/27s were built, and in the 1990s the type was in service with 20 air forces. The service debut of the MiG-23/27 was not without its share of problems, though, many accidents in the early days having resulted from failure of the wing sweep mechanism.

MIKOYAN-GUREVICH MIG-27L FLOGGER-J

Specification
Type: battlefield support aircraft
Crew: 1
Powerplant: one 10,000kg (22,046lb) thrust Tumanskii R-27F2M-300 turbojet
Performance: max speed 2445km/h (1520mph); service ceiling 18,290m (60,000ft); combat radius 966km (600 miles)
Dimensions: wing span 13.97m (45ft 10in) spread and 7.78m (25ft 6in) swept; length 16.71m (54ft 10in); height 4.82m (15ft 9in)
Weight: 18,145kg (40,000lb) loaded
Armament: one 23mm (0.91in) GSh-23L cannon; underwing pylons for various combinations of air-to-air missiles and offensive stores

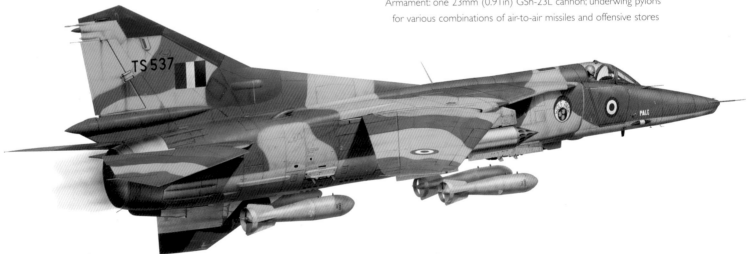

NO. 9 'WOLFPACK' SQUADRON INDIAN AIR FORCE, HINDAN, 1990
The Indian Air Force's MiG-27s were designated MiG-27L. The first aircraft were assembled from Soviet-supplied kits by Hindustan Aeronautics Ltd, but at a later stage in the programme major Indian sub-ssemblies were incorporated. In Indian Air Force service, the type is known as Bahadur (Valiant).

Panavia Tornado

The variable-geometry Tornado was the result of a 1960s requirement for a strike and reconnaissance aircraft capable of carrying a heavy and varied weapons load and of penetrating foreseeable Warsaw Pact defensive systems by day and night, at low level and in all weathers. To develop and build the aircraft, a consortium of companies was formed under the name of Panavia; it consisted principally of the British Aircraft Corporation (later British Aerospace), Messerschmitt-Bölkow-Blohm (MBB) and Aeritalia, as well many subcontractors. Another consortium, Turbo-Union, was formed by Rolls-Royce, MTU of Germany and Fiat to build the Tornado's Rolls-Royce RB-199 turbofan engines.

The first of nine Tornado IDS (Interdictor/Strike) prototypes flew in Germany on 14 August 1974, aircrews of the participating nations having been trained at RAF Cottesmore in the United Kingdom, which received the first Tornado GR.1s in July 1980. The Royal Air Force (RAF) took delivery of 229 GR.1 strike aircraft, the Luftwaffe 212, the German Naval Air Arm 112, and the Aeronautica Militare Italiana (Italian Air Force) 100. RAF and Italian Tornados saw action in the 1991 Gulf War.

The Tornado GR.1A is a variant with a centreline reconnaissance pod, deliveries beginning in 1990, while the GR.4, armed with Sea Eagle anti-shipping missiles, is an anti-shipping version; the GR.4A is the tactical reconnaissance equivalent. Forty-eight Tornado IDS were delivered to Saudi Arabia. The Tornado GR.Mk 1A was developed to meet the RAF's reconnaissance needs in the 1990s and beyond. It retains virtually full air-to-ground strike capability, although the 23mm (0.91in) Mauser cannon were deleted to make room for the recce pod. The GR.Mk 1A also served with No. 2 Squadron, also at Marham.

PANAVIA TORNADO GR.MK 1A

Specification

Type: tactical reconnaissance aircraft

Crew: 2

Powerplant: two 7292kg (16,075lb) thrust Turbo-Union RB.199-34R
   Mk 103 turbofan engines

Performance: max speed 2337km/h (1452mph); service ceiling
   15,240m (50,000ft); combat radius 1390km (864 miles)

Dimensions: wing span 13.91m (45ft 7in) spread and 8.6m (28ft
   2.5in) swept; length: 16.72m (54ft 10in); height 5.95m (19ft
   6.25in)

Weight: 27,216kg (60,000lb) loaded

Armament: up to 9000kg (19,840lb) of stores; Vinten Linescan
   infrared sensors and TIALD (Thermal Imaging and Laser
   Designator)

No. 13 Squadron, Royal Air Force RAF Marham, Norfolk, early 1990s

183

MiG-27 Flogger vs Panavia Tornado

THE MiG-27 AND THE TORNADO IDS had much in common. Both featured variable-geometry wings, and both were optimized for airfield attack. The difference was in their numbers – defence against a blistering, low-level strike by waves of Floggers would have proved difficult, if not impossible.

The MiG-23 saw extensive operational service during the Soviet Union's operations in Afghanistan. The Flogger-G variant carried flare/chaff launchers mounted on the upper fuselage, these being used to decoy infrared-guided, shoulder-launched anti-aircraft missiles, such as the American Stinger, of which considerable numbers were acquired by rebel forces. The Mujahideen had no air power of any kind, but Floggers were sometimes engaged by Pakistan Air Force F-16s when they were attacking ground targets in the vicinity of the Afghan–Pakistan border, and at least two MiG-23s are reported to have been shot down in air combat.

One MiG-23 pilot received the Soviet Union's highest award. He was Colonel Anatolij Levchenko, who flew 188 missions during the Afghan conflict. His last was on 27 December 1986. Having attacked traffic on the Salang Pass, his aircraft was hit by anti-aircraft fire from an AAA battery. Unable to eject, he dived his aircraft into the battery, destroying it and enabling the rest of his squadron to complete their mission unopposed. Levchenko was posthumously awarded the Gold Star of a Hero of the Soviet Union.

Against aircraft such as the Tornado interdictor/strike aircraft, the Flogger might have proved a lethal weapon.

BELOW: *The MiG-27 would have been in the European front line had the Cold War turned hot.*

ABOVE: *A Tornado GR.1 of the RAF carrying the Hunting JP.233 Airfield Attack Weapon System, long-range tanks, ECM pods and Sidewinder missiles.*

At the height of the Cold War period, the huge numbers of Floggers in service with the Warsaw Pact air forces was of great concern to NATO, as the type might have saturated the sky over the battlefield and established local air superiority. At that time, NATO had limited intelligence about the aircraft, and some western pilots were dismissive of it, claiming that the F-4 Phantom (the principal NATO type then in service) could easily deal with it. It was only when the pilot of a Syrian MiG-23 defected to Israel and western experts were able to analyse the Flogger that the type came to be seen as an extremely effective fighter, in some cases able to outperform the F-15s and F-16s that were entering service in the early 1980s. Against aircraft such as the Tornado interdictor/strike aircraft, forced to operate in daylight as well as at night because of urgent wartime requirements, the Flogger might have proved a lethal weapon.

Iraqi Airfields

Airfield attack was one of the roles of the MiG-23/27, a task that was also the primary concern of NATO's Panavia Tornado GR.1 IDS (Interdictor/Strike) force. During the Gulf War of 1991, Tornados of the RAF, Royal Saudi Air Force and Italian Air Force were given the task of neutralizing the Iraqi airfields, as well as attacking petrol, oil and lubricant installations.

The RAF Tornado GR.1s made their airfield attacks using the JP233 Low Latitude Airfield Attack System, the technique being to make diagonal bomb-runs across runways, in ordet to isolate Iraqi aircraft in their hardened shelters. RAF Tornados carried the Sky Shadow electronic countermeasures (ECM) pod, and in some cases were also assisted by USAF Wild Weasel Phantom F-4Gs. The flight to the target was made on autopilot, with the pilot taking over manually for the final pass at very low level, pulling the aircraft up a

little during the run over the target to ensure the necessary clearance on weapons release and ready to take evasive action against SAM or anti-aircraft gunfire.

The Iraqi command, control and communications centres, fixed SS-1C Scud missile sites, chemical/biological warfare production storage sites, rocket propellant plants, other military factories and airfields were all hit during this phase. Of 30 Iraqi main operating airfields, 25 had been heavily attacked by 23 January 1991, and the Iraqi Air Force's sortie rate had fallen from a daily average of over 200 before the onset of the campaign to about 40.

In the later stages of the campaign, RAF Tornado GR.1s, lacking their own laser-designator pod, operated alongside Buccaneers of the Lossiemouth Strike Wing which were equipped with Pave Spike laser designator pods, the Buccaneer illuminating the target – often a hardened aircraft shelter, bridge or missile silo – and guiding the bombs after release by the Tornado. Two Tornados equipped with the GEC Ferranti TIALD (Therman Imaging/Airborne Laser Designator) were deployed to the Gulf and used operationally in interdiction attacks.

SA-3 Attacks

TIALD was the only targeting pod to offer thermal imaging and TV as prime sensors. These could be selected in flight to provide 24-hour all-weather capability. This self-contained system had many advantages compared with tactics involving a dedicated laser-designator like the Buccaneer, flying as part of a package of aircraft carrying laser-guided bombs.

In one instance, while flying as part of such a package, a Tornado was lost when its crew, their heads down in the cockpit and with a lot of voice chatter in progress between the other aircraft in the group, failed to receive warning of a missile threat until it was too late. The Tornado was hit by two SA-3 missiles in rapid succession; the pilot ejected and was taken prisoner, but the navigator was killed. Such are the perils of interdiction.

Boeing AH-64 Apache

Originally developed by Hughes, the AH-64 Apache has been produced under the McDonnell Douglas and McDonnell Douglas Helicopters banners and is now a Boeing product, following the 1997 merger of the two aerospace giants. The first YAH-64 flew in September 1975 and, after a long evaluation, was selected for production as the AH-64A Apache, which entered US Army service in April 1986.

The Apache offered a significant capability improvement over the AH-1 Cobra with its sophisticated night vision and target acquisition/designation system and laser-guided Hellfire missiles. The helmet-mounted sighting system is linked to the powerful Chain Gun cannon under the nose, allowing the pilot (in the aft seat)

or co-pilot/gunner to aim the gun by looking at it. The A model Apache was exported to Israel, Egypt, the UAE, Saudi Arabia and Greece. In the 1991 Gulf War it flew the first missions in the conflict and destroyed large numbers of Iraqi vehicles.

Lessons from the war led to the development of the AH-64D, most but not all of which are fitted with the Longbow millimetre-wave radar in a mast-mounted radome. A new radar-guided version of the Hellfire allows firings from outside a line-of-sight position and identification and selection of targets at much greater ranges than previously. The US Army is to upgrade 500 of its 800-plus AH-64As to Longbow standard.

BOEING AH-64D LONGBOW APACHE

Specification
Type: attack helicopter
Crew: 2
Powerplant: two 1342kW (1800hp) General Electric T700-GE-701C turboshaft engines
Performance: max speed 293km/h (182mph); Hovering ceiling in ground effect 4172m (13,690 ft); range 428km (300 miles)
Dimensions: main rotor diameter 14.63m (48ft 0in); fuselage length 14.97m (49ft 1.5in); height 4.66m (15ft 3.5in)
Weight: 9525kg (21,000lb) loaded
Armament: one M230 Chain Gun 30mm (1.18in) cannon with 1200 rounds; 2841kg (6263lb) of ordnance, including unguided rockets and AGM-114 Hellfire missiles

1ST BATTALION, 14TH AVIATION (TRAINING) BRIGADE, US ARMY TRAINING AND DOCTRINATION COMMAND ALABAMA, 1996
This aircraft, 90-0423, was an AH-64A rebuilt as the fourth of six development AH-64Ds, and first flew as such in October 1993. It was later given the new serial 98-5083 and assigned to the 1st Battalion of the 14th Aviation (Training) Brigade (1/14 AVN) at Fort Rucker. The AH-64D has been exported to the Netherlands, Singapore and the United Kingdom.

Mil Mi-24 'Hind'

The Mil Mi-24, given the Nato reporting name Hind, was the first helicopter to enter service with the Soviet Air Force as a dedicated assault transport and gunship. Its missions included direct air support, anti-tank, armed escort and air-to-air combat.

The helicopter, which can carry eight fully armed troops, was used extensively during the Soviet involvement in Afghanistan in the 1980s. The Russians deployed significant numbers of Hinds to Europe and exported the type to many developing countries.

The Hind-A fuselage consisted of a large, oval-shaped body with a glassed-in cockpit, tapering at the rear to the tail boom. The Hind-D fuselage featured nose modification with tandem bubble canopies and a chin-mounted turret. The swept-back tapered tail fin had a rotor on the right on some models, with tapered flats on a boom just forward of the fin. External stores were mounted on underwing external stores points. Each wing had three hardpoints for a total of six stations. The Hind's wings provided 22– 28 per cent of its lift in forward flight. Nearly all of the older Hind-A, Hind-B and Hind-C variants were upgraded or modified to Hind-D or Hind-E standard.

MIL MI-24 HIND-D

Specification

Type: assault helicopter

Crew: 2

Powerplant: two Klimov (Isotov) TV3-117 Series III turboshaft
engines each rated at 1641kW (2200hp)

Performance: max speed 310km/h (192mph); service ceiling 4500m
(14,765ft); range 750km (466 miles)

Dimensions: rotor diameter 17.30m (56ft 9in); length 17.51m (57ft
5.5in); height 4.44m (14ft 6.25in)

Weight: 12,500kg (27,557lb) loaded

Armament: one four-barrelled 12.7mm (0.50in) rotary gun in
remotely controlled undernose turret; various combinations of
anti-armour missiles, rocket pods, gun pods etc

16TH AIR ARMY, GROUP OF SOVIET FORCES, GERMAN DEMOCRATIC REPUBLIC, EARLY 1980S
The early model Mi-24 Hind-A was deployed to East Germany in strength in 1974, equipping two helicopter assault regiments at Parchim and Stendahl. The improved Hind-D began to reach the frontline units by 1976; it was supplanted and all but replaced by the Mi-24V Hind-E from 1979. Almost all the Hind-Ds had been replaced by the time the Russians withdrew from Germany in 1992.

BOEING AH-64 APACHE VS MIL MI-24 'HIND'

ON THE NIGHT of 16/17 January 1991, several hours before the start of Operation Desert Storm – the Allied offensive against Iraq – eight McDonnell Douglas AH-64 Apache helicopters of the US 101st Airborne Division flew northward at low level into the desert darkness.

The helicopters were heavily laden with extra fuel tanks, Hellfire air-to-surface missiles, 70mm (2.75in) rockets and 30mm (1.18in) ammunition. Accompanying them, for navigational purposes, was a USAF special operations CH-53. The Apaches' mission was to penetrate deep inside Iraq and destroy two key radar sites, opening a corridor for the Allied strike aircraft assigned to key targets in the Baghdad area.

The helicopter teams also launched 100 70mm (2.74in) rockets and strafed the targets with 4000 rounds of 30mm (1.18in) ammunition before leaving the area.

Apache Mission

The mission involved a round trip of 1758km (1092 miles), and was flawless. The Apaches split into two attack groups in the target area, popping up to 30m (100ft) at the last moment to launch a total of 15 laser-guided Hellfires, all of which hit the two radar sites. The helicopter teams also launched 100 70mm (2.74in) rockets and strafed the targets with 4000 rounds of 30mm (1.18in) ammunition before leaving the area. The attack had lasted less than two minutes.

On the return journey, the Apaches landed at a desert rendezvous called Cobra Base to take on fuel pre-positioned there by a US Army CH-47 'Fat Cow' helicopter. This was a time-consuming operation, and it was well into the following morning by the time the force headed for the Saudi Arabian border. En route, the CH-47, which was equipped with the ALQ-144 infrared countermeasures system, detected an Iraqi SAM launch and took evasive action using chaff and flares. The missile nevertheless homed in and blew away the helicopter's aft landing gear. Despite this damage, the CH-47 managed to reach its base safely.

While still in Iraqi air space, the Apaches, accompanied by Blackhawk, Chinook and Kiowa helicopters that had been positioned forward as a backup force, attacked any targets that they could find. One Apache and one Blackhawk were lost to enemy ground fire.

This remarkable operation, which lasted 15 hours from start to finish, including the time spent on the ground, highlighted the amazing versatility of the Apache – and left actual and potential enemies in no doubt about what its phenomenal firepower could achieve.

Hinds in Afghanistan

Ten years before the conflict in Iraq, the Russians had already demonstrated the value of the attack helicopter in Afghanistan, where

BELOW: The Apache has provided NATO with an awesome helicopter attack capability. Seen here is the AH-64D Longbow Apache, with mast-mounted radar.

the heavily-armed Mil Mi-24 Hind first saw combat, about 250 being deployed. A US Army observer of the Russian involvement in Afghanistan commented at the time that:

'The Hind is an extremely lethal weapon, with machine guns or cannon in the nose turret and up to 192 unguided missiles under its stub wings. It has room for eight to twelve ground troops and their equipment in the fuselage, and it is widely used by the Soviets for punitive and search-and-destroy missions. The Hind has also been used to provide close air support for ground troops, to strike Afghan villages (sometimes in conjunction with fixed-wing aircraft), and to conduct armed-reconnaissance missions to detect and attack guerrilla groups.

'Convoy protection is also provided by other Hinds that range ahead of the column to detect and strike guerrillas'

'Due to its heavy armour, the Hind is nearly impervious to guerrilla small arms unless the guerrillas can fire down at the helicopters using weapons positioned high on the sides of mountains.

'The Hind has only three known vulnerable points: the turbine intakes, the tail rotor assembly, and an oil tank inexplicably but conveniently located beneath the red star on the fuselage.

'The terrain in Afghanistan has had considerable influence on the use of the Hind. Many of the narrow roads in Afghanistan snake

ABOVE: *The Mil Mi-24 Hind would have caused serious problems for NATO's armour had there ever been an armed confrontation during the later period of the Cold War.*

through valleys overlooked by steep, tall mountains. Such terrain provides perfect ambush situations. As a result, whenever a Soviet troop column or supply convoy moves into guerrilla territory, it is accompanied by Hinds whose pilots have developed a standard escort tactic. Some Hinds hover over the ground convoy, watching for guerrilla activity, while others land troops on high ground ahead of the advancing column. These troops secure any potential ambush positions and provide flank security until the column has passed; they are themselves protected against guerrilla attack by the Hinds that inserted them and subsequently hover overhead. Once the convoy passes their position, the troops are picked up and reinserted farther along the route. Convoy protection is also provided by other Hinds that range ahead of the column to detect and strike guerrillas that may have concentrated along the route.

'Other information on Hind tactics indicate that a closer relationship between air and ground arms has been a major aim of the Soviet force development. Hinds are the primary Soviet close air support weapon in Afghanistan. They not only strike enemy forces in contact with Soviet troops but sometimes carry out attacks as much as twenty to thirty kilometres forward of the forward edge of battle area.'

Grumman F-14 Tomcat

Although often regarded as the ultimate 'superfighter', the F-14 Tomcat is nearing the end of its career with the US Navy. Many famous squadrons were disbanded in the 1990s, and others have since made the transition to the F/A-18F Super Hornet for the fleet defence role. Despite various avionics upgrades, the F-14 retains the AIM-7 Sparrow for medium-range hitting power, unlike most other US fighters which now employ the longer-range AIM-120 AMRAAM. The Tomcat's combination of cannon, Sidewinder, Sparrow and Phoenix missiles covers threats at all ranges.

GRUMMAN F-14A TOMCAT

Specification

Type: carrier-based interceptor fighter

Crew: 2

Powerplant: two 96.78kN (21,750lb thrust) Pratt & Whitney TF30-P-414A afterburning turbofan engines

Performance: max speed 2485km/h (1544mph); service ceiling over 15,240m (50,000ft); ferry range 3800km (2360 miles)

Dimensions: wing span 19.54m (64ft 1.5in); length 19.10m (62ft 8in); height 4.88m (16ft 0in)

Weight: 33,724kg (74,349lb) loaded

Armament: one M61 Vulcan 20mm (0.79in) cannon; maximum ordnance of 6577kg (14,500 lb), including two AIM-9, four AIM-7 Sparrow and four AIM-54 Phoenix air-to-air missiles

FIGHTER SQUADRON 111 'SUNDOWNERS', CARRIER AIR WING 15US NAVY, NAS MIRAMAR, 1990S

Fighter Squadron 111 (VF-111) was redesignated from VA-154 in 1959 and subsequently flew the F-11F Tiger, F-8 Crusader and F-4 Phantom, scoring several kills with the latter two types in Vietnam. The squadron became famous in those colourful days of US naval aviation for its red and white shark's mouth on the nose and sunburst on the rudder or tail fin. In 1978, the squadron made the transition from the F-4J to the F-14A, and took its Tomcats to sea aboard the USS *Kitty Hawk* in May 1979.

Remaining as part of Carrier Air Wing 15 (CVW-15), the squadron flew from the Pacific Fleet carriers *Kitty Hawk* and *Carl Vinson* for the following 16 years. When not on cruise, the squadron was based at Naval Air Station Miramar near San Diego. During the 'Sundowners' Tomcat period, the US Navy toned down its colour schemes and markings to reduce visual and infrared detection ranges. All colour disappeared and the famous shark's mouth and sunburst became all but invisible on VF-111's aircraft, although small areas of colour occasionally reappeared on the commanding officer's F-14. VF-111 was the victim of post–Cold War cutbacks and disbanded in 1995.

Sukhoi Su-22 'Fitter'

In the early 1960s, the Sukhoi bureau redesigned the Su-7, giving it a more powerful engine, variable-geometry wings and increased fuel tankage. In this guise it became the Su-17/20 Fitter C, which was unique among combat aircraft in being a variable-geometry derivative of a fixed-wing machine. It was an excellent example of a remarkable Russian talent for developing existing designs to their fullest extent.

The development of the Fitter-C was a facet of the Russians' practice of constant development, enabling them to keep one basic design of combat aircraft in service for 30 or 40 years and foster long-term standardization. Also, the use of the same production facilities over a long period of time helped greatly to reduce costs, which is why the Soviet Union was able to offer combat types on the international market at far more competitive rates than the West.

The Su-22 was an updated version with terrain-avoidance radar and other improved avionics. A principal Su-22M user was the Syrian Arab Air Force, which took delivery of some 50 aircraft from 1978; another important user was Vietnam. The Su-22 remains in service with former Warsaw Pact air forces, such as the Czech Republic and Slovakia.

SUKHOI SU-22MF FITTER-K

Specification

Type: fighter-bomber

Crew: 1

Powerplant: one 11,250kg (24,802lb) thrust Lyulka AL-21F-3 turbojet

Performance: max speed 2220km/h (1380mph); service ceiling 15,200m (49,865ft); combat radius 675km (419 miles)

Dimensions: wing span 13.80m (45ft 3in); length 18.75m (61ft 6in); height 5m (16ft 5in)

Weight: 19,500kg (42,990lb) loaded

Armament: two 30mm (1.18in) cannon; nine external pylons with provision for up to 4250kg (9370lb) of stores

JAGDBOMBERGESCHWADER 77 'GERHARD LEBERECHT VON BLÜCHER' LUFTSTREITKRÄFTE, LAAGE, ROSTOCK, 1980s ·
Two East German units were armed with the Su-22M; the other was a naval wing, Marinefliegergeschwader 28 'Paul Wieczoreck'. As well as performing the tactical reconnaissance mission, East German Fitter crews were trained to use S-25L laser-guided rocket projectiles and the Kh-58U (As-11 Kilter) anti-radar missile in the defence suppression role.

GRUMMAN F-14 TOMCAT VS SUKHOI SU-22 'FITTER'

THE FIRST TIME that Grumman's big naval fighter leaped into the world's headlines was on 19 August 1981, when two aircraft of Fighting Squadron VF-41, piloted by Commander Henry Kleeman and Lieutenant Lawrence Muczynski, destroyed two Libyan Air Force Su-22 Fitters over the Mediterranean.

The Tomcats were launched from the aircraft carrier USS *Nimitz* at 04.05 GMT to patrol an area 111km (69 miles) north of the Libyan coast over the Gulf of Sirte. Fifteen vessels of the United States Sixth Fleet, including the carriers *Nimitz* and *Forrestal*, were conducting a missile-firing exercise in the southern Mediterranean at the time. Although the exercise area was clearly defined and the standard international warning issued several days earlier, no fewer than 35 patrols of Libyan aircraft had approached the zone and six aircraft had actually infringed it. The Libyans had been intercepted and turned back by Sixth Fleet Tomcats

Interception

On this occasion, the Tomcat patrol flown by Kleeman and Muczynski was one of several tasked with protecting the perimeter of the exercise area against potentially hostile incursions. At 15.20, while orbiting at 6096m (20,000ft), Kleeman's Radar Intercept Officer (RIO) picked up a radar contact some 74km (46 miles) to the south and heading in their direction. The fighter controller directed both Tomcats to

investigate and they turned south, with Kleeman in the lead and Muczynski 2.5km (1.5 miles) to the rear and slightly higher.

The two radar returns continued to close head-on with the Tomcats, and shortly the weapons officers of both American aircraft reported that their equipment had locked on to transmissions from Soviet-made SRD-5M 'High Fix' air interception and fire-control radars operating in the I-Band. This type of radar was known to be contained in the Fitter's air intake centrebody, and provided the Americans with the first indication of the type of aircraft they were about to encounter.

He waited 10 seconds until his target had crossed the sun, then fired an AIM-9L Sidewinder from a range of about 300m (1000ft).

BELOW: *The Grumman F-14 Tomcat provided the US Navy with the most effective fleet air defence system in the world, working in conjunction with the E-2 Hawkeye surveillance aircraft.*

ABOVE: *Sukhoi Su-22 'Fitter' of the Czech Air Force. Czech and Polish Fitters now regularly exercise with aircraft of other NATO air forces, and prove tough opponents.*

Just before the Fitters came into visual range, at about 13km (8 miles), the Tomcats started a hard counter-break to starboard to cancel out the Libyans' already marginal missile launch window. The Fitters were visual at between 10 and 11.3km (6 and 7 miles) and the Americans saw that they were flying in close formation, with wingtips about 150m (500ft) apart, at about two o'clock on a reciprocal heading. The Tomcat pilots turned again to keep the Fitters in sight and rendezvous with them, and as Kleeman passed 150m (500ft) above and about 300m (1000ft) in front he saw one of the Fitters launch an AA-2 Atoll infra-red homing missile from its starboard pylon. He told Muczynski that they were being fired on and continued a very hard left turn across the Fitters' tails, keeping them in sight all the while and causing the Atoll to break lock as its seeker reached its gimbal limits.

Evasive Manoeuvres
Both Tomcats had broken hard left, and now Kleeman saw the lead Fitter – the one that had fired the Atoll – enter a climbing left-hand turn towards Muczynski and pass through the loop of the American's maximum-rate turn, still climbing. As his wingman rolled out of the turn and went after the lead Fitter, Kleeman reversed his own turn, rolling out to the right in pursuit of the Libyan wingman. He waited 10 seconds until his target had

crossed the sun, then fired an AIM-9L Sidewinder from a range of about 300m (1000ft). The missile struck the Fitter in the tailpipe area, causing the Libyan pilot to lose control, and he ejected within five seconds.

The two Fitters had been destroyed by a combination of superior tactics, superior weapons and vastly superior aircraft.

Muczynski, meanwhile, had also fired a Sidewinder from about 700m (2300ft), and this too destroyed its target. The pilot of the second Fitter was not seen to eject. The time from the first radar contact to the kills was under 60 seconds. Enthusing about the F-14, one Sixth Fleet Tomcat pilot commented that: 'We've got a great interceptor, a great fleet air defence fighter, and a close-in dogfighter as well, with a weapons fit that spans the spectrum and a real long loiter time. We proved that in the Mediterranean, there, off the coast of Libya. We were doing CAPs [Combat Air Patrols] 24 hours round the clock, with a loiter time on station of up to three hours. As soon as they'd seen what the aircraft could do, the Libyans had a great respect for the aircraft as a whole and particularly the weapons systems.'

The combat over the Gulf of Sirte proved the point. The two Fitters had been destroyed by a combination of superior tactics, superior weapons and vastly superior aircraft. From the moment they had first been detected by the Tomcats' radar, the Libyans had stood little chance of inflicting damage on their opponents.

General Dynamics F-111

The early career of the F-111 was hugely controversial due to its protracted development and the failure of the F-111B version, which was intended for the US Navy's fleet defence role. The F-111A of the US Air Force (USAF) first flew in December 1964 and made its combat debut in Vietnam in 1968. The initial deployment was notable for its 50 per cent loss rate, but the F-111, nicknamed the 'Aardvark', soon proved the most effective long-range strike platform, using its terrain-following radar to navigate to and attack important targets at night and in bad weather.

The F-111 had no internal bomb bay, but could carry a very wide range of conventional and nuclear ordnance, including almost all the precision-guided weapons in the US inventory. The F-111F differed from the F-111E in having the Pave Tack installation. This large underfuselage pod allowed the aircraft to designate the target for its own laser-guided bombs (LGBs). In the 1991 Gulf War, the F-111F proved a far more effective tank buster than the F-16, destroying over ten times as many Iraqi vehicles, mainly by night using LGBs.

GENERAL DYNAMICS F-111F

Specification
Type: variable-geometry tactical bomber
Crew: 2
Powerplant: two 116kN (25,100lb thrust) Pratt & Whitney TF30-P100 afterburning turbofan engines
Performance: max speed 2338km/h (1453mph); service ceiling 17,267m (56,650ft); range 5848km (3634 miles)
Dimensions: wing span (spread) 19.20m (63ft); length 22.4m (73ft 6in); height 5.18m (17ft)
Weight: 44,884kg (98,950lb) loaded
Armament: up to 11,600kg (25,000lb)

524TH FIGHTER SQUADRON, 27TH FIGHTER WING AIR COMBAT COMMAND, UNITED STATES AIR FORCE, CANNON AFB, NEW MEXICO, 1993
The 'CC' tailcode identifies this F-111F as based at Cannon Air Force Base, the main stateside home for 'Aardvarks' from 1969 until 1998. F-111F 70-2396 was assigned to the 492nd TFS, 48th TFW, at Lakenheath, England, in the mid-1980s and was launched as part of Operation El Dorado Canyon, the raid on Libya in April 1986. When F-111s were replaced in Europe by F-15Es in 1992, 70-2396 was reassigned to the 27th FW at Cannon; in January 1996 it was placed in desert storage.

Sukhoi Su-24 'Fencer'

In 1965, the Soviet government instructed the Sukhoi design bureau to begin design studies of a new variable-geometry strike aircraft in the same class as the General Dynamics F-111. One of the criteria was that the new aircraft must be able to fly at very low level in order to penetrate increasingly effective air defence systems. The resulting aircraft, the Su-24, made its first flight in 1970, and deliveries of the first production version, the Fencer-A, began in 1974.

Several variants of the Fencer were produced, culminating in the Su-24M Fencer-D, which entered service in 1986. It features an advanced nav/attack targeting system which, combined with the

Kaira-24 laser ranger/designator, enables the use of laser-guided and TV-guided weapons. Navigation and radio communication systems were also upgraded. The addition of an in-flight refuelling system greatly improved the aircraft's range and flexibility.

The Su-24MR is a tactical reconnaissance version. The Su-24MK is the export variant of the Su-24M which was developed for friendly Arabian nations. Reportedly 20 aircraft were exported to Syria, 15 to Libya, and 24 to Iraq. There are almost no differences between the Su-24MK and the original Su-24M. The Ukrainian Air Force also inherited two regiments of Su-24s.

SUKHOI SU-24 FENCER-D

Specification

Type: interdictor/strike aircraft
Crew: 2
Powerplant: two 11,250kg (24,802lb) thrust Lyulka AL-21F3A
  turbojets
Performance: max speed 2316km/h (1439mph); service ceiling
  17,500m (57,415ft); combat radius 1050km (650 miles)
Dimensions: wing span 17.63m (57ft 10in) spread and 10.36m
  (34ft) swept; length 24.53m (80ft 5in); height 4.97m (16ft 0in)
Weight: 39,700kg (87,520lb) loaded
Armament: one 23mm (0.91in) GSh-23-6 six-barrelled cannon; nine
  external pylons with provision for up to 8000kg (17,635lb) of
  stores

149TH BOMBER AIR DIVISION, 67TH BOMBER AIR REGIMENT, SIVERSKIY, POLAND, 1985

GENERAL DYNAMICS F-111 VS SUKHOI SU-24 'FENCER'

BOTH THE USA AND USSR appreciated the importance of the long-range, low-level, all-weather interdictor/strike aircraft. But while the F-111 was designed to operate singly, the Su-24 'Fencer' adopted different tactics.

In 1972 the F-111 was the most sophisticated interdictor in the world, and one which had defied all its early critics to become a key weapon in the West's arsenal. To describe a low-level flight in the extraordinary machine is a challenge in itself, as will be seen from this extract from an article written by American aviation author Ernest K. Gann, who flew in an F-111A in 1971:

'As you sink down from the heights, the mountains become ever more imposing and you remember a wager made the night before. If during the TFR (Terrain-Following Radar) run you manage to resist

reaching for the stick and taking over from the automatic pilot, you will win two martinis … here are the 11,000ft [3350m] mountains approaching from directly ahead at a mere 553 miles per hour [890km/h] and you are looking up at them from a vantage of 200ft [60m]. You indulge in some erratic swallowing and glance furtively at

BELOW: Once initial problems with its wing sweep mechanism had been overcome, the F-111 proved to be a superb strike aircraft. This F-111 is an aircraft of the 20th TFW, Upper Heyford.

Wheeler (Colonel Tom Wheeler, Chief of F-111 Acceptance at Fort Worth) who is not looking out at all but is thoughtfully studying an old aviation chart, vintage 1935…

ABOVE: The Sukhoi Su-24 'Fencer' was the Russian equivalent of the F-111, but the tactics it employed were different. Fencers operated in 'packages', with fighter escort.

'…the autopilot levels the nose and you slither across the rumpled surface like a giant manta ray searching for food.'

'As if cushioned softly against the face of a mountain, the One-Eleven rises with the slope … there is a saddle in the mountain ahead … trees higher than eye level, rocks, boulders, great chunks of very abrasive stuff off both wing tips. Wheeler reaches for a knob. "Do you prefer your ride to be soft, medium or hard?" Your hand is curved like the talons of an eagle exactly one half-inch ahead of the stick … The One-Eleven slips through the saddle and starts down the backside of the mountain, still at 200ft [60m] and just under the speed of sound … Just as you are resigned to continuing straight through the bottom of the valley on the direct route to Peking, the autopilot levels the nose and you slither across the rumpled surface like a giant manta ray searching for food.'

In Vietnam, the F-111s operated singly and achieved impressive results in their 'blind' first-pass attacks on pinpoint targets, which often lay in the middle of densely populated areas. As one F-111 pilot put it in an interview with Air Force magazine: 'It takes real discipline to come up over these mountains, as we did at night, out on top of the cloud layer in the moonlight. We'd see those jagged peaks all around us poking through the cloud tops, and we'd have to put the nose down back into that mist. And as we went down the moonlight would fade, and the cloud get darker, and we'd know we were descending far below those peaks and were depending on our radars and our autopilots – and with Hanoi coming up, I wouldn't say I wasn't worried.

'One night, when the weather was very bad, I was in cloud for the last eleven minutes before bombs away. That means at the lowest level of the whole flight, at 250 or 200 feet [75 or 60m] going up and down the hills, we didn't see a thing outside the cockpit, not even

after the bombs left us. For me, this thing was really remarkable. Even now I can't explain how fantastic it was … the confidence I gained in the airplane, it made a believer out of me. Given a choice on a night strike of going in Hi or going in Lo, I'll take Lo every time. And I'll go anywhere in the F-111.'

Doubtless the crews of Russia's F-111 equivalent, the Sukhoi Su-24 'Fencer', have similar confidence in the ability of their own aircraft. Russian operating procedures and tactics differ from those of the USAF, and have been steadily refined since the Russian Air Force absorbed the lessons of the Gulf War of 1991. On exercises, the Su-24s operate in cells of four aircraft, making saturation attacks on targets rather than attacking individually.

'Given a choice on a night strike of going in Hi or going in Lo, I'll take Lo every time. And I'll go anywhere in the F-111.'

The usual mix of aircraft on a deployment exercise might include six Tupolev Tu-95 bombers, ten Su-24 attack aircraft and four Sukhoi Su-27 escort fighters, these being supported by twelve Il-78 flight refuelling tankers, one A-50 AWACS and two airborne command posts. On one exercise, Voskhod-93, which began on 18 May 1993, a mix of aircraft described above departed from three airfields in western Russia at 01.00 hours local time, heading for the Amur training area in the far east. The ten Su-24s refuelled twice during the 8000-km (5000-mile) flight, which was accomplished in twelve and a half hours, while the Su-27s refuelled at airfields en route. Full readiness was achieved straight after the transfer, attacks against simulated targets by the Su-24s being coordinated from an Il-62 command post. The exercise lasted two days, the aircraft returning to their home bases on 19 May.

Tupolev Tu-22M 'Backfire'

Allocated the NATO reporting name 'Backfire', the Tupolev Tu-22M first flew in 1971, reached initial operational capability (IOC) in 1973 and, during the years that followed, replaced the Tu-16 Badger in Soviet service. The mission of the new bomber, peripheral attack or intercontinental attack, became one of the most fiercely contested intelligence debates of the Cold War, and it was a long time before the true nature of the threat it posed – anti-shipping attack – became known.

The original design (Backfire-A) underwent major modifications and re-emerged as the Tu-22M2 Backfire-B. About 400 Tu-22Ms were produced, 240 of them being M-2s/3s. The M3 (Backfire-C) variant had reduced defensive armament and the flight refuelling probe was deleted; a reconnaissance version, the Tu-22MR, entered service in 1985, and the Tu-22ME is the latest of the attack variants.

The variable-geometry Tu-22M Backfire's design was based on that of the earlier Tu-22 Blinder, which had many shortcomings and which saw operational service in Afghanistan during the Soviet intervention there.

TUPOLEV TU-22M 'BACKFIRE'

Specification

Type: maritime strike aircraft

Crew: 4

Powerplant: two 20,000kg (44,092lb) thrust Kuznetsov NK-144 turbofans

Performance; max speed 2125km/h (1321mph); service ceiling 18,000m (59,055ft); range 4000km (2485 miles)

Dimensions: wing span 34.30m (112ft 6in) spread and 23.40m (76ft 9in) swept; length 36.90m (121ft 11in); height 10.80m (35ft 5in)

Weight: 130,000kg (286,596lb) loaded

Armament: one 23mm (0.91in) GSh-23 twin-barrel cannon in radar controlled tail barbette; up to 12,000kg (26,455lb) of stores in weapons bay, or one S-4 missile, or three AS-16 missiles

924TH RECONNAISSANCE AIR REGIMENT NORTHERN FLEET, OLENYA, RUSSIA, 1998
The 924th Reconnaissance Air Regiment is sometimes referred to as the 924th Missile Carrier Regiment. Its role during the Cold War would have been to attack Nato ships in the North Atlantic and North Sea, or any naval unit that was approaching the Russian coast. To do this, large numbers of Backfires would have been deployed to attack Nato naval forces, using the Kh-22M (AS-4 Kitchen) air-to-surface missile. Backfires also serve with the Northern Fleet's 574th Air Reconnaissance Regiment, and with units of the Black Sea Fleet. Seen here is a Tu-22M3 Backfire-C of the 924th Reconnaissance Air Regiment.

Rockwell B-1B

Designed to replace the B-52 and FB-111 in the low-level penetration role, the Rockwell B-1 variable-geometry supsersonic bomber prototype flew on 23 December 1974, and on 2 December 1976 the US Air Force (USAF) was authorized to proceed with production of the aircraft. In June 1977, however, President Jimmy Carter, in a nationwide television address, reversed this decision and stated that the B-1 would not be produced, but on 2 October 1981 President Ronald Reagan's new US administration took the decision to resurrect the supersonic bomber programme.

The operational designation of the supersonic bomber, 100 of which were to be built for Strategic Air Command, was to be B-1B. The two prototypes already built, and which had undergone a substantial evaluation programme, were now to be known as B-1As. The first B-1B flew in October 1984, and the first operational B-1B was delivered to the 96th Bomb Wing at Dyess Air Force Base on 7 July 1985. The last B-1B was delivered on 2 May 1988, since when the type has taken part in offensive operations in the Balkans and elsewhere. The B-1B equips five USAF squadrons assigned to the 8th Air Force, and two of the Air National Guard.

ROCKWELL B-1B

Specification

Type: strategic bomber

Crew: 4

Powerplant: four 13,962kg (30,780lb) thrust General Electric F101-GE-102 turbofans

Performance: max speed 1328km/h (825mph); service ceiling 15,240m (50,000ft); range 12,000km (7455 miles)

Dimensions: wing span 1.67m (136ft 8in); length 44.81m (147ft); height 10.36m (34ft)

Weight: 216,634kg (477,000lb) loaded

Armament: up to 38,320kg (84,500lb) of Mk 82 or 10,974kg (24,200lb) of Mk 84 iron bombs in the conventional role, 24 SRAMs, 12 B-28 and B-43 or 24 B-61 and B-83 free-fall nuclear bombs, eight ALCMs on internal rotary launchers and 14 more on underwing launchers, and various combinations of other underwing stores; low-level operations are flown with internal stores only

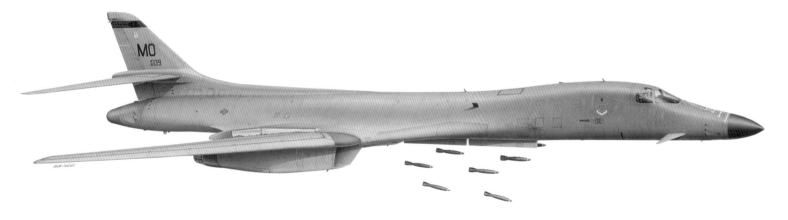

34TH BOMB SQUADRON, 366TH WING, UNITED STATES AIR FORCE, ELLSWORTH AIR FORCE BASE, SOUTH DAKOTA, 1990S
The 366th Wing, to which this B-1B belongs, is the USAF's rapid deployment air intervention wing, which also comprises F-16Cs, F-15C/Es and KC-135R tankers. Known as 'The Gunfighters', the wing's function is to deploy at very short notice for operations in any part of the world.

TUPOLEV TU-22M VS ROCKWELL B-1B

For both the former Cold War adversaries, the road to developing a successful supersonic bomber was long and hard. Eventually both the USA and USSR got the formula right with the Tu-22M and B-1B.

The Tupolev Tu-22M and the Rockwell B-1B were both intended to perform specific roles, yet the operational reality proved to be far different. The Tu-22M3 'Backfire-C' was optimised for low-level attack missions against NATO carrier battle groups, with support from AWACS platforms; the first aircraft were delivered to the 185th Guards Heavy Bomber Aviation Regiment, and 268 Tu-22M3s were built before production ceased in 1993. Its principal anti-shipping weapon originally was the Kh-22 (NATO reporting name 'Kitchen') which could be armed with either a conventional or nuclear (3.5kT) warhead, but later on up to six Kh-15P nuclear-tipped air-to-surface missiles could be carried on an internal rotary launcher. Soviet tactics envisaged saturating a NATO battle group with as many attacking aircraft as possible, with up to seven Backfires from each strike package having the aircraft carrier as their principal target. The Backfire could also operate in the air-to-air role against NATO early warning aircraft.

Exceptional Design

The Backfire's combat debut, however, took place not over the North Atlantic, but over the arid mountain terrain of Afghanistan. In January 1988, 16 aircraft of the 402nd Heavy Bomber Regiment deployed to an air base in Turkestan for operations against the Mujaheddin, attacking mountain strongholds with bombs of up to 3000kg (6614lb). The final Afghan missions were flown early in 1989, but the Backfire saw further action during the Chechen conflict in 1995, attacking targets in the Grozny area.

...16 aircraft of the 402nd Heavy Bomber Regiment deployed to an air base in Turkestan for operations against the Mujaheddin, attacking mountain strongholds with bombs of up to 3000kg (6614lb).

The Tu-22M is an exceptionally well-designed aircraft. The fuselage design comprises the forward crew stations, a central weapons bay, a rear engine compartment, and a pair of air intakes and tunnels working their way around the weapons bay to the engines. The only serious flaw in the original design was that the side-mounted air

BELOW: An early-model Tu-22M Backfire seen at Monino Air Museum, near Moscow. The Backfire remains a very effective anti-shipping strike aircraft, armed with stand-off weapons.

intakes created unacceptable airflow turbulence over the fin and rudder at high angles of attack; this problem was solved by increasing the size of the dorsal fin ahead of the rudder, the additional fin volume being used to store extra equipment and fuel cells.

There was a time, in the early stage of its evolution, when the future of the Tu-22M seemed uncertain, but production orders were assured after a series of demonstrations were carried out before senior Soviet politicians in 1971. One of these involved an attack by a single aircraft on a simulated tank regiment with a full load of 500kg (1102lb) bombs. The target was destroyed and the politicians were impressed, even when shrapnel ripped through the reviewing box, narrowly missing them.

The B-1B made its combat debut in 1998, when aircraft carried out bombing missions against Iraq in support of Operation Desert Fox.

Afghanistan and Iraq

Although conceived for the nuclear attack role, America's Rockwell B-1B, like the Backfire, found its operational application in the long-range conventional bombing role, having undergone a Conventional Mission Upgrade Programme. The first stage of this upgrade (designated Block-B) was completed in 1995 and gave the aircraft an improved synthetic aperture radar, as well as upgrading other elements of the avionics suite. A further (Block-C) upgrade in 1997 updated the aircraft's software to permit the delivery of various cluster bomb combinations.

The B-1B made its combat debut in 1998, when aircraft carried out bombing missions against Iraq in support of Operation Desert Fox,

ABOVE: *The Rockwell B-1B Lancer might never have been developed had it not been for President Ronald Reagan, who resurrected the programme after its cancellation.*

undertaken because of Iraq's repeated infringements of the 'No-Fly Zone' and missile attacks on Coalition aircraft. Six B-1Bs took part in Operation Allied Force in the former Yugoslavia in 1999, in support of NATO operations in Kosovo, and eight more saw action in Operation Enduring Freedom, the bombing of terrorist strongholds in Afghanistan, others were employed during offensive operations against Iraq in 2003. In 2001, a B-1B of the 20th Bomb Wing, operating from Diego Garcia in the Indian Ocean against targets in Afghanistan, was lost over the sea through a technical malfunction, the four crew members being saved.

The B-1B has an effective escape system. Each crew member sits on a Weber ACES II ejection seat, unlike the crew of the B-1A, who sat inside a jettisonable capsule. In an emergency, this capsule could be separated from the fuselage to descend under three parachutes, similar to those used to lower the Apollo space capsules. Impact was cushioned by air bags, which also served as flotation bags in the event of a landing on water. However, in October 1974 it was announced that the B-1B would have standard ejection seats. Each crew member has a knob which can be used to set the ejection sequence to Auto or Manual; the normal setting is Auto, in which either pilot can initiate an ejection sequence that leads to all four crew members being rapidly ejected. Any seat not in Auto mode is instantly bypassed, the sequence going on to the next. In the Manual mode, any crew member can initiate only his or her own ejection.

McDonnell Douglas F-15 Eagle 🇺🇸

The United States Air Force (USAF) and various aircraft companies in the United States began discussions on the feasibility of an advanced tactical fighter to replace the F-4 Phantom in 1965. Four years later it was announced that McDonnell Douglas had been selected as prime airframe contractor for the new aircraft, then designated FX; as the F-15A Eagle, it flew for the first time on 27 July 1972, and first deliveries of operational aircraft were made to the USAF in 1975.

The tandem-seat F-15B was developed alongside the F-15A, and the main production version was the F-15C. The latter was built under licence in Japan as the F-15J. The F-15E two-seat dedicated strike/attack variant was supplied to Israel as the F-15I and to Saudi Arabia as the F-15S. Saudi Arabia also purchased a further 62 F-15C/D aircraft to replace its BAe Lightning F.Mk 53 interceptors, which had been withdrawn from use. In all, the USAF took delivery of 1286 F-15s (all versions), Japan 171, Saudi Arabia 98 and Israel 56.

F-15s saw much action in the 1991 Gulf War, and Israeli aircraft were in combat with the Syrian Air Force over the Bekaa Valley in the 1980s. F-15s have also been operational over the Balkans and other trouble spots.

MCDONNELL DOUGLAS F-15C EAGLE

Specification
Type: air superiority fighter
Crew: 1
Powerplant: two 10,885kg (23,810lb) thrust Pratt & Whitney F100-PW-220 turbofans
Performance: max speed 2655km/h (1650mph); service ceiling 30,500m (100,000ft); range 5745km (3570 miles) with conformal fuel tanks
Dimensions: wing span 13.05m (42ft 9in); length 19.43m (63ft 9in); height 5.63m (18ft 5in)
Weight: 30,844kg (68,000lb) loaded
Armament: one 20mm (0.79in) M61A1 cannon; four AIM-7 or AIM-120 and four AIM-9 air-to-air missiles

318TH FIGHTER INTERCEPTOR SQUADRON, TACTICAL AIR COMMAND, UNITED STATES AIR FORCE, WASHINGTON, 1990S
The 318th Fighter Interceptor Squadron (FIS) converted to the F-15C from the Convair F-106A in 1983. The squadron was deactivated in 1989, its Eagles being assigned to the Oregon Air National Guard.

Mikoyan-Gurevich MiG-25 'Foxbat'

The prototype MiG-25 was flown as early as 1964 and was apparently designed to counter the projected North American B-70 bomber, with its Mach 3.0 speed and ceiling of 21,350m (70,000ft). The cancellation of the B-70 left the Foxbat in search of a role; it entered service as an interceptor in 1970 with the designation MiG-25P (Foxbat-A), its role now redefined as being capable of countering all air targets in all weather conditions, day or night, and in dense hostile electronic warfare environments.

The MiG-25P continues to serve in substantial numbers and constitutes part of the Russian S-155P missile interceptor system. Variants of the MiG-25 are also in service in the Ukraine, Kazakhstan, Azerbaijan, India, Iraq, Algeria, Syria and Libya. The MiG-25R, MiG-25RB and MiG-25BM are derivatives of the MiG-25P. The MiG-25R, as its suffix implies, is a reconnaissance variant, while the MiG-25RB has a high-level bombing capability against area targets.

This version is fitted with a reconnaissance station, aerial camera, topographic aerial camera, the Peteng sighting and navigation system for bombing programmed targets, and electronic countermeasures (ECM) equipment, which includes active jamming and electronic reconnaissance systems. The MiG-25BM variant has the capability to launch guided missiles against ground targets, and to destroy area targets, targets with known coordinates, and enemy radars.

The MiG-25P's enormous main radar, code-named 'Fox Fire' by Nato, is a typical 1959 technology set. It uses thermionic valves (vacuum tubes) and puts out 600kW of power to burn through enemy jamming.

MIKOYAN-GUREVICH MIG-25P FOXBAT-A

Specification

Type: interceptor

Crew: 1

Powerplant: two 10,200kg (22,487lb) thrust Tumanskii R-15B-300 turbojets

Performance: max speed 2974km/h (1848mph); service ceiling 24,383m (80,000ft); combat radius 1130km (702 miles)

Dimensions: wing span 14.02m (45ft 11in); length 23.82m (78ft 1in); height 6.10m (20ft)

Weight: 37,425kg (82,508lb) loaded

Armament: four underwing pylons for various combinations of air-to-air missile

SAKHALOVKA INTERCEPTOR WING, SOVIET AIR DEFENCE FORCES, VLADIVOSTOK, RUSSIA 1967

F-15 Eagle vs MiG-25 'Foxbat'

Israeli and Syrian combat aircraft had been involved in a series of skirmishes over Lebanese territory since 1979, and in the course of these actions Israeli F-15s encountered MiG-25 Foxbats for the first time.

Since the F-15 had been designed to counter the MiG-25 in the air superiority role in the first place, the results of these actions, which were firmly in the F-15's favour, attracted a lot of attention. The Israelis reported that the Foxbat was fast at high altitude but that its manoeuvrability was poor, as was the visibility from the cockpit. At medium and low altitudes the heavy MiG-25's speed fell away markedly and its handling qualities were sluggish.

'The pilots behaved as if they knew they were going to be shot down...'

Israeli Superiority

The MiG-23 'Flogger', according to the Israelis, was a much better proposition, but the Syrian tactics left a lot to be desired. A senior Israeli Air Force officer, speaking about the summer 1982 air battles

BELOW: *Wherever it has been called upon to fight, the F-15C has proved to be a superlative air superiority fighter.*

over the Bekaa Valley, said that: 'The pilots behaved as if they knew they were going to be shot down and waited to see when it was going to happen and not how to prevent it, or how to shoot us down. This was strange, because in the 1973 war the Syrians fought aggressively. This time it was different, so it was difficult to compare the aircraft. They could have flown the best fighter in the world, but if they flew it the way they were flying, we would have shot them down in exactly the same way. It wasn't the equipment at fault, but their tactics. Look at the area of operations and the restrictions we had. We couldn't enter Syria. They were only two minutes from their bases, while we were between ten and forty minutes from base; some of our aircraft had to come from Ouvda down in the Negev. Most of the kills, 85 to 90 per cent, were in the Bekaa Valley, less than a minute from the Syrian border. It meant we only had two minutes from them crossing to crossing back if they only wanted to sweep the Bekaa area. If we didn't succeed in two minutes then we couldn't follow them across the border. That was a difficult situation for us. Maybe for them as well... They fired missiles, they fought, but in a

peculiar way. I didn't mean they were sitting ducks, but in our view they acted without tactical sense. Maybe in their view the best tactic was to get away from – I don't know what. But the results show it was very strange.'

Aerial Clashes

Israel invaded the Lebanon on 4 June 1982 and the first Syrian loss occurred on 7 June, when a MiG-29R 'Foxbat' was destroyed during a high-level reconnaissance mission.

> ## Of the 102 Israeli aircraft lost in that conflict, 39 were shot down by SAMs, and AAA accounted for the rest.

The Israelis have always refused to say what shot it down, but it was probably one or more F-15s armed with Sparrow long-range air-to-air missiles. Four more MiGs (MiG-21s or -23s or both) were shot down on the following day, but the major air battle over the Bekaa started on 9 June, when Israeli A-4 Skyhawks, F-4 Phantoms and Kfirs launched the first big attacks on Syrian SAM and artillery sites east of Beirut. It was the first time the Kfir had been in action and a superlative aircraft it proved to be, both in the air-to-air and air-to-ground roles.

ABOVE: *The MiG-25 'Foxbat' was no use as an air superiority fighter, lacking the necessary manoeuvrability, and was adapted to the high-speed, high-level reconnaissance role.*

During the Yom Kippur war of 1973, the Israeli Air Force had been unable to establish air superiority over the west bank of the Suez Canal because of the high density of modern Egyptian surface-to-air missile (SAM) sites and radar-controlled anti-aircraft artillery (AAA). Of the 102 Israeli aircraft lost in that conflict, 39 were shot down by SAMs, and AAA accounted for the rest. During the invasion of the Lebanon, therefore, SAM and AAA sites were singled out for high-priority attacks at an early stage. The Israeli strike aircraft used electronic warfare and deception techniques to get through to the sites, which were destroyed one by one from very low level with 'iron' bombs. Many of the batteries were knocked out as they were being moved from one site to another and were consequently vulnerable to air attack; the Syrians had relied on fighter combat air patrols (CAP) to defend their weapons during the mobile phase and committed large numbers of aircraft, hoping to establish air superiority by weight of numbers. In fact, the air superiority scales were tilted the other way because of the better skill and tactics of the Israeli pilots – and aircraft like the superlative F-15.

Lockheed Martin F-16 Fighting Falcon

The F-16 Fighting Falcon, originally designed by General Dynamics and now produced by Lockheed Martin, is the world's most prolific combat aircraft, with more than 2000 in service with the United States Air Force (USAF) and a further 2000 in service with 19 other air forces around the world.

The F-16 had its origin in a USAF requirement of 1972 for a lightweight fighter and first flew on 2 February 1974. It carries an advanced GEC-Marconi HUDWACS (HUD and Weapon Aiming Computer System) in which target designation cues, as well as flight symbols, are shown on the head-up display. The HUDWAC computer is used to direct the weapons to the target, as designated on the HUD. There are five ground-attack modes and four air-combat modes. The F-16's underwing hardpoints are stressed for manoeuvres up to 9g, enabling the aircraft to dogfight while still carrying weaponry.

The F-16B and F-16D are two-seat versions, while the F-16C, delivered from 1988, featured numerous improvements in avionics and was available with a choice of engine. F-16s have seen action in the Lebanon (with the Israeli Air Force), in the Gulf Wars and in the Balkans. The type has been upgraded constantly to extend its life well into the 21st century.

LOCKHEED MARTIN F-16C FIGHTING FALCON

Specification

Type: air superiority, strike and defence suppression aircraft

Crew: 1

Powerplant: either one 10,800kg (23,770lb) thrust Pratt & Whitney F100-PW-200 or one 13,150kg (28,984lb) thrust General Electric F110-GE-100 turbofan

Performance: max speed 2142km/h (1320mph); service ceiling 15,240m (50,000ft); combat radius 925km (525 miles)

Dimensions: wing span 9.45m (31ft); length 15.09m (49ft 6in); height 5.09m (16ft 8in)

Weight: 16,057kg (35,400lb) loaded

Armament: one General Electric M61A1 multi-barrelled cannon; seven external hardpoints for up to 9276kg (20,450lb) of ordnance

52ND TACTICAL FIGHTER WING, USAFE, SPANGDAHLEM AIR BASE, GERMANY 1990S
The F-16C shown here was the personal aircraft of Brigadier-General Glenn A. Proffitt II, Officer Commanding the 52nd Tactical Fighter Wing (TFW), which took over the 'Wild Weasel' defence suppression role following the retirement of the F-4G Phantom in the 1990s.

Mikoyan MiG-29 'Fulcrum'

The MiG-29 (Nato code-name 'Fulcrum') was developed to meet a requirement for a lightweight fighter to replace MiG-21s, MiG-23s and Su-17s in the battlefield air superiority and ground-attack roles. The first prototype flew in October 1977, and deliveries to Soviet Frontal Aviation began in 1983. The powerful pulse-Doppler radar is backed up with a passive infrared search-and-track (IRST) system. This can detect, track and engage a target while leaving the radar in a non-emitting mode. The IRST sensor is mounted in front of the windscreen. For close-in engagements, a helmet-mounted sight can be used to cue infrared-homing missiles onto an off-boresight target.

MIKOYAN MiG-29 FULCRUM-A

Specification

Type: air superiority and defence aircraft

Crew: 1

Powerplant: two 81.39kN (18,298lb thrust) Klimov/Leningrad RD-33 afterburning turbofan engines

Performance 2445km/h (1519mph); service ceiling 17,000m (55,775ft); combat radius 750km (466 miles)

Dimensions: wing span 11.36m (37ft 3.25in); length 17.32m (56ft 10in); height 4.73m (15ft 6.2in)

Weight: 18,500kg (40,785lb) loaded

Armament: one GSh-301 30mm (1.18in) cannon; maximum stores of 3000kg (6614lb)

968TH ISTREBEITEL'NYI AVIATSIONNY POLK, 16TH AIR ARMY, SOVIET FRONTAL AVIATION, NOBITZ (ALTENBURG), GERMAN DEMOCRATIC REPUBLIC, 1990S

Until the early 1990s, significant Soviet forces were based with the 16th Air Army in East Germany. The 968th Istrebeitel'nyi Aviatsionny Polk (IAP, or Fighter Aviation Regiment) was based at Altenburg, near Leipzig, for a brief period. The 968th's Fulcrums replaced a regiment of MiG-27 'Floggers', which in turn had replaced Su-24 'Fencers' in 1989. The particular squadron that operated this MiG-29 is unknown, but it was the only one to wear a squadron badge at Altenburg and flew earlier-production Fulcrums than its sister units. The winged star badge originated with Yak fighters in World War II. In April 1992, the 968th IAP withdrew to Lipetsk in Russia. Altenburg is now a civil airport, served by budget airline Ryanair, among others.

F-16 FIGHTING FALCON VS MiG-29 'FULCRUM'

THE COMBAT PROWESS of the F-16 first came to the public's attention on 7 June 1981, when eight aircraft of the Israeli Air Force made a long-range low-level precision attack on Iraq's Osirak nuclear reactor near Baghdad.

The Israelis claimed that the reactor, which was then in the process of construction, was to be used to produce weapons-grade plutonium in connection with Iraq's military programme (which, as later events revealed, it undoubtedly was). It was scheduled to come into operation in the late summer of 1981, and according to Israeli sources it would have provided Iraq with the means of producing up to five 20-kiloton nuclear bombs. The Israeli Air Force was instructed to destroy the reactor, and an air strike was planned to take place at 06.30 hours local time on a Sunday to minimize civilian casualties. Fighter escort for the operation, code-named Opera, was to be provided by six F-15s.

The F-16s went in at very low level and completely destroyed the French-built 70mW reactor with 454kg (1000lb) bombs; fifteen out of the sixteen dropped hit the target. One French civilian was killed.

Consummate Fighter

The aircraft took off from Etzion, near Eilat, and flight-refuelled before heading across Jordan at low level and then continuing over the barren northern territory of Saudi Arabia. The pilots reported sporadic and inaccurate anti-aircraft fire as they crossed the border into Iraq, but no further opposition was encountered during the remainder of the operation; even though the heavily camouflaged reactor site was protected by SAMs, none was launched.

The strike pilots had no difficulty in locating the target; abortive rocket attacks had been made on the site by Iranian F-4 Phantoms, and Iran had been willing to provide photographic intelligence. The F-16s went in at very low level and completely destroyed the French-built 70mW reactor with 454kg (1000lb) bombs; 15 out of the 16 dropped hit the target. One French civilian was killed.

In the following year Israeli F-16s were in action over the Lebanon's Bekaa Valley, the Israeli pilots claiming the destruction of 44 Syrian MiGs for no loss. In the late 1980s, the F-16 saw action with the Pakistan Air Force. Between 1986 and 1989, PakAF F-16 pilots claimed to have shot down eight Soviet and Afghan aircraft (four Su-22s, two MiG-23s, one Su-25 and an An-26) which violated Pakistani air space during anti-guerrilla operations.

BELOW: The F-16 Fighting Falcon has been the subject of numerous upgrades, which will keep it a viable combat aircraft for many years to come.

During Operation Desert Storm in 1991, 249 F-16s flew 13,340 ground-attack sorties against chemical and conventional weapons manufacturing and storage facilities, as well as participating in airfield attacks and the hunt for mobile Scud missiles. F-16s were not responsible for any Iraqi air combat losses during the first Gulf War, but in December 1992/January 1993 they used AMRAAM missiles to shoot down two Iraqi MiG-23s that violated the no-fly zones.

On 12 April, 1993, USAF F-16s shot down four Serbian Super Galebs that had bombed the town of Bujogno. Since then, F-16s have been a cornerstone of NATO peacekeeping operations, and were used extensively in the second Gulf War.

Combat Problems

Despite its excellent agility and weapons systems, the MiG-29 Fulcrum has not fared as well as the F-16 in combat situations, a situation that may be attributed to the quality of its pilots.

> ### In the second Gulf War, Iraqi MiG-29s stood uselessly on their airfields, unable to take off because their pilots were elsewhere.

The 'Fulcrum' saw action in the Gulf War of 1991, but the limited number in Iraqi service were flown by inexperienced pilots and very few combat sorties were mounted. The type also saw action over

ABOVE: *When it first appeared in public, western aviation experts were amazed by the MiG-29's ability to perform combat manoeuvres never seen before – such as the tail slide, designed to break a Doppler radar lock.*

Serbia against much larger numbers of NATO aircraft, and in Eritrea against Ethiopian Su-27 'Flankers'.

Much of the F-16's success in Iraq and Serbia was doubtless due to the fact that allied forces had taken the initiative and established complete air supremacy at a very early stage, giving the MiG-29s little or no chance to respond. In the second Gulf War, Iraqi MiG-29s stood uselessly on their airfields, unable to take off because their pilots were elsewhere. In the case of the Serbian MiG-29s, these aircraft were 15 years old and lacked spares, and when they went into action some of their vital systems failed to function. Ten were destroyed, six in air combat and four on the ground. MiG-29s were used to a limited degree during Soviet operations in Afghanistan. It would have been interesting to see the outcome of a clash between these aircraft and Pakistan AF F-16s, but the MiGs did not operate near the Pakistan border, so no confrontation ever took place.

MiG-29s form the backbone of Syria's air defences. The principal operating base is Saiqal, where the MiG-29 is flown by Nos 697, 698 and 699 Squadrons. Syrian pilots are competent and experienced, and have learned much in the years since the conflict over the Bekaa, when they suffered repeated and humiliating defeats at the hands of the Israelis.

Mikoyan MiG-29 'Fulcrum'

MIKOYAN MIG-29 FULCRUM-A

Specification

Type: air superiority and defence aircraft

Crew: 1

Powerplant: two 81.39kN (18,298lb) Klimov/Leningrad RD-33
afterburning turbo fan engines

Performance: max speed 2445km/h (1,519mph);
combat radius 750km (466 miles); service ceiling 17000m (55,775ft)

Dimensions: span 11.36m (37ft 3.25in); length 17.32m (56ft 10in);
height 4.73m (15ft 6.2in)

Weight: loaded 18,500kg (40,785lb)

Armament: one GSh-301 30mm (1.18in) cannon, maximum stores
of 3000kg (6,614lb)

237TH GVRADEYSKAYA TSENTR POKAZA AVIATSIONNY TEKNIKI, AIR FORCES MOSCOW MILITARY DISTRICT, KUBINKA, RUSSIA,
EARLY 1990S.

The 234th Istrebeitel'nyi Aviatsionny Polk (Fighter Aviation Regiment) flew Lavochkin fighters during the Great Patriotic War, as World War II is known in Russia. In 1952, it was redeployed to Kubinka near Moscow to replace units sent to Korea. Kubinka has long been used for demonstrating advanced combat aircraft to national and foreign leaders. Its personnel were the first in the Soviet Union to fly solo and jet aerobatic displays, and led May Day and other fly-pasts over Moscow from 1946. The success of these demonstrations led to the awarding of the coveted 'Guards' title and the right to display the Guards banner on the unit's aircraft.

Post-war Soviet and Russian unit histories remain largely obscure, but it seems the 234th was later redesignated the 237th GTsPAT (Gvradeyskaya Tsentr Pokaza Aviatsionny Tekniki, or Guards Aircraft Demonstration Centre), named after Ivan Kozhedub. Kozhedub was the leading Soviet ace of the war, with 62 victories, and later became leader of the Soviet air units in Korea. By 1989, the flying unit at Kubinka was designated the 237th Composite Air Regiment and its 1st Squadron received the Su-27 'Flanker', leading to the formation in 1991 of the Russian Knights display team. The 237th's MiG-29 unit also formed a display team from its complement of 'Fulcrums', and this became known as the 'Swifts'. The MiG-29 makes an exceptional aerobatic platform with its ability to fly at high angle-of-attack and its relatively light weight combined with powerful engines. Both teams have made a number of foreign visits and demonstrations in Europe and beyond. The 237th is Russia's main aerobatic school and is equipped with Su-24 and Su-25 attack aircraft as well as MiG and Sukhoi fighters.

McDonnell Douglas F/A-18 Hornet

While the F-14 replaced the Phantom in the naval air superiority role, the aircraft that replaced it in the tactical role (with both the US Navy and US Marine Corps) was the McDonnell Douglas F-18 Hornet. First flown on 18 November 1978, the prototype Hornet was followed by 11 development aircraft.

The first production versions were the fighter/attack F/A-18A and the two-seat F/A-18B operational trainer; subsequent variants are the F/A-18C and F/A-18D, which have provision for AIM-120 air-to-air missiles and Maverick infrared missiles, as well as an airborne self-protection jamming system. The aircraft also serves with the Canadian Armed Forces as the CF-188 (138 aircraft). Other customers are Australia (75), Finland (64), Kuwait (40), Spain (72) and Switzerland (34). Total US deliveries, all variants, were 1150 aircraft.

The Hornet first saw combat during the Libyan confrontation of 1986, when the type flew ship-to-shore strikes and defence suppression missions. The type featured prominently in Operation Desert Storm in 1991, where it flew the bulk of US Navy/US Marine Corps (USMC) offensive operations, and has since taken part in many Nato peacekeeping operations, notably in the Balkans.

MCDONNELL DOUGLAS F/A-18A HORNET

Specification

Type: tactical strike aircraft

Crew: 1

Powerplant: two 7264kg (16,000lb) thrust General Electric F404-GE-400 turbofans

Performance: max speed 1912km/h (1183mph); service ceiling 15,240m (50,000ft); combat radius 1065km (662 miles)

Dimensions: wing span 11.43m (37ft 6in); length 17.07m (56ft); height 4.66m (15ft 3in)

Weight: 25,401kg (56,000lb) loaded

Armament: one 20mm (0.79in) M61A1 Vulcan cannon; external hardpoints with provision for up to 7711kg (17,000lb) of stores

MARINE FIGHTER ATTACK SQUADRON 314 'BLACK KNIGHTS', CARRIER AIR WING 13, USS CORAL SEA, MEDITERRANEAN, 1986
Operating from the USS *Coral Sea*, the Hornets of Marine Fighter Attack Squadron 314 (VMFA-314) were engaged in attacks on Libyan surface-to-air missile sites during Operations El Dorado Canyon and Prairie Fire in 1986. The units usual VW tail code was replaced by AK, denoting its inclusion within Carrier Air Wing 13 (CVW-13) aboard the *Coral Sea* for this deployment.

MiG-29 'Fulcrum' vs F/A-18 Hornet

THE ROYAL AUSTRALIAN AIR FORCE is a principal user of the Hornet, operating a fleet of 55 F/A-18s and 16 F/A-18B aircraft.

In 1999, the Australian Defence Force initiated a programme to upgrade the fleet with more advanced avionics, including improved radios, mission computer, global positioning system and other refinements, such as the replacement of the existing APG-65 radar with the much more advanced APG-73, a state-of-the-art system that performs both air-to-air and air-to-ground functions. The RAAF's Hornets are operated by No. 75 Squadron, based at Tindal, in the Northern Territory, and No. 77 Squadron at Williamtown in New South Wales. Both squadrons frequently send detachments on exercise to New Zealand, and multi-national air exercises are held every couple of years with the air forces of Malaysia, Singapore and the United States, with Britain occasionally taking part. It was the Iraq war of 2003, however, that gave the Australian Hornets their first real taste of combat.

Iraq Deployment

In February 2003, 14 RAAF F/A 18 Hornets deployed to Al Udeid air base in Qatar for operations in Iraq. It was the first overseas

BELOW: This Czech Air Force MiG-29 was photographed at RAF Fairford in 1993.

combat deployment of Australian fighter aircraft since July 1953, when Gloster Meteor F.8s of No. 77 Squadron flew their last sorties in Korea. Combat operations in Iraq began on 20 March and ended on 27 April, by which time the Australian Hornets had flown 350 combat sorties and dropped 122 laser-guided bombs.

'There is a clear possibility that if the MiG-29 capability had been developed to its full potential, it would have outclassed the F/A-18.'

The missions flown ranged from interdiction to air defence and close air support and included operations with the Australian SAS and various commando units. Numerous missions were also flown in support of US Marines involved in heavy street fighting in Baghdad and Tikrit. The Hornets returned to Australia in May.

The chance to see how the MiG-29 and the Hornet fared in combat against one another came during exercises held under the five-power defence agreement that involves Malaysia, Singapore, Australia, New Zealand and the United Kingdom. The MiG-29s in question are operated by the Royal Malaysian Air Force, whose acquisition of the Russian type prompted an Australian defence official to remark that:

ABOVE: *The F/A-18 Hornet has provided the United States Navy and some air forces with a potent strike aircraft. This one is seen about to 'hook the wire' aboard a US carrier.*

'The most potent threat facing the RAAF and its allies in the region is likely to come from variants of the Russian MiG-29 'Fulcrum' and Su-27/30 'Flanker'. These are big, fast, highly manoeuvrable fighters with excellent air-to-air missiles. In a WVR [Within Visual Range] dogfight they are formidable opponents. When the MiG-29 entered service in Malaysia in the mid-1990s it was a much more capable aircraft than had been operated in the region previously, but the capability provided by the MiG-29 at the time did not match its potential. There is a clear possibility that if the MiG-29 capability had been developed to its full potential, it would have outclassed the F/A-18.'

Aerial Competition

During the five-power air exercises, there were indications that the RMAF MiG-29s did indeed outclass the F/A-18. In a series of practice air engagements at medium and close range, the MiGs succeeded in shooting down all the participating Hornets. The Malaysians were using AA-10, AA-11 and AA-12 missiles against the Australians' AIM-9 Sidewinder and AIM-7 Sparrow missiles. According to some reports, resulting from observing live firings of missiles against unmanned aerial targets, the AIM-11 Archer

missile has a longer range, better warhead and better IR sensor than the AIM-9.

...flown by highly capable pilots such as those of the Royal Malaysian Air Force, the MiG-29 would beat most aircraft.

Other observers pointed out that any comparison between the F/A-18 and MiG-29 in this context was probably unfair, as the Australian aircraft were operating in the attack role and were heavily laden, whereas the MiG-29s were operating in clean configuration. In these circumstances, and flown by highly capable pilots such as those of the RMAF, the MiG-29 would beat most aircraft.

Until the mid-1990s, Australia's F/A-18s had the only beyond-visual-range air combat capability in South-East Asia, and the RAAF's Hornets and F-111s gave it unrivalled strike and air support capability. Since then, the picture has changed dramatically, and very swiftly. The introduction of modern combat aircraft into the air forces of South East Asia, and upgrades to older types, have eroded or eliminated the substantial capability enjoyed by the RAAF in the region as recently as 10 years ago. Modern equipment is supplied by both East and West, but it is Russia, which offers huge reductions on its combat aircraft deals, which is likely to be the principal supplier.

Lockheed Martin F-22 Raptor

In September 1983, the USAF awarded Advanced Tactical Fighter (ATF) concept definition study contracts to six American aerospace companies. Of these, two – Lockheed and Northrop – were selected to build demonstrator prototypes of their respective proposals. Each produced two prototypes, the Lockheed YF-22 and the Northrop YF-23. The Lockheed proposal was selected, and the first definitive F-22 flew on 7 September 1997. The second prototype first flew on 29 June 1998. By late 2001, there were eight F-22s flying.

The F-22 combines many stealth features. Its air-to-air weapons, for example, are stored internally; three internal bays house advanced short-range, medium-range and beyond-visual-range air-to-air missiles. Following an assessment of the aircraft's combat role in 1993, it was decided to add a ground-attack capability, and the internal weapons bay can also accommodate 454kg (1000lb) GBU-32 precision guided missiles.

The F-22 is designed for a high sortie rate, with a turnaround time of less than 20 minutes, and its avionics are highly integrated to provide rapid reaction in air combat, much of its survivability depending on the pilot's ability to locate a target very early and kill it with a first shot. The F-22 was designed to meet a specific threat, which at that time was presented by large numbers of highly agile Soviet combat aircraft, its task being to engage them in their own airspace with beyond-visual-range weaponry. It will be a key component in the Global Strike Task Force, formed in 2001 to counter any threat worldwide. The United States Air Force (USAF) requirement is for 438 aircraft.

LOCKHEED MARTIN F-22 RAPTOR

Specification

Type: advanced tactical fighter

Crew: 1

Powerplant: two 15,872kg (35,000lb) thrust Pratt & Whitney F119-P-100 turbofans

Performance: max speed 2335km/h (1450mph); service ceiling 19,812m (65,000ft); combat radius 1285km (800 miles)

Dimensions: wing span 13.1m (43ft); length 19.55m (64ft 2in); height: 5.39m (17ft 8in)

Weight: 27,216kg (60,000lb) loaded

Armament: AIM-9X and AMRAAM air-to-air missiles; GBU-32 Joint Direct Attack Munition and other advanced weapons

UNITED STATES AIR FORCE, EDWARDS AFB, 2000s

Sukhoi Su-27 'Flanker'

The Sukhoi Su-27 is a dual-role aircraft; in addition to its primary air superiority task, it was designed to escort Su-24 'Fencer' strike aircraft on deep-penetration missions. The prototype, designated T-10, flew for the first time in May 1977, the type being allocated the code name 'Flanker' by Nato.

Full-scale production of the Su-27P Flanker-B air defence fighter began in 1980, but the aircraft did not become fully operational until 1984. Like its contemporary, the MiG-29 'Fulcrum', the Su-27 combines a wing swept at 40 degrees with highly swept wing root extensions, underslung engines with wedge intakes, and twin fins. The combination of modest wing sweep with highly swept root extensions is designed to enhance manoeuvrability and generate lift, making it possible to achieve quite extraordinary angles of attack.

The Su-27UB Flanker-C is a two-seat training version, while the Su-27K Flanker-D is a navalized version, serving in small numbers aboard the Russian carrier *Kutnetzov* (formerly *Tbilisi*). The Su-27 serves with the air forces of China, where it is designated J-11, and Vietnam, and some were inherited by states such as Belarus and Kazakhstan, created by the collapse of the Soviet Union. The Su-30K export version of the Flanker is operated by No. 24 Squadron of the Indian Air Force.

SUKHOI SU-27 FLANKER-B

Specification

Type: air superiority fighter and long-range interceptor

Crew: 1

Powerplant: two 12,500kg (27,557lb) thrust Lyulka AL-31M
turbofans

Performance: max speed 2500km (1500mph); service ceiling
18,000m (59,055ft); combat radius 1500km (930 miles)

Dimensions: wing span 14.70m (48ft 2in); length 21.94m (71ft 11in);
height 6.36m (20ft 10in)

Weight: 30,000kg (66,138lb) loaded

Armament: one 30mm (1.18in) GSh-3101 cannon; 10 external
hardpoints with provision for various combinations of air-to-air
missiles

582ND GUARDS FIGHTER AIR REGIMENT, FOURTH AIR ARMY, FRONTAL AVIATION, CHOJNA, POLAND, 1990
The 582nd Guards Fighter Air Regiment was one of two Poland-based Su-27 units withdrawn to Russia in 1992 as part of the general withdrawal of Russian forces from former Warsaw Pact countries. The aircraft illustrated here, of the 582nd Guards Fighter Air Regiment, is Sukhoi Su-27 Flanker-B 'Blue 24'.

F-22 Raptor vs Su-27 'Flanker'

Despite Russian attempts to produce an operational interceptor that would provide an effective counter to America's Lockheed Martin F-22 Raptor, the Sukhoi Su-27 'Flanker' remains the F-22's main adversary in the long-range interceptor role.

The F-22's main advantage is that it combines many stealth features. It is also designed for a high sortie rate, having a turn-round time of less than 20 minutes, and its avionics are highly integrated to provide rapid reaction in air combat, much of its survivability depending on the pilot's ability to locate a target very early and kill it with a first shot.

The F-22 was designed to meet a threat that was very real: the USAF's latest fighter, the F-16, had entered service in 1979, and in the decade that followed the Russians introduced no fewer than five fighter-attack types, their missions all neatly dovetailing into one another to provide excellent operational integration. The Sukhoi Su-24 'Fencer,' with its all-weather, low-level penetration capability, greatly enhanced the Soviet ability to carry out deep strikes into NATO territory; the Su-25 'Frogfoot' ground-attack

aircraft quickly proved itself to be an excellent close-support fighter in Afghanistan; the MiG-29 'Fulcrum' and the Su-27 'Flanker' were a match for NATO aircraft in the air superiority role, as well as having a substantial ground attack capability; and the MiG-31 'Foxhound', developed to counter US bombers armed with cruise missiles, brought a new dimension to the Soviet air defence system.

The Russians clearly had the ability to develop an aircraft in the F-22 class, and there were serious concerns that they would do so first.

BELOW: *The F-22 represents the third generation of Lockheed stealth design, allowing it to advance much closer to a target before firing, giving it a far higher kill probability.*

ABOVE: *The basic variant of the Su-27 'Flanker' is without peer as a long-range interceptor, while advanced derivatives look set to dominate Russian military aviation into the 21st century.*

Of all these new Soviet types, it was the Su-27 'Flanker' that came as the most profound shock to NATO analysts. Between 1986 and 1988, one of the Su-27 development aircraft, designated P-42, was prepared for a series of world record attempts, challenging previous records set up by a specially-stripped McDonnell Douglas F-15E Strike Eagle. The P-42 was stripped of all radar, armament and operational equipment and lightened for its record attempts.

Among the 27 world records set by the P-42 between 1986 and 1988 were five absolute time-to-height records previously held by the F-15. These included a staggering 15,000m (49,210ft) climb in 70.33 seconds, almost seven seconds faster than the Strike Eagle.

Su-27 Developments
The Russians clearly had the ability to develop an aircraft in the F-22 class, and there were serious concerns that they would do so first.

Then came the breakup of the Soviet Union, with its attendant economic problems, and it soon became clear that, as well as striving to develop an F-22-class aircraft (the MiG-MFI), they were also applying new technology to existing designs to make them viable into the next century. The trend was exemplified in the Sukhoi Su-37, a single-seat fighter and ground attack aircraft developed from the Su-27/35 and incorporating three-dimensional vectoring nozzles to give it super-agility. For example, the Su-37 can pitch up rapidly beyond the vertical, perform a tight 360-degree somersault within its own length, and pull out to resume level flight with no height loss.

The Su-27 'Flanker' is a very dangerous adversary indeed. In certain circumstances, it can detect, locate and identify its targets without using radar, using a multi-spectral suite of sensors.

The Russians therefore appear to have succeeded in producing aircraft that will perform much of the F-22's mission at a fraction of the cost, putting them within reach of many nations that hitherto could afford only cheap multi-role aircraft and creating a dangerous imbalance of power. In the Far East, China, despite an apparently growing rapprochement with the West, remains a perceived threat to the stability of the Pacific Basin. Not only is she armed with modern combat types like the Su-27, but also her ambitions are backed up by a powerful nuclear capability.

The Su-27 'Flanker' is a very dangerous adversary indeed. In certain circumstances, it can detect, locate and identify its targets without using radar, using a multi-spectral suite of sensors, which avoids giving away its presence to enemy radar warning receivers.

But the 'Flanker' is much more than just a long-range bomber destroyer. Airshow audiences have watched transfixed as Su-27s have performed manoeuvres which no western combat aircraft can duplicate, demonstrating safe handling characteristics in the extreme corners of the flight envelope. This gives an Su-27 pilot unparalleled agility in a low-speed fight, and allows him to 'point' the nose far away from the direction of flight to aim his weapons in an off-axis snap-shot.

Lockheed F-117 Nighthawk 🇺🇸

The F-117A 'Stealth' aircraft began life in 1973 as a project called 'Have Blue', launched to study the feasibility of producing a combat aircraft with little or no radar and infrared signature. Two Experimental Stealth Tactical (XST) 'Have Blue' research aircraft were built and flown in 1977 at Groom Lake, Nevada (Area 51). The evaluation of the two Have Blue aircraft led to an order for 65 production F-117As. Five of these were used for evaluation, and one crashed before delivery. Its first flight in June 1981 and entered service in October 1983.

F-117As of the 37th Tactical Fighter Wing played a prominent part in the 1991 Gulf War, making first strikes on high-priority targets; since then, they have been used in the Balkans and Afghanistan. The last of 59 F-117As was delivered in July 1990. The F-117's primary role is to attack high-value command, control and communications targets. Such targets include leadership bunkers, command posts and air defence and communications centres.

LOCKHEED F-117A NIGHTHAWK

Specification

Type: fighter-bomber

Crew: 1

Powerplant: two 4899kg (10,800lb) thrust General Electric F404-GE-F1D2 turbofan engines

Performance: max speed Mach 0.92; service ceiling classified; range classified

Dimensions: wing span 13.20m (43ft 4in); length 20.08m (65ft 11in); height 3.78m (12ft 5in)

Weight: 23,814kg (52,500lb) loaded

Armament: provision for 2268kg (5000lb) of stores on rotary dispenser in weapons bay, including the AGM-88 HARM anti-radiation missile, AGM-65 Maverick air-to-surface missile, GBU-19 and GBU-27 optronically guided bomb, BLU-109 laser-guided bombs, and B61 free-fall nuclear bomb

49TH FIGHTER WING, UNITED STATES AIR FORCE, HOLLOMAN AIR FORCE BASE, NEW MEXICO, 1992
The 49th Fighter Wing has a long and distinguished record. Activated on 18 August 1948 at Misawa, Japan, with F-51 Mustangs and F-80 Shooting Stars, it rearmed with F-84 Thunderjets, with which it carried out many notable ground-attack missions during the Korean War. Armed successively with the F-86 Sabre, F-100 Super Sabre, F-105 Thunderchief and F-4 Phantom, it saw combat in Vietnam in 1972. It used F-15A Eagles from 1977–92, when it rearmed with the F-117A.

Northrop Grumman B-2 Spirit

Development of the B-2, originally known as the Advanced Technology Bomber (ATB), was begun in 1978 and the US Air Force (USAF) originally wanted 133 examples; however, by 1991, successive budget cuts had reduced this to 21 aircraft. The prototype flew on 17 July 1989, and the first production B-2 was delivered to the 393rd Bomb Squadron of the 509th Bomb Wing at Whiteman Air Force Base, Missouri, on 17 December 1993.

In designing the ATB, Northrop decided on an all-wing configuration from the outset. The all-wing approach was selected because it promised to result in an exceptionally clean configuration for minimizing radar cross-section, including the elimination of vertical tail surfaces, with added benefits such as span-loading structural efficiency and high lift/drag ratio for efficient cruise. Outboard wing panels were added for longitudinal balance, to increase lift/drag ratio and to provide sufficient span for pitch, roll and yaw control.

The original ATB design had elevons on the outboard wing panels only, but as the design progressed additional elevons were added inboard, giving the B-2 its distinctive 'double-W' trailing edge. The aircraft is highly manoeuvrable, with fighter-like handling characteristics. In addition to the 'stealth' properties of its design, the B-2 is coated with radar-absorbent materials.

NORTHROP GRUMMAN B-2A SPIRIT

Specification

Type: strategic bomber

Crew: 4

Powerplant: four 8618kg (19,000lb) thrust General Electric F118-GE-110 turbofans

Performance: max speed 764km/h (475mph); service ceiling 15,240m (50,000ft); range 11,675km (7255 miles)

Dimensions: wing span 52.43m (172ft); length 21.03m (69ft); height: 5.18m (17ft)

Weight: 181,437kg (400,000lb) loaded

Armament: 16 AGM-129 Advanced Cruise Missiles, or alternatively 16 B.61 or B.83 free-fall nuclear bombs, 80 Mk 82 227kg (500lb) bombs, 16 Joint Direct Attack Munitions, 16 Mk84 907kg (2000lb) bombs, 36 M117 340kg (750lb) fire bombs, 36 CBU-87/89/97/98 cluster bombs, and 80 Mk36 304kg (560lb) or Mk 62 sea mines

393RD BOMB SQUADRON, 509TH BOMBARDMENT WING, UNITED STATES AIR FORCE, WHITEMAN AIR FORCE BASE, MISSOURI, MID-1990S

The 509th Bombardment Wing, which began life as the 509th (Composite) Bomb Group, was formed in 1944 to drop the world's first atomic bombs. Since then, it has pioneered the operational use of new strategic weapons and systems for the USAF.

F-117 Nighthawk v B-2 Spirit

THE F-117 AND B-2 'STEALTH' aircraft were designed to penetrate undetected into the airspace of the former Warsaw Pact. When they went to war, it was in a far different environment – but the weaponry that confronted them was mostly Russian in origin.

The F-117A first came to the attention of the general public in 1989, when one example bombed Rio Hato airfield in support of the American invasion of Panama. It captured the public's attention, however, two years later, during the operations against Iraq in January 1991.

One of the biggest problems confronting those responsible for planning the Allied air interdiction campaign against Iraq was to make an accurate intelligence assessment of Iraq's military capability. The building of an overall intelligence picture had been left largely to the US Central Intelligence Agency, which relied heavily on intelligence provided by Israel. Since it was in Israel's own interest to paint as gloomy a picture as possible of Iraq's military power, the end result was that the Iraqi capability to wage a high-technology war was greatly over-estimated, and this

BELOW: the unmistakeable shape of the F-117 Nighthawk, whose true configuration and capabilities were kept secret for years.

affected the choice of targets and the method of attack in the early stages of the war.

The main priorities of the air interdiction phase of Desert Storm were to destroy Iraq's capability to wage war with nuclear, chemical and biological weapons, to neutralize her air force's major airfields, and to disrupt the country's command, control and communications systems, to render them ineffective. This phase assumed the proportions of a strategic air war against industrial as well as military objectives.

F-117As have been used operationally in support of NATO operations in Kosovo, and in Operation Iraqi Freedom in 2003.

The main weapons used against the command, control and communications systems, whose primary sites were in built-up areas, were the Lockheed F-117As of the 37th Tactical Fighter Wing and

ABOVE: The fact that every worker on the B-2 programme had to undergo a security vetting process increased the cost of developing the aircraft by 10–15 per cent.

the General Dynamics AGM-109 Tomahawk cruise missile. The F-117As were armed with laser-guided BLU-109 BLU-109 900kg (2000lb) high explosive bombs.

More than 20 F-117As were deployed to Saudi Arabia and these bombed all their assigned targets on the first night of offensive operations. Pilots made good use of their aircraft's ability to remain undetected in the target area for lengthy periods while targets were verified. The pilots were also aided by the climate; the night on which the war began was clear and dark, with a new moon in its early phase – the best conditions for the night vision equipment and for the 'smart' weapons carried by the strike aircraft.

Since then, F-117As have been used operationally in support of NATO operations in Kosovo, and in Operation Iraqi Freedom in 2003.

The USAF unit responsible for the service introduction of America's other stealth bomber, the Northrop B-2, was the 509th Bomb Wing, which has been responsible for the operational development of new strategic weapons systems ever since its B-29s dropped the first atomic bombs on Japan in 1945.

The B-2 flew its first combat mission on 24 March 1999, when two aircraft made a 31-hour non-stop sortie from Whiteman Air Force base, Missouri, to attack targets in the former Yugoslavia in support of Operation Allied Force. Six B-2s were assigned to this operation, and in the course of 45 sorties they dropped 656 Joint Direct Attack Munitions (JDAMS) on their objectives. These missions, which required multiple air-to-air refuellings, were extremely exhausting for the crews.

The 509th Bomb Wing's B-2s subsequently took part in Operation Enduring Freedom in 2001, attacking targets in Afghanistan. Six missions were flown in the first three days of the conflict, the B-2s taking off from Whiteman AFB, flying direct to Afghanistan with the support of air refuelling tankers, and then recovering to Diego Garcia in the Indian Ocean, where the bombers were turned around and assigned fresh crews. They then flew a second mission to Afghanistan before returning to Whiteman AFB. Each sortie, including time spent on the ground, lasted seventy hours on average.

The B-2 flew its first combat mission on 24 March 1999, when two aircraft made a 31-hour non-stop sortie from Whiteman Air Force base, Missouri, to attack targets in the former Yugoslavia in support of Operation Allied Force.

During operational trials, B-2 crews have regularly flown sorties of 30 hours or more, and in flight simulator conditions the limit has been pushed to 50 hours, the pilots taking it in turn to sleep on a makeshift bed.

As for the aircraft themselves, around 50 percent of the B-2 fleet is serviceable at any one time. Unserviceability problems are usually caused by inability to meet the stringent 'stealth' requirements, the radar-absorbent skin needing frequent treatment to remove any blemishes.

Accurate target intelligence remains crucial to all 'stealth' operations. The lack of it caused acute embarrassment in May 1999, during Operation Allied Force, when a B-2 crew mistakenly dropped JDAMs on the Chinese Embassy in Belgrade.

Index

AIRCRAFT